GRAMMARS
OF THE
URBAN GROUND

GRAMMARS OF THE URBAN GROUND

Ash Amin and Michele Lancione, editors

Duke University Press / Durham and London / 2022

Designed by Matthew Tauch
Typeset in Alegreya by Westchester Publishing Services

Library of Congress Cataloging-in-Publication Data
Names: Amin, Ash, editor. | Lancione, Michele, editor.
Title: Grammars of the urban ground / Ash Amin and
Michele Lancione, editors
Description: Durham : Duke University Press, 2022. | Includes
bibliographical references and index.
Identifiers: LCCN 2021041695 (print)
LCCN 2021041696 (ebook)
ISBN 9781478015710 (hardcover)
ISBN 9781478018339 (paperback)
ISBN 9781478022954 (ebook)
ISBN 9781478092643 (ebook other)
Subjects: LCSH: Sociology, Urban. | City planning—Political
aspects. | Marginality, Social—Political aspects. | BISAC: SOCIAL
SCIENCE / Sociology / Urban | SOCIAL SCIENCE / Human Geography
Classification: LCC HT151 .G667 2022 (print) | LCC HT151 (ebook) |
DDC 307.76 dc23/eng/20211201
LC record available at https://lccn.loc.gov/2021041695
LC ebook record available at https://lccn.loc.gov/2021041696

Cover art: Photograph by Michele Lancione, 2019.

This title is freely available in an open access edition made
possible by a generous contribution from the British Academy.

CONTENTS

ACKNOWLEDGMENTS

We are grateful to the authors for their willingness to write chapters in the spirit of this book. Their cooperation has greatly enhanced the cohesion and clarity of the project. We also thank the British Academy for its enthusiasm in hosting a series of workshops in 2018 and 2019 on new urban grammars, from which this book germinated, and for facilitating its open access. Philip Lewis and Desislava Stoichkova created the opportunity and believed in the need to open new ways of "thinking the urban." We are also indebted to Courtney Berger at Duke University Press for her support and encouragement, to Chen Qu for invaluable help in tying together references and bibliographies, and to the two referees who offered valuable suggestions to strengthen the manuscript.

THINKING CITIES FROM THE GROUND

Introduction

The twentieth-century urban grammar of abstraction, models, plans, and grand theory falls short of encapsulating and addressing contemporary urban complexity and agency. Like amalgams (De Boeck 2015), cities are entanglements of bodies, nature, things, technologies, infrastructures, and institutions, with the relations of assembly doing much of the work under the radar of the inherited language of urban analysis and planning. Cities have also become the gathering points of global networks of organization, flow, and connectivity, formed through the intersecting velocities, accelerations, and pause-points of transnational production, finance, migration, tourism, culture, climate, and political influence, all defying assumptions of urban territorial enclosure and integrity. If urban life is shaped and governed through these folds of time and space, if in this condition of relational co-presence and nodal connectivity the quintessentially "urban" comes to the fore, a nonbinary language capable of capturing this ontology is required.

For one, as repeatedly argued by decolonial scholars of cities in the South, this means rejecting the one-model-fits-all (Western) tradition of urban theorizing, which has for so long silenced other ways of thinking the urban and which lacks critical capability. When we say "critical" we mean an approach that refuses to take things for granted (Marcuse 2009), including *its way of thinking and theorizing*. Even the field of critical urban studies, no longer a marginal voice, struggles with this precept, while cities continue to escape and defy the fixed categories of theory, entreating them to be constantly reexamined. Criticality in urban thinking requires working with plural analytics and concepts, placing them in continual dialogue with each other, then being prepared for their unsettlement by new ontological developments.

The field of critical urban studies has sought to stay close to the urban ground from diverse perspectives, ranging from political economy and political ecology to post-structuralist, feminist, queer, black, and decolonial thought. In this effort over the last three decades, baseline concepts capturing formative processes and powers have been mobilized to read the twists and turns of urban life as it unfolds and accretes, in an attempt to acknowledge and examine the entanglements and relations that make cities and city life. A conscious effort has been made to hold in view the complex relationship between scales, structural formation and everyday praxis, human as well as nonhuman agency, and the varied power dynamics undergirding these relations. Any inclination to force the empirical into the precepts of an abstract model or explanatory paradigm has ceded to the desire to bring it to the surface of theoretical enquiry, and of political praxis. If the call within critical urbanism for a complex understanding of the city was inclined in early years to silence relations and histories in search of the baseline, today it looks to write the multiplicity of the urban into its theorization.

The scope of our collective intervention with this book, then, is to take stock of at least some of the multiplicity, and to offer a potential reading of its ongoing journey. This is not an attempt to renew or revise what we might call critical urban studies, but instead to present a reflection at the *crossroads* (Simone 2010), around a particular modality of "thinking cities" that has emerged in recent years, renewing the language of critical urban thinking. A new generation of scholars is coming up, strengthened by calls for more-nuanced and more-political urban epistemologies (Oswin 2018; Roy 2020), founded on the double move that the canons of urban theory need jostling from below, and that the agentic power of cities demands an evolving, yet deeply grounded and relational, account and politics of the urban (Lancione and McFarlane 2021).

This to us seems a common orientation across the diverse strands of contemporary critical urbanism, including the "ontological turn" (see below) in which we locate our own thinking and work more explicitly indebted to Marxian political economy, political ecology, and feminist, queer, and critical-race thought. What cuts across these approaches is an increased attention to relational thinking, to situated and yet always translocal formations, and to processes involving nonhuman agencies. Far from offering theoretical homogeneity and methodological clarity, such inclinations signal at a minimum the vitality of an entire field of enquiry ("the urban") trying both to challenge its past assumptions and, crucially for us, *to look for a language of complex formations*. The shared double move of rewording urban theory and reworlding the urban ground raises important questions about the meaning of "critical" enquiry: What constitutes the "political" in forms of urban enquiry that both center a critique of urban knowledgeproduction and are committed to the multiplicity of city lives? Are there traces, across the strands and their locations, of a common grammar of at least shared, or sharable, intents? And, crucially, on what basis can distillations of process and project be made, without falling back into the trap of twentieth-century essentialist taxonomies that often generalized the Western, white, and male gaze, with effects that go well beyond the remit of "urban scholarship" (de Sousa Santos 2016; Bhambra et al. 2018)?

Rather than any search for unifying theory, the shared impulse behind these questions seems to be a desire to stay close to the grounds of urban life, through its various scales and relations, and to experiment with conceptual lexicons that allow for a richer, and more profoundly critical, exploration of city-making and urban struggles. This openness is more than a desire to work with and through the simple fetish of "everyday life" or to map the phenomenological as seen. It is to find ways of getting at immanent processes and tendencies, open to how knowledge about the ground is produced and also to the possibility that the political economies and ecologies of cities as composites are interactively formed and chronologically accreted, requiring a relational and excavational critique of essentialist thinking (Stengers 2005). For example, if cities are envisaged as amalgams of financial, informational, and human flow, of the more-than-human, of multiple sources of authority, then how this assemblage makes social and material life becomes the matter of political attention and its sites become the passage points of political action. The challenges of urban address are wrested from the language of urban deliberation and territorial control and placed in the language of opportunities presented by urban process, bending toward a politics of making its practices visible and alterable through sustained ontological interventions.

This book is an attempt to sketch the elements of a grammar of the urban ground, building both on critical traditions of thought and on the ontological turn in urban studies so as to identify formative impulses and mechanisms that could also be altered for reparative action and just outcomes. It aims to move beyond siloed categories such as urban "economy," "society," and "politics," which ignore the horizontal, connective, and aggregative forces of city-making that efforts to improve urban lives, agencies, and environments must negotiate. For this task, we have selected voices who in recent years have done much of the work of thinking from the ground and interpreting its grammars, attempting to work at the precise juncture of immanent force and expressible manifestation. Before summarizing their contributions, however, we briefly recall the genealogy of the turn in critical urbanism that this book encapsulates, to then reflect on why the choice of motifs from the urban ground is of conceptual and practical value.

Ontological Turns and Political Grounds

"The city is a *mediation* among mediations," "an *oeuvre*," wrote Henri Lefebvre, aiming to emphasize the manufactured nature of the city (2008, 101). This includes its scripting. In writing about the city, in (re)presenting it, urban scholars contribute to its creation and reproduction, which is why the question of *critical grammars for the city* is so important. In adopting, explicitly or implicitly, a particular urban lexicon, scholars become part of that "mediation among mediations," opening up as well as foreclosing opportunities for engaging, appropriating, and experimenting with what's at stake in the city. Indeed, the large number of journals, books, and articles dedicated to urban policy analysis and intervention is a clear sign of the will to power over the urban oeuvre. Policies are ranked, benchmarked, bought, sold, and implemented without much thought given to questions of validity, applicability, and reach (McCann 2013). And this work sustains a lucrative industry of academic knowledge-production (Flyvbjerg 2001; McCann 2008; Allen and Imrie 2010). Another consequence is the tendency to search for those core urban structures and processes that are decipherable from a singular theorization of the urban.

Centering the urban ground in ways of talking, writing, and theorizing about cities offers no easy answer to the conceptual (and political) limitations of extant thinking, nor does doing so mean to elude the question of "mediations." It is, on the contrary, a way to get closer to what "mediations" actually are in the immanent life of our global urban world, whether they be they matters of financial circulation or of everyday affective orientations. Centering the "ground" of city life in critical urban thinking means, in other words, to stay close to the instantiation of urban processes, the nexuses where modalities of life (including its suppression in diverse ways) take form, unfold, and irradiate well beyond their immediate topographical limits. Given that nexuses are always multifaceted—in that they can be matter existing of bodies, places, and relational spaces—looking for *grammars of the urban ground* means expanding the conceptual vocabulary to incorporate a situated and heterodox lexicon of and for the "city." The "political," in such an enterprise, lies not only in finding a language for complex formations, but also in looking for the generative possibilities of such a grammar to promote emancipatory ways of managing urban life.

Crucially, a certain attentiveness to what we might call the "urban ground" has always been present in critical urban scholarship. Urban land is one of these grounds, as the work of David Harvey or, more recently, Raquel Rolnik has clearly shown (Harvey 1985; Rolnik 2019). Here the land itself is shown to turn into a nodal point—a fix, to use Harvey's words—through which a particular modality of urban development (estate-based, financially wired, and profit-oriented) has not only been made possible but even encouraged to flourish. Its political economy has seen the flattening of state and independent regulation of the urban estate, to make for corporatist and financial translocal speculation. Extensive commodification in this way has created "mundane" terrains for capital profiteering—for example, technocratic rent management to ensure new levels of immediate extraction of financialized value, and the systematic removal of land from the long-term housing market in the name of short-term and high-return profit-making (which has latterly escalated to the extensive Airbnbization of dwellings in tourist cities worldwide).

Marxian political economy has done much to reveal the urban estate and all that it sustains as both the agent and the effect of diverse modalities of capitalist extraction and regulation. In the same way, a cognate political ecology has shown how the metabolic infrastructures and natures of cities have succumbed to the logic of capital (Heynen et al. 2006; Bulkeley et al. 2014; Castán Broto 2019), subsuming an ever-expanding material environment on which huge concentrations of people depend for survival, and producing class, racial, and other forms of dispossession and violence (Perry 2013; Shabazz 2015; Gibbons 2018; Roy 2019). In a similar vein, feminist urban thinking has always taken the grounds—of patriarchal homes and planning—as the prime locus to build a critique and to craft a progressive political language of and for the "city" (Massey 1994; Katz 1996;

Kern 2020). These tendencies alone show that an optic from the "ground" of urban life is not a recent discovery, and owes much to materialist analysis of the city maturing since the 1970s. Yet, recent years have also seen the arrival of other theorizations of the urban ground—less economistic, more situated, and erring toward immanent forces and dialectic relations rather than structural impositions. One prominent development has been the interpretation of the ground of cities as being "ordinarily" differentiated, thereby challenging assumptions about how urbanity (and capital) work across geographies and scales (Robinson 2005; Roy and Ong 2011). There is now a conspicuous literature on comparative urbanism advocating also a "southern" knowledge attentive to contextual histories and local processes and wary of totalizing theory from the experience of (some) northern cities (Roy and Crane 2015; Bhan 2016; Oswin 2020).

If this turn began to acknowledge the variegations and complexities of urban life—across scale and place (Massey 1993)—and to signal a "compositional" approach that should "not take things for granted" (Marcuse 2009), it also produced a foray into diverse bodies of post-structuralist thought that can only be gathered as plural voices in critical urbanism, rather than as a coherent body of theory. But, as indicated above, we would claim for them a common interest to make visible and speak from compositional arrangements close to the urban surface. We see the turn toward words such as "assemblage," "complexity," or "relationality" as being united in stressing the importance of getting closer to the entanglements (re)producing the urban and in understanding their ontological status: if not as all-powerful "structures" then as forces-in-relation and sociomaterial mediations (Gibson-Graham 2014; Amin and Thrift 2016) with considerable political agency across the spectrum of urban life (McFarlane 2011; Lancione 2016; Datta 2012; Simone and Pieterse 2017). In this ontological turn the "political" neither evaporates nor evades a critique of capital, as its critics from political economy are wont to claim. Instead, it is tacked from a "minor" and "molecular" perspective, which looks to the machinery of everyday orderings that make people, things, and nature subjects of, and subjugated to, capitalism, and from which change could be organized. As two often misinterpreted philosophers of this ontological turn put it, "molecular escapes and movements would be nothing if they did not return to the molar organizations to reshuffle their segments, their binary distributions of sexes, classes, and parties" (Deleuze and Guattari 1987, 219).

The ontological turn looks to "social theory in an altogether different way," proposing "horizontality versus verticality, self-organization versus structuration, emergence versus transcendence, attention to ontology as opposed to epistemology" (Escobar 2007, 106). Three traits are worth recalling to situate the critical thinking and grammars of the urban ground that this book seeks to encapsulate. The first is a reading of the social that is open to immanence, uneasy about enclosing relational developments into specific ontological categories or treating them as matters of cause and effect (Deleuze and Guattari 1987; Massumi 1992; Buchanan 1997; Bonta and Protevi 2004). In urban analysis, this implies focusing on how the city, in its many entanglements, emerges in their makings and always in excess of the givens of social categorization (Amin and Thrift 2002; Latour 2005). The second trait is a "post-human" sensibility of seeing the "social" as the yield of humans and non-humans in interaction, with neither being prominent over the other but only affecting each other (Ahmed 2007; Stewart 2007; Anderson 2014). This is close to what Graham Harman has called an object-oriented ontology, asserting that objects have an autonomous existence vis-à-vis human thought, which itself must be considered as one of the "objects" making up the world (Harman 2009), and it adds to Arturo Escobar's appeal to work with multiple ontological possibilities to design and inhabit a plural world (Escobar 2018). The third trait is an interest in a politics-of-becoming based on the terms of assemblage and encounter (Foucault 1980), thus repositioning, for example, traditionally understood a priori abstractions of class, gender, and race as infractions meted out and contested in the melee of their lived intersections both with each other and with more-than-human material (Grosz 1993; Stengers 2010).

This approach has been taken up with some vigor in urban scholarship troubled by the gap between the actual and pretheorized city (derived for the most part from Western cities deemed to be paradigmatic). An initial thrust came from readings of cities as relational topologies, rather than as topographies contained within their administrative boundaries. Doreen Massey (1994) and Saskia Sassen (2002), expanding on contributions that showed the urban-land nexus to be shaped remotely as well as structurally (Harvey 1985; Castells 1990), opened urban scholarship to the plural geographies—local, global, interregional, historical—shaping city life. Then, in 2002 one of us (Amin) and Nigel Thrift explored the potential of the ontological turn by interpreting cities as a "mechanosphere" of intersecting infrastructures, later followed by writing conjecturing cities as assemblages, atmospheres, and more-than-human entities (Whatmore 2002; Farías and Bender 2010; McFarlane 2011). In more recent years, new lines of thinking have emerged, sharing a similar interest in post-human articulations and processes. They delve into the everyday makeshift conditions of neighborhoods by urbanites to inhabit seemingly underregulated cities (Simone 2004; Simone and Pieterse 2017), into the intricacies of urban infrastructures shaping social subjectivity and experience in differentiated ways (Chattopadhyay 2012; Larkin 2013; Amin and Thrift 2016), and into urban marginality refracted through the lens of history, material occupancy, and political organization (Vasudevan 2015; Lancione 2016; Roy 2017; Thieme 2017; Truelove 2018).

The amassing body of assemblage thinking in urban studies has not escaped tokenistic uses of its concepts to deliver descriptive, ahistoric, and power-free accounts of the urban. At other times, enthusiasm for the more-than-human has tended to neglect questions related to entrenched social inequalities and injustices, not to mention the critical insights of long-established traditions in political economic, feminist, critical-race, and queer thinking. Yet, combined with the latter, the ontological turn reinforces a genuinely critical urbanism of the sort outlined at the start of this chapter, attending to the relational and material structuration of everyday urban life, disclosing the discriminations and power asymmetries of the urban "mechanosphere," and opening a ground for a politics of renegotiation of the urban through the circuits that constitute it, with the understanding that these circuits are never purely technical. We are not suggesting a carefree merger of conceptual positions, but instead some trade of ideas between them. The insights, for example, of a conceptual toolkit honed to untangle racial dispossession in the contemporary urban cannot be folded into the language of "assemblages." Yet, the latter's interest in material infrastructures, multiple ontologies of everyday life, and sites of affective labor can help to widen understanding of racialized exclusions of interest also to the former (Amin 2012). Similarly, while work on the political economy of urban land grab might not look into the embodied experience of housing precarity, without understanding the latter there can be no test of the lived effects of diverse models of political economy (Lancione 2018; Weheliye 2014).

We are interested in showing how disparate grammars can—and very productively—be held together in their shared commitment to the immanent urban ground, taken as a space of not one but many performative logics, played out in the workings of sociotechnologies and infrastructures, markets and institutions, land and real estate, environmental processes, and bodily encounters, to name just a few sites. Thus, we would expect, as in this book, a situated critique of capital, of gender, race, sexual and colonial violence, and of material and environmental arrangements. We would expect an eschewal of theoretical unity, abstraction, and overconfidence, and an openness to conceptual pluralism, experimentation, and renewal. We would expect a sensibility of more than words and humans, of the "make+shift" (Vasudevan 2015), acknowledging the nonverbal, provisional, and experimental nature of city life.

Ultimately, acknowledging the polivocality of urban sociomaterial processes is key to the *grammars* we are signaling in this book, and it requires a double move. First, it means "writing the city into the urban." We borrow this expression from Pushpa Arabindoo, who, in introducing an event that took place at Institut d'Études Avancées de Paris to celebrate the fifty years of Lefevbre's *La Révolution Urbaine*, invited scholars to get closer to the city in order to be able to write about it. Arabindoo's invitation is to harness the "theoretical potential of the urban" through an attentiveness to the "ethnographic insights of the city" (Arabindoo 2018). It gets us once again to get "out there," in the way of the Chicago School (Park 1936; Lindner 2006), but this time with a firmer grasp of the place of political economy, epistemic framing, scholarship of the "margins," and assemblage thinking. Such writing cannot retrofit the city into an image of the urban, but can only find clarity in the messiness of interconnections, junctures, and those friction points making up life in different places. It must be attentive to local specificities and processes, it must use theory as a compass, and it must be careful in making urban comparisons across geographies (Lancione and McFarlane 2016). Writing the city into the urban in this way requires being attentive to the "multiplicity of story lines" (Simone and Pieterse 2017) that fold together machinic tendencies and lived practices. The authors here exemplify this kind of attentiveness to the urban ground, questioning what urban theory does and how, and staying close to the particularities of situated city life.

Secondly, "writing the city into the urban" means informing urban praxis without pretensions of oversight. The language of urban intervention is cast out of the mold of working the grain, making fine adjustments, finding epistemic collaborators, avoiding grand designs, and, above all, exposing policy fashions such as neoliberal techno-driven entrepreneurialism (as is clear in much of the "smart city" charade) that sharpen inequalities and exclusions. A grammar of the urban ground, as the authors in this volume show, commits to the opportunities of "make+shift," while at the same time is concerned about the situated and transversal forms of violence that demand more than prosaic alterations. Light years away from a nontemporal, nongeographical, and "fuzzy" language of capitalist subjections (Deleuze and Guattari 1987), it offers a nonprescriptive lexicon that can be appropriated, explored, and adapted by actors who try daily to alter city workings and dynamics. Some of the authors of this book are already doing this kind of work, and we hope that the style and ethos of their work herein will invite further interlocutors: urban scholars and activists looking for ways of sensitively intervening in the weft and warp of urban functioning, provisioning, living, belonging, and survival, using those as the access points for a molecular and molar politics of justice and sustainability (Katz 2017).

Post-categorical Urbanism

Staying close to the ground requires a form of what we might call "post-categorical thinking," so as to open a space to "think the city" beyond the categories of received wisdom (Lancione 2016). There can be little point in engaging in the intersectional, transversal, ethnographic, and vernacular—the composite and the experienced—if the rich material yielded is then flattened by limiting categorizations. This is not to reject the latter in absolute terms. Categories are often appropriated and filled with new meaning, as subaltern groups have been doing for some time (think, for instance, how meanings of the notion "queer" have evolved). The post-categorical thinking that we have in mind has more to do with what can emerge when the norm is interrupted, and when experiments are free to flow. This is a form of a posteriori thinking: an opening that exceeds and surpasses standardized definitions, which may well be enclosed into new definitions, but that is about the event of an opening in the first place. This means suspending the urge to compartmentalize evidence, and instead to make for a degree of lexical ambiguity or pluralism.

A first step might be to commit to urban detailing, listing what goes on within the meshwork of urban-making and unmaking and being guided by the enforcements of the sociotechnical networks. This form of tracing seeks rigor, detail, and orientation, not comprehensive statement, building the elements of a lexicon to speak about urban complexity in ways that provide the bare marking of immanent urban processes. Such bare marking then permits urban detailing to enter into dialogue with the precepts of a critical urbanism interested in the asymmetries of political economy, bodily differentiation, and more-than-human assembly. This form of ground-up theorizing indexed to certain precepts of power opens conceptual and political possibilities, rather than reducing them to paradigmatic givens. Seemingly mundane and "neutral" things such as infrastructures, affective atmospheres, material arrangements, but also sociocultural practices, are set free to speak and, when filtered through the precepts of power, permit unseen or silenced political machinations and propositions to come to the fore (McFarlane and Silver 2017; Thieme et al. 2017; Lancione 2019). Thinking post-categorically—of allowing oneself to inhabit the space of multiple grammars of the urban ground—is about intervening in the writing and speaking of "the city" so as to alter assumed ways of *containing* it. Let us, for example, examine how the categories of urban economy, welfare, and governance can be reimagined.

Consider how the received categories of urban economy are forced open by the ground material of urban value generation, distribution, and reproduction together with the making of the everyday economy in between political economy, makeshift practices, and infrastructural provision. Staple categories such as urban "supply" and "demand," "scale and scope," "competitive advantage," and "formality and informality" cede to a narrative of value generation that would recognize the interdependencies of sociality, organization, infrastructures, and urban property. Accordingly, new value circuits press for recognition in the urban economic calculus, as do unrecognized interdependencies of value creation. A different kind of supply-side economics emerges, one attending to the powers of infrastructure, the performances of technology, the circulations of passion, the differentials of social performativity, and the heavy weight of legal and property relations: all nuances of how the city works as a sociotechnical and cultural arrangement that both enables and disables economic life, unevenly shaping its allocations and rewards. A politics of infrastructure, sentiments, tenure, and conduct inserts itself into the calculus of urban economic management, and of struggles for economic justice informed by grassroots organization manifest in all but the most corporatized segments of an urban economy (from the makeshift and informal to the cooperative and circular).

A similar disruption of the given categories of urban welfare is forced by attending to actual dwelling practices: to how humans and nonhumans in interaction make and meet the everyday ends. This is not to deny the categories of class, gender, race, or any other form of classification that typically correlates with inequalities of social provisioning and recognition. Instead, it is to interrogate these classifications through an analysis of the lived material practices of urban inhabitation, subtly shifting the focus toward the urban constitution of well-being and its differentials through the dwelling of urban material—the interdependencies of technology, biology, habitat, infrastructure, and their contextual histories. Such a grammar of the urban social based on the composites of dwelling opens the ground for an associated *politics of the composites*. Over and above interventions around the quantities and qualities of housing, schooling, health care, jobs, and green spaces, a politics of the composites might attend to topological influences on welfare such as urban size, sprawl, and density, to the mediations of supply, service, and housing infrastructures, to the many informal curative practices of city dwellers toward each other and their environments, to the myriad micro-fascisms that spoil social life, and, in general, to delving into the daily matter of welfare.

In the grammars of this book, urban politics finds itself sandwiched between top-down efforts to manage urban complexity and bottom-up efforts to claim the city on the behalf of particular interests, between varieties of managerialism and varieties of interest politics. Both bend toward altering conduct by adjusting the frames of governance, representation, and participation—that is, the "rules" of political power and responsibility in the city. An attention to the grammars of the urban ground bends toward a politics of adjustment of the lively agencies-in-relation that produce the distortions and discriminations of everyday life and reward in the repetitions of instituted routine. Its interventions veer toward altering the terms and means by which the powers of the urban mechanosphere operate, recursively, to discriminatory ends. Its language becomes that of intervening in the pinch points and strategic nodes of critical urban networks, enabling the public and popular control of infrastructures, habitats, and neighborhoods, drawing on law and political assemblies to reorder city material workings, and acknowledging the agency of manifold actants involved in a city's constitutive fabric (Easterling 2014; Amin and Thrift 2016).

Lexical Openings

In assembling this book, we asked our authors to start from these broader entry points of urban economy, welfare, and governance, and then to show what a nondogmatic, open, and critical urban epistemology might look like. We invited colleagues who, we believe, have decisively contributed in the past decades to push the boundaries of urban theory along the lines we have identified in this introduction. We asked them to vivify the meanings of value creation, well-being, and agency. And from such rein-sertion of the city both as a *topology* (for example, its scale or density) and *from below* (detailing city-making) into various domains of urban life, we asked them to propose a new way of thinking and dealing with the city *from within* (reimagining city-politics). The variety of styles, settings, geographies, and urban assemblages analyzed in the book were chosen purposefully to offer a number of orientations and opportunities for scholars, practitioners, policy-makers, and activists intrigued by the chance of rethinking the way cities can be studied ground-up and organized plurally, beyond what is still taught in many urban theory courses around the globe. Their propositions are very much about writing the urban political, where the language used to encapsulate what it is to be done by whom constitutes an operational opening. The language itself is key in keeping urban politics on the move, pressing to recognize and attain more, reach out further, and close the gap between the real and the desired.

In this spirit, we open the book with Natalie Oswin's reflections on the relationship between queer thinking and urban theory. Exploring the treat-ment of sexuality in Burgess and Park's foundational work on the city of Chicago, Oswin reminds us that no grammar is really ever "new": the grav-itational pull of "old" debates and frames is always there, cutting through or feeding back, even when that takes a contested form. In looking through this history, one can see how the relationship between (hetero)normative (and categorical) urban thought and queer thinking is more than a simple matter of oppositions. Perhaps what is needed is not *yet another* theory: that is, not a Queer Urban Theory naming a radical queer urban sensibility. This is because what Oswin, following but also reworking Park and Burgess, calls "social junk"—a "capitalist surplus composed of gendered, sexualized, racialized, and classed . . . waste" that traditionally is contained, silenced by, and sanitized within the canon of urban studies—does not require a new theory in its name, but instead needs a "queering" move that makes space for lateral, nonpresumptive ways of thinking the urban. As we note in this introduction, such a move is about fostering forms of post-categorical thinking that suspend *explanation* in favor of a lexicon carved out from the grounds, to crack the ceiling of overly ordered theory and practice. Oswin signals that the *queering* of urban thinking requires an ear not only to the post-categorical but also to the "multi-modal," which is situated in a trans-versal "urban undercommons."

In chapter 2, Ananya Roy brings to the fore a foundational aspect of thinking cities from the ground of "social junk." Building on the turn toward "southern" urban theorizing, in which she has had a prominent role, Roy addresses the methods of "reworlding" urban inquiry. If it must include the fundamental work of foregrounding colonial lineages, it also must engage in "the task of resituating the cities of the global North in the long history of racial capitalism, including slavery, settler-colonialism, and imperialism," she suggests. To this end, Roy introduces the notion of "racial banishment" so as to foreground the "structuring processes of racial capitalist and settler logics of spatial settlement and expulsion" in explaining urban displacement using the language of gentrification or eviction. In adopting the language of "banishment" and its underpinnings in racial capitalism, she proposes a contrasting grammar to understand—and act on—enduring forms of urban dispossession. This shift is deeply political. It is about exposing the epistemic violence of concepts and methodologies "that persistently obscure the forms of racialized dispossession through which the American metropolis has been built." It is about showing how the way in which concepts are built reflects the kind of urban political they can both reveal and deal with (de Sousa Santos 2016): in today's context, exposing how the consequences of racial banishment are occluded yet exacerbated by grammars of austerity management and large-scale biological threat such as COVID-19 (Lancione and Simone 2020).

In the third chapter, Colin McFarlane unpacks the political economy of another keyword, *density*—widely understood as a foundational urban principle. He proposes a double move so as to recenter urban density from a decolonial, processual, and comparative perspective. He argues the need to decouple *density* from celebratory staples derived from emblematic (northern) forms of urban agglomeration, so that "an alternative archive of knowledge about urban density" can be produced from multiple lived experiences revealing how densities are "at once vital for remaking the city, and increasingly at risk all over the urban world." This *force of density* is proposed by McFarlane as a key component of making the urban political, shifting "density" away from being an a posteriori phenomenon to register and replicate, toward attending to "density's knowledge politics" and its situated possibilities in specific historic settings, citing evidence from his extensive fieldwork in cities such as Mumbai and Hong Kong. From the ground of experience, density returns as a heterogeneous category activated in the efforts of various urban subjects in contested ways, offering yet another example of the valence of writing the city back into urban theory *in order to* open new avenues of practice. Here, policy is not called to "act upon" but rather "to learn from, in a concerted and ongoing way, the heterogeneity of dense lived urbanisms that already exist in the city, and to attempt to augment those."

In a similar vein, in chapter 4 Nigel Thrift refashions the contours of another urban keyword—*size*—steering us clear of magical formulations of possibility or disablement arising out of "bigness" in contemporary city life. Cities around the globe, he observes, have seen not only ballooning populations but also amplifications arising from their insertion in a myriad of larger and larger world-spanning communication networks. Size has become ontological and formative, but in far from clear or straightforward ways. Thrift delves into the cultural paradoxes of urban scaling up and out, one being the challenge of standing out "from the urban crowd in an era in which standing out from the crowd has become an insistent predicate to action." He notes how the pursuit of originality has now become a mass pursuit by urbanites with the means of "making life into a series of peak experiences . . . something close to a sacred mission," with cities being expected to feed and be measured by the experience of "intensity." These cultural shifts, for Thrift, challenge conventional understandings of urban innovation premised on the amassment of culture and creativity, since originality is "the result of heavily contingent and contextual interactions, the outcomes of which are often decided only in the moment." In-the-moment fashioning, with significant repercussions, requires "other words for processes that unfold in cities that will always—always—be partially unknowable," and necessitates an urban vocabulary with words reaching out into the unknown and the uncertain.

In chapter 5, Mariana Valverde unpacks both the power and the contingency of law, which too often is viewed in urban studies as being remote and fixed in the arena of urban governance. She argues that the legal forms chosen by actors in specific situations—"property forms, land tenure forms, contracts, municipal legal tools, national laws—encourage certain ways of living and acting together, often in invisible and/or unintended ways, while discouraging others." These are ways that are never "wholly predictable or inevitable" both because of the variety of legal pathways that could be chosen and because of the politics of consensus and conflict surrounding a legal course of action. Valverde examines a diverse set of legal forms enacted by private and public interests to show how the detail of action and sociopolitical enrollment shapes outcomes in unpredictable directions (one example being a gated community using a contractual option to tax itself to build a swimming pool that will also benefit neighboring communities, serving "the same purpose as a municipal swimming pool, even if it is privately owned and privately built"). Valverde's chapter underscores the value of seeing how "legal structures and legal tools have a 'constitutive effect' on social life including civic habits of urban citizenship."

These first five chapters refine and expand our earlier entreaty for grammars of the ground by reimagining some of the staples of contemporary urbanism and the urban canon. The remaining chapters take this thinking further, more explicitly foregrounding detailed ethnographic material. In choosing to present our authors' contributions this way, we editors obviously do not intend to create a distinction between more "theoretical" and more "empirical" material. All the accounts presented here are focused on the dynamic compositions of the urban grounds: some authors decided to center their reflections and theorizations spurring from the latter, while others preferred to stay closer to narrating the unfolding of everyday assemblages. Both these strategies (and many others, we are sure!) are valid ways of experimenting with grammars of the urban ground that are attentive both to a foundational critique of urban knowledge-production and to the multiplicitous and contested nature of the assemblage we call "urban."

The authors' accounts, based in most cases on their decades of direct engagement with urban formations and struggles around the world, are rooted in composite—atmospheric, materialist, processual, and "lively"—readings of urban infrastructures, histories, and entrenched inequalities. The conceptual language exceeds that of "critical urban theory" and assemblage urbanism. Yet, like the latter, in bringing together and tracing the everyday formations of more-than-human urban life *in order to* better understand and oppose embedded and contingent power unbalances, each chapter with its own signature words offers a prime example of how thinking with the language of the ground opens "queer" insights and motivations.

Teresa Caldeira's chapter on everyday life in the peripheries of São Paulo, Brazil, is informed by her more than forty years of fieldwork in the city on practices of autoconstruction, the gender politics of LGBTQ+ activists, and youth art and digital expression. Her resulting text foregrounds the concept of *transitoriness* to encapsulate the social dynamic of time, everyday rhythm, and aspiration in that enormous city. According to Caldeira, the new social dynamic—particularly among the youth—is less oriented toward a "certain desired and anticipated future that is supposed to be better or more advanced or developed," or toward "settling down" and investing in "fixed spaces." Like the subjects in AbdouMaliq Simone in chapter 10, the youth in São Paulo seem to be living *through* their city, in constant circulation, deploying a series of "lateral moves" to get along in an environment that has lost the capacity to propose a clear pathway. These movements are a strategy (against institutionalized repression) but they also signal "a certain relationship to the city: a relationship of exploration, conquest and possession, even if only temporary"—in short, a refusal to stay put. Crucially, Caldeira's chapter shows how *transitoriness* has now become the "organizing logic of the everyday" whose grammar is in dire need of being wrested from that of the authoritarian forces looming large in the Brazilian political landscape.

In chapter 7 Filip De Boeck, again based on his decades of work in the streets of Kinshasa, the Democratic Republic of the Congo, presents how the simple word and object *hole* (as in a hole in a pockmarked street) vies for analytical and political attention, used commonly by residents to describe infrastructural degradation but also new openings amid the closures and ruinations of that postcolonial city. The city, as De Boeck it, is "no longer the steady, stable, impenetrable, and leveled horizontality of the modernist urban ground but instead opens up a much more bumpy and even incoherent landscape in which the underground of the hole literally becomes foreground and surface, the very center of the vortex that the city is." In this situation, the language of the "hole" describes the "shady deals" that residents have to make to survive, the sideways moves into "often uncharted spatial, social, and mental territory that the city obliges them to make," and the literal opportunities presented to make a transaction (such as makeshift market stalls around potholes to offer goods to slowed down and diverted traffic). So much for so many hangs around the literal and figurative topography of the "hole," which is barely noticed in urban writing but is so essential to grasp, according to De Boeck, so as to encapsulate life lived on the street and to bring it to public attention with the help of texts, photographs, and art projects making the invisibilities tangible.

In another novel slant on the affordances of infrastructure, Caroline Knowles in chapter 8 takes a street view to look into how finance capital and its plutocracy, so central to many primary cities, are materially sustained in central London. Adopting an "operational approach" involving a ground ethnography of walking around and getting close up to people and things, Knowles covets "a grainier and more practical grasp of infrastructure for its human, algorithmic, and material textures, operations and micro-mechanisms" so as to expose "some of its less obvious compositional mechanisms as they unfold empirically in the everyday heave of city life." In the case of London's money machine and its subjects, this approach brings into view "a slightly ragged female labor force in cheap clothes eating hasty lunches," "the human and technological security operations that contain, regulate, and exclude the atmospheres of quiet entitlement exchanged over lavish lunches or practiced in a daytime yoga class," even the "elaborate domestic operations supporting wealthy lifestyles." Complex entanglements are revealed, as is the enjoined and *fragile* labor of the assemblage of software, buildings, cultural practices, and many more elements that are involved in maintaining what Knowles calls London's plutocratic life and its excesses. If the fine grain of such exposure can be extracted, according to her, a resulting politics denormalizing the assemblages "places their construction in question, exposes them to the public gaze, suggests things could have been otherwise, shows that particular political decisions and actions, rather than others, were in play, that things need not be as they are, they could, in fact be quite different."

In chapter 9, Tatiana Thieme and Edgar Pieterse propose a critical reflection on everyday economies in urban Africa, in particular what counts as "work." They show how "the notions and everyday practices of work in African cities have consistently countered ideals of large-scale industrial wage employment," especially among the youth, now defying staple outlines for labor market entry and engagement. Looking beyond silencing mainstream economic categories opens the possibility of narrating *how* the economy there is felt and lived, and how it could be better sustained rather than subsumed. Thieme and Pieterse propose an *affirmative vocabulary*, able to encompass actual logics and knowledges of making a living, but they also recognize everyday struggles of *"doing business"* and *"tending to matters of social justice."* In conducting extensive ethnographic work with Mathare youths in Nairobi, the authors propose an idea of a just economy that is based on *radical social enterprise*, exemplified by progressive youth projects combining income generation with a social mission. Such acknowledgments alert us to affirmative capacity in everyday economic arrangements in a raft of cities as involving far more than mere survival. They speak to "the imperative to phase out an industrial and linear economic approach, recognize the prevalence of a post-wage era, and become the driving force (for better or worse) of digital platforms."

Similarly, AbdouMaliq Simone in chapter 10 builds on his long-standing lexicon of everyday negotiations and improvisations in cities of the Global South, to name the pathways—both ubiquitous and necessary—taken by dwellers engaging in nonlinear navigation of their cities, livelihoods, and aspirations. Simone draws from his archive of ethnographic evidence to trace the fugitive *lateral moves* and circulations through which residents in various cities make ends meet, with the "growing sense that livelihood is not secured through a continuous, incremental 'upward' trajectory." Citing tactics in Jakarta, Simone notes that a key disposition is that of comparison, based on "maximum exposure" to one's own increasingly complex and volatile surroundings. Residents elect not to pin things down and refuse "to provide accounts, either to oneself or to others, about how one's life course at any particular moment connects to those of others." Comparison, especially among the competing middle classes, stems less from having a fixed point of reference than from keeping things in circulation, *deforming*, as Simone puts it, the temporalities and spatialities of one's own life in attunement with those of Jakarta at large. With this turn he brings into view an urban praxis of "maximum exposure" to other circulations in order to seize opportunities of living and inhabiting the city that would not be otherwise possible: a behavioral version of the sociotechnologies that support London plutocrats, as Knowles details in chapter 8.

All the contributions in this collection recover the neglected or occluded "edge" as the urban heartland, proposed explicitly as a term in the last chapter by Suzanne Hall as a relation to power from which the everyday and its subjects can push back. Based on her extensive research on migrant businesses operating in the streets of South London, though regularly ignored by local authorities always looking to large retail for urban regeneration, Hall argues that "from the street we learn of different vocabularies of making work and repurposing space," requiring an "engagement with the edge as neither a peripheral nor minority condition, but as a space from which to push back, refute, and reconfigure." In such "edge territories," we see how "the combined systemic violations of state and market have disproportionate impact, and where intersections of 'race,' class, and locale surface the discriminatory impacts of dispossession." But she also shows how occupants "acquire improvisational repertoires to contend with the permanence of inequality and uncertainty," their "densely invested interiors . . . a form of everyday politics, sustained in the frictions and promises of social interaction and the wide array of cultural expression." While London—and, for that matter, many other large cities in the world—languish under austerity, having been abandoned by the "high capital" that once served them, microbusinesses improvise to sustain livelihoods and ways of life: shunned by the formal powers, people are calling out for recognition.

Conclusion

The lexicon of this book—made of junk, racial banishment, densities and scales, legal forms, transitoriness, saturations, infrastructures, deformations, edges, and affirmatory vocabularies—comes out of an effort, on the part of theorists and activists alike, to write back the grounds of the city into the *urban* in ways that are committed to social justice and radical change. The "political" here lies both in the subtle conceptual work of displacing policy-redundant "city buzz" (and related "theory") and in the effort to narrate how the ecologies and biopolitics making up the ground of urban life "become political": not simply in the sense of being matters of collective concern but in the sense of being part of, and therefore of shaping, everyday praxis of urban contestation. We believe the commitment to these two points, reflected also in a more discursive style of writing, is what characterizes innovative urban thinking today.

We have chosen to fashion a post-categorical vocabulary attuned to material practices and lived cultures in the city. Its concepts bring us closer to junctures and intersections, rework master concepts such as density and size, and begin to point at an urbanism worked in and through the assemblages of everyday experience. They point at a politics of radical adjustment, in the dual sense of being rooted and subaltern. We believe these efforts—of pushing established boundaries and ways of doing urban scholarship—are more important now than ever. The challenges and deep restructurings brought forward by COVID-19 around the globe, along with the likely austerity-mode to which many urban and national agencies will turn in years to come (RHJ Editorial Collective 2020), require our giving close attention to ground processes: both those annihilated by this and future crises, and those that will fight back, silently, from the enmeshments of the lived city. We see this book as offering a space to engage with some of the grammars needed to rethink urban process and the grounded politics of urban change.

References

Ahmed, Sara. 2007. *The Cultural Politics of Emotion*. London: Routledge.
Allen, Chris, and Rob Imrie, eds. 2010. *The Knowledge Business. The Commodification of Urban and Housing Research*. Farnham: Ashgate.
Amin, Ash. 2012. *Land of Strangers*. Cambridge: Polity Press.
Amin, Ash, and Nigel Thrift. 2002. *Cities, Reimagining the Urban*. Cambridge: Polity Press.

Amin, Ash, and Nigel Thrift. 2016. *Seeing Like a City*. Cambridge: Polity Press.

Anderson, Ben. 2014. *Encountering Affect: Capacities, Apparatuses, Conditions*. Farnham: Ashgate.

Arabindoo, Pushpa. 2018. "Writing the City [into the Urban]. Workshop Precis." Paris: Institut d'études avancées de Paris.

Bhambra, Gurminder K., Dalia Gebrial, and Kerem Nişancıoğlu, eds. 2018. *De-Colonising the University*. London: Pluto Press.

Bhan, Gautam. 2016. *In the Public's Interest: Evictions, Citizenship, and Inequality in Contemporary Delhi*. Geographies of Justice and Social Transformation 30. Athens: University of Georgia Press.

Bonta, Mark, and John Protevi. 2004. *Deleuze and Geophilosophy: A Guide and Glossary*. Vol. 37. Edinburgh: Edinburgh University Press. https://doi.org/10.1111/j.1475-4762.2005.655c.x.

Buchanan, Ian. 1997. "The Problem of the Body in Deleuze and Guattari, Or, What Can a Body Do?" *Body and Society* 3, no. 3: 73–91. https://doi.org/10.1177/1357034X97003003004.

Bulkeley, Harriet, Vanesa Castán Broto, and Gareth A. S. Edwards. 2014. *An Urban Politics of Climate Change: Experimentation and the Governing of Socio-Technical Transitions*. London: Routledge.

Castán Broto, Vanesa. 2019. *Urban Energy Landscapes*. Cambridge: Cambridge University Press. https://doi.org/10.1017/9781108297868.

Castells, Manuel. 1990. *The Informational City: A New Framework for Social Change*. Toronto: Centre for Urban and Community Studies.

Chattopadhyay, S. 2012. *Unlearning the City: Infrastructure in a New Optical Field*. Minneapolis: University of Minnesota Press.

Datta, Ayona. 2012. *The Illegal City: Space, Law and Gender in a Delhi Squatter Settlement*. Farnham: Ashgate.

De Boeck, Filip. 2015. "'Divining' the City: Rhythm, Amalgamation and Knotting as Forms of 'Urbanity.'" *Social Dynamics* 41, no. 1: 47–58. https://doi.org/10.1080/02533952.2015.1032508.

Deleuze, Gilles, and Felix Guattari. 1987. *A Thousand Plateaus*. New York: Continuum.

Easterling, Keller. 2014. *Extrastatecraft: The Power of Infrastructure Space*. London: Verso.

Escobar, Arturo. 2007. "The 'Ontological Turn' in Social Theory: A Commentary on 'Human Geography without Scale,' by Sallie Marston, John Paul Jones II and Keith Woodward." *Transactions of the Institute of British Geographers* 32, no. 1: 106–111. https://doi.org/10.1111/j.1475-5661.2007.00243.x.

Escobar, Arturo. 2018. *Designs for the Pluriverse: Radical Interdependence, Autonomy, and the Making of Words*. Durham, NC: Duke University Press.

Farías, Ignacio, and Thomas Bender, eds. 2010. *Urban Assemblages: How Actor-Network Theory Changes Urban Studies*. London: Routledge.

Flyvbjerg, Bent. 2001. *Making Social Science Matter: Why Social Inquiry Fails and How It Can Succeed Again*. Cambridge: Cambridge University Press.

Foucault, Michel. 1980. *Power/Knowledge: Selected Interviews and Other Writings 1972–1977*. Edited by C. Gordon. London: Harvester Press.

Gibbons, Andrea. 2018. *City of Segregation: 100 Years of Struggle for Housing in Los Angeles*. London: Verso.

Gibson-Graham, Julie Katherine. 2014. "Rethinking the Economy with Thick Description and Weak Theory." *Current Anthropology* 55, no. 9: 147–153.

Grosz, Elizabeth, 1993. "A Thousand Tiny Sexes: Feminism and Rhizomatics." *Topoi* 12, no. 2: 167–179.

Harman, Graham. 2009. *Prince of Networks: Bruno Latour and Metaphysics*. Melbourne: Re.Press.

Harvey, David. 1985. *The Urbanization of the Capital: Studies in the History and Theory of Capitalist Urbanization*. Baltimore: Johns Hopkins University Press.

Heynen, Nik, Maria Kaika, and Erik Swyngedouw, eds. 2006. *In the Nature of Cities: Urban Political Ecology and the Politics of Urban Metabolism*. New York: Routledge.

Katz, Cindi. 1996. "Towards Minor Theory." *Environment and Planning D: Society and Space* 14, no. 4: 487–499.

Katz, Cindi. 2017. "Revisiting Minor Theory." *Environment and Planning D: Society and Space* 35, no. 4: 596–599. https://doi.org/10.1177/0263775817718012.

Kern, Leslie. 2020. *Feminist City*. London: Verso.

Lancione, Michele, ed. 2016. *Rethinking Life at the Margins: The Assemblage of Contexts, Subjects and Politics*. London: Routledge, Taylor and Francis.

Lancione, Michele. 2018. "The Politics of Embodied Precarity: Roma People and the Fight for the Right to Housing in Bucharest, Romania." *Geoforum* 101: 182–191.

Lancione, Michele. 2019. "Weird Exoskeletons: Propositional Politics and the Making of Home in Underground Bucharest." *International Journal of Urban and Regional Research* 43, no. 3: 535–550. https://doi.org/10.1111/1468-2427.12787.

Lancione, Michele, and Colin McFarlane. 2016. "Life at the Urban Margins: Sanitation Infra-Making and the Potential of Experimental Comparison." *Environment and Planning A* 48, no. 12: 2402–2421. https://doi.org/10.1177/0308518X16659772.

Lancione, M., and C. McFarlane, eds. 2021. *Global Urbanism: Knowledge, Power and the City*. New York: Routledge.

Lancione, Michele, and AbdouMaliq Simone. 2020. "Bio-Austerity and Solidarity in the COVID-19 Space of Emergency." *Society and Space Magazine*. https://www.societyandspace.org/articles/bio-austerity-and-solidarity-in-the-covid-19-space-of-emergency.

Larkin, Brian. 2013. "The Politics and Poetics of Infrastructure." *Annual Review of Anthropology* 42: 327–343.

Latour, Bruno. 2005. *Reassembling the Social*. Oxford: Oxford University Press.

Lefebvre, Henri. 2008. *Writing on Cities*. Edited by Eleonore Kofman and Elizabeth Lebas. Oxford: Blackwell Publishing.

Lindner, Robert. 2006. *The Reportage of the Urban Culture: Robert Park and the Chicago School*. Cambridge: Cambridge University Press.

Marcuse, Peter. 2009. "From Critical Urban Theory to the Right to the City." *City* 13, no. 2–3: 185–197. https://doi.org/10.1080/13604810902982177.

Massey, Doreen. 1993. "Power Geometry and a Progressive Sense of Place." In *Mapping the Futures: Local Cultures, Global Change*, edited by John Bird, Barry Curtis, Tim Putnam, and Lisa Tickner. London: Routledge.

Massey, Doreen. 1994. *A Global Sense of Place*. Minneapolis: University of Minnesota Press.

Massumi, Brian. 1992. *A User's Guide to Capitalism and Schizophrenia: Deviations from Deleuze and Guattari*. Cambridge, MA: MIT Press.

McCann, Eugene. 2008. "Expertise, Truth, and Urban Policy Mobilities: Global Circuits of Knowledge in the Development of Vancouver, Canada's 'four Pillar' Drug Strategy." *Environment and Planning A* 40, no. 4: 885–904. https://doi.org/10.1068/a38456.

McCann, Eugene. 2013. "Policy Boosterism, Policy Mobilities, and the Extrospective City." *Urban Geography* 34, no. 1: 5–29. https://doi.org/10.1080/02723638.2013.778627.

McFarlane, Colin. 2011. *Learning the City: Knowledge and Translocal Assemblage*. Oxford: Wiley Blackwell.

McFarlane, Colin, and Jonathan Silver. 2017. "The Poolitical City: 'Seeing Sanitation' and Making the Urban Political in Cape Town." *Antipode* 49, no. 1: 125–148. https://doi.org/10.1111/anti.12264.

Oswin, Natalie. 2018. "Planetary Urbanization: A View from Outside." *Environment and Planning D: Society and Space* 36, no. 3: 540–546. https://doi.org/10.1177/0263775816675963.

Oswin, Natalie. 2020. "An Other Geography." *Dialogues in Human Geography* 10, no. 1: 9–18. https://doi.org/10.1177/2043820619890433.

Park, Robert E. 1936. "Human Ecology." *The American Journal of Sociology* 42, no. 1: 1–15.

Perry, Keisha-Khan. 2013. *Black Women against the Land Grab: The Fight for Racial Justice in Brazil*. Minneapolis: University of Minnesota Press.

RHJ Editorial Collective. 2020. "Covid-19 and Housing Struggles: The (Re) Makings of Austerity, Disaster Capitalism, and the No Return to Normal." *Radical Housing Journal* 2, no. 1: 9–28.

Robinson, Jennifer. 2005. *Ordinary Cities: Between Modernity and Development*. London: Routledge.

Rolnik, Raquel. 2019. *Urban Warfare: Housing Under the Empire of Finance*. New York: Verso.

Roy, Ananya. 2017. "Dis/Possessive Collectivism: Property and Personhood at City's End." *Geoforum* 80 (March): A1–11. https://doi.org/10.1016/j.geoforum.2016.12.012.

Roy, Ananya. 2019. "Racial Banishment." In *Keywords in Radical Geography: Antipode at 50*. New York: Wiley-Blackwell.

Roy, Ananya. 2020. "'The Shadow of Her Wings': Respectability Politics and the Self-Narration of Geography." *Dialogues in Human Geography* 10, no. 1: 19–22. https://doi.org/10.1177/2043820619898899.

Roy, Ananya, and Emma Shaw Crane, eds. 2015. *Territories of Poverty: Rethinking North and South*. Georgia: University of Georgia Press.

Roy, Ananya, and Aihwa Ong, eds. 2011. *Worlding Cities: Asian Experiments and the Art of Being Global*. London: Wiley-Blackwell.

Sassen, Saskia. 2002. *Cities in a World Economy*. London: Sage.

Shabazz, Rashad 2015. *Spatializing Blackness: Architectures of Confinement and Black Masculinity in Chicago*. Chicago: University of Illinois Press.

Simone, AbdouMaliq. 2004. *For the City Yet to Come: Changing African Life in Four Cities*. Durham, NC: Duke University Press.

Simone, AbdouMaliq. 2010. *City Life from Jakarta to Dakar: Movements at the Crossroads*. London: Routledge.

Simone, AbdouMaliq, and Edgar Pieterse. 2017. *New Urban Worlds: Inhabiting Dissonant Times*. Cambridge: Polity Press.

Sousa Santos, Boaventura de. 2016. *Epistemologies of the South: Justice Against Epistemicide*. London: Routledge.

Stengers, Isabelle. 2005. "The Cosmopolitical Proposal." In *Making Things Public: Atmospheres of Democracy*, edited by Bruno Latour and Peter Weibel, 994–1003. Cambridge, MA: MIT Press.

Stengers, Isabelle. 2010. *Cosmopolitics I*. London: University of Minnesota Press.

Stewart, Kathleen. 2007. *Ordinary Affects*. Durham, NC: Duke University Press.

Thieme, Tatiana. 2017. "The Hustle Economy: Informality, Uncertainty and the Geographies of Getting By." *Progress in Human Geography*, February, 0309132517690039. https://doi.org/10.1177/0309132517690039.

Thieme, Tatiana, Michele Lancione, and Elisabetta Rosa. 2017. "The City and Its Margins: Ethnographic Challenges across Makeshift Urbanism: Introduction." *City* 21, no. 2: 127–134. https://doi.org/10.1080/13604813.2017.1353331.

Truelove, Yaffa. 2018. "Negotiating States of Water: Producing Illegibility, Bureaucratic Arbitrariness, and Distributive Injustices in Delhi." *Environment and Planning D: Society and Space* 36, no. 5: 949–967. https://doi.org/10.1177/0263775818759967.

Vasudevan, Alexander. 2015. *Metropolitan Preoccupations: The Spatial Politics of Squatting in Berlin*. London: Wiley-Blackwell.

Weheliye, Alexander. 2014. *Habeas Viscus: Racializing Assemblages, Biopolitics, and Black Feminist Theories of the Human*. Durham, NC: Duke University Press.

Whatmore, Sarah. 2002. *Hybrid Geographies: Natures Cultures Spaces*. London: Sage.

NATALIE OSWIN

SOCIAL JUNK

'What makes queer urban theory different? What does it bring to the fore?' These are the questions that the editors of this collection asked me to reflect on. There is no "queer urban theory," though. Not in a formal sense. To be clear, there is queer theory, there is urban theory, and there is a long-standing body of intellectually and politically important scholarship that connects the two. But there is no "queer urban theory." Queer scholarship is rarely explicitly acknowledged or engaged by urban theorists. It is off (or at least way out in the remote suburbs of) the urban canonical map, and it has little overt impact on or influence within urban studies. "Queer urban theory" is simply not a sanctioned scholarly subfield. I therefore especially appreciate the editors' interest in including a chapter on queer thought in this effort to advance an urban "grammar of grammars." Like them, I believe that engaging with multiple critical urban grammars is crucial for opening up "opportunities for engaging, appropriating, and experimenting with what's at stake in the city" (Amin and Lancione, introduction). Queer must be in this lexicon. For sexuality is an "especially dense transfer point for relations of power" (Foucault 1978, 103) and, as such, "there are very general social crises that can only be understood from a position critical of the sexual order" (Warner 1991, 6).

But while I am all in for a multi-modal critical urban theory that reshuffles the landscape from below, I sound a note of caution and care in this chapter. As mentioned, queer thought on the urban and urbanization is not *new* but *sidelined*. Further, urban theory as effectively "straight" (and cisgender and white and male and Western) theory casts a long, problematic shadow. So, while there is no "queer urban theory" per se, queerness is not a void within urban theory. Instead, it is a residue, an elision, a shadowy presence. The queer, indeed the non-normative of various description, is everywhere within mainstream urban thought and praxis—as prop, as foil, as a problem in need of correction, as object out of place. In other words, though a minor ingredient, queer theory has been in the mix for a long time already. Its grammar, like all grammars, is dynamic and contested and contoured by multiple forces, and any effort to recuperate it for radical ends must know and grapple with its travels.

In what follows, I chart a tradition of queer urban studies as it emerged out of a dominant grammar, that of *The City*, the 1925 collection of essays by the Chicago School sociologists Robert Park and Ernest Burgess. Still widely taught today as "foundational" to urban theory, and reissued for a second time in 2019 (the first reissue was in 1967), this text is not only ripe for queer analysis. Its authors played a pivotal, paradoxical, and widely unrecognized role in spurring on queer and other critical "underdog" scholarship on the urban and urbanization that exist today. This text's role in the history of queer and urban studies as both facilitator and foil, I argue, shows that while there is no "queer urban theory" per se, queer aims may in fact be better met without one.

The City as Laboratory

In 1938, the famed Chicago School sociologist Ernest Burgess posed the following "true" or "false" exam question to students in his "social pathology" course: "In large cities, homosexual individuals tend to congregate rather than remain separate from each other" (Heap 2003, 467). This course was popular and offered regularly, and I will bet that he asked this question, or versions of it, many times over many years. I am also willing to wager that similar questions appear on exam scripts in urban studies courses to this day, and that, like Burgess, the scholarly questioners reward a tick in the "true" box. Now, as throughout the history of urban studies, LGBTQ+ politics, people, subcultures, and movements are not explicitly mentioned all that often within urban studies scholarship. When they are, in what we might refer to as "canonical" or "mainstream" urban studies, at least, the mention often consists of nothing more than an effort to pin down or locate "queer" within that urban morphological feature "the gay village." And then that's that; the sexuality and gender identity components of the course are considered complete, with only the barest of coverage despite the existence of huge bodies of literature that tell us so much more about queer ontologies and epistemologies of the urban and urbanization.[1]

Or so it seems. Sexuality and gender identity, in fact, run throughout all our urban studies courses and texts, particularly in the moments when queer lives and scholarship are highlighted, to be sure, but more importantly (and with great consequence for those "queer moments") also when they do not. And the work of Burgess and his collaborator, Park, plays an outsized role in creating this reality.

Consider Burgess and Park's "concentric zone" model (see figure 1.1). It is a staple within the urban studies canon and curriculum, consisting of five simple circles, laid out to purportedly portray how cities are carved up into functional bands of social and economic significance. As Robert Sampson states in his foreword to the 2019 edition of *The City*, this model is not without critique: "The concentric zone is a perennial punching bag . . . because it seems too simple and schematic" (Sampson 2019, ix). "But," Sampson continues, "Burgess himself said the concentric zone was but an ideal type that did not describe every city." He then quotes Andrew Abbott (whom he describes as "one of the Chicago School's strongest defenders"): "when we read a classic, we ignore the old ideologies and the odd phrases in order to focus on . . . the perennial, the permanent, the enduring" (Sampson 2019, x). I agree that we can learn a great deal from the endurance of the "concentric zone" model. I strongly disagree, however, that we should ignore its offenses. These, I argue, are crucial to understanding not just the model, but also urban studies' relationship to queerness, and much else.

The "concentric zone" model most commonly referred to today, as indeed it has been referred to for some years, is that depicted in figure 1.1. It is not a standalone depiction, however. In *The City*, another version appears four pages later, and this second version is that from which the first version is derived. In it (reproduced here as figure 1.2), text is overlaid on the circles, describing the "moral regions" of the city, the "black belt," the "slum," the "bright light area," and so on. Regardless of how subsequent scholars read the "concentric zones" and put them to use, this image illuminates its intellectual underpinnings. These are encapsulated in the following words, of Park's, in a chapter of *The City* about what he calls "juvenile delinquency":

> Our great cities, as those who have studied them have learned, are full of junk, much of it human, i.e., men and women who, for some reason or other, have fallen out of line in the march of industrial progress and have been scrapped by the industrial organization of which they were once a part. . . . In fact, the slum areas that invariably grow up just on the edge of the business areas

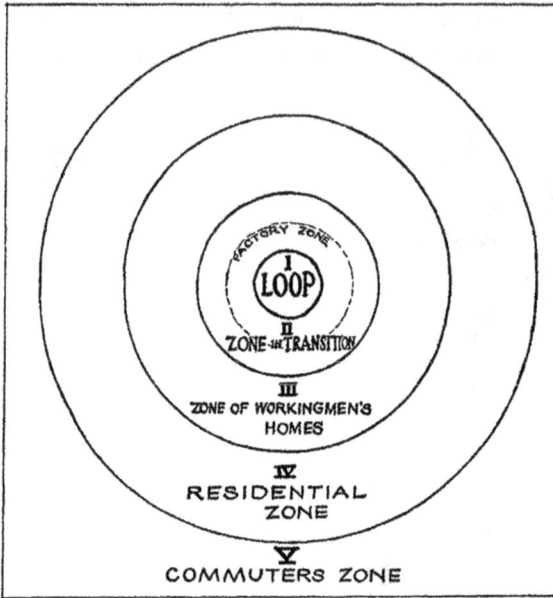

1.1 "The growth of the city." Source: Robert E. Park and Ernest W. Burgess, *The City* (2019 [1925])

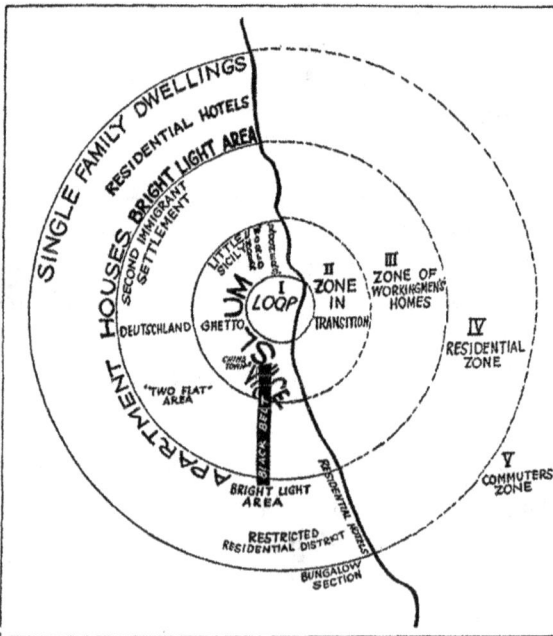

1.2 "Urban areas." Source: Robert E. Park and Ernest W. Burgess, *The City* (2019 [1925])

of great cities, areas of deteriorated houses, of poverty, vice, and crime, are areas of social junk (Park and Burgess 2019 [1925], 109).

Burgess and Park, like other "foundational" urban theorists who are also still widely taught (such as Georg Simmel and Louis Wirth), were centrally troubled by "social disorganization" in the city. They understood capitalist urbanization as a profoundly disruptive social force. They saw the city as "a product of nature, and particularly of human nature," indeed as "the natural habitat of civilized man" (Park and Burgess 2019 [1925], 2), and "in a chronic condition of crisis" (22). They state: "Under the disintegrating influences of city life most of our traditional institutions, the church, the school, and the family, have been greatly modified" (24). Park and Burgess's aim, in *The City* and in their wider body of work, was thus to study the city as a site of "unstable equilibrium" (22). They saw it as a "laboratory or clinic in which human nature and social processes may be conveniently and profitably studied" (46).

Study it they did. They and their students sorted the "social junk," cataloging "social type" after "social type." As Dennis Judd states: "An outpouring of studies of hobos, the homeless, 'taxi-dance' halls, gangs, prostitutes, ethnic and racial ghettos, and other groups and lifestyles documented the human behavior nurtured within the 'ecological crucible' of Chicago" (Judd 2001, 5). Park and Burgess and the many others working under their influence thus laid out a new "science" of urban studies. As Judd continues: "Any one of the studies might have seemed merely descriptive and studiously empirical, but for the Chicago researchers a larger picture emerged that revealed the deleterious effects of urban life" (2011, 6). This was highly impactful and field-defining work. Mary Jo Deegan notes: "The University of Chicago towered over the intellectual and professional landscape of sociology from 1892 until 1942. It reputedly trained over half of all sociologists in the world by 1930" (Deegan 2001, 11). Indeed, its studies have "long been cited as founding frameworks for sociological inquiry into the urban dynamics of race, ethnicity, delinquency and crime" (Heap 2003, 458), and, notably, not without considerable critique (a point I will return to below).

Lesser known, in part because most of the work is unpublished, many of Park and Burgess's students conducted work on homosexuality in the city. The sociologist Chad Heap (2003) examines this work, which is archived in the Burgess Papers at the University of Chicago. He discusses early Chicago School studies of homosexuality within student work on "the effects of mass publications [like newspapers and romance magazines] on sexual practices and ideas," in "an unpublished 'Glossary of Homosexual Terms' compiled by students at the university during the 1930s," and also in a "series of graduate theses and undergraduate research papers documenting a range of early twentieth-century urban social types" including "the homosexual" (Heap 2003, 474). As both Heap and the queer theorist Gayle Rubin (2002) note, this work was considered "remarkable" and "pioneering" for its day, as it was an early and unprecedented effort within American sociology not to study "homosexuals" as a biologically driven "species" but rather to "situate sexuality in a social context" (Heap 2003, 459). It unfortunately did largely still stigmatize "the homosexual," though. As Heap notes, "while Burgess argued that heterosexuality and homosexuality were both products of dynamic social relations, his research—and that of his students— continued to differentiate between these two practices by associating the former with sexual normativity and respectability and the latter with social pathology" (2003, 477, fn. 9).

Nonetheless, this work opened a door. While Michel Foucault is widely known as *the* scholar who challenged medicalized explanations for "homosexuality," as Gayle Rubin notes, "the work of establishing a social science approach to sex, of producing ethnographic studies of contemporary sexual populations, and of challenging the privileged role of psychiatry in the study of human sexuality was mostly accomplished by sociologists" (Rubin 2002, 21). After World War II, and especially in the 1950s and 1960s, the Chicago School tradition of urban ethnography continued. But, quoting Rubin again: "the post–World War II cohort did more than add to the literature on diverse concentrations of urban delinquents. Several of its members also developed a pervasive critique of the prevailing assumption that something was intrinsically wrong with deviants and misfits" (Rubin 2002, 26). By 1963, Erving Goffman published *Stigma: Notes on the Management of Spoiled Identity*, in which he challenged "the attitudes we normally have toward a person with a stigma." He continues, "By definition, of course, we believe the person with a stigma is not quite human. On this assumption we exercise varieties of discrimination, through which we effectively, if often unthinkingly, reduce his life chances" (Goffman 1963, 5). In 1967, Howard Becker, in the journal *Social Problems*, wrote: "When do we accuse ourselves and our fellow sociologists of bias? I think an inspection of representative instances would show that the accusation arises . . . when the research gives credence, in any serious way, to the perspective of the subordinate group in some hierarchical relationship. . . . We provoke the suspicion that we are biased in favor of the subordinate parties . . . when we tell the story from their point of view" (quoted in Rubin 2002, 26). Deviance studies thus began to be fractured, as some scholars started to shed the language of the "delinquent" for the language of the "underdog." This was a pivotal move, since the plight of social subjects within the social sciences (as everywhere else) depends, as the legal scholar Janet Halley clarifies, "not on who we are but how we are thought" (Halley 2000, 67).

The door opened wider still as deviance studies morphed into queer theory, among other impacts. The queer theorist Heather Love follows Rubin in re-narrating academic histories of queer studies that overlook its connections to deviance studies. Love states: "In its embrace of a politics of stigma and its reliance on a general category of social marginality, queer theory borrowed its account of difference from deviance studies" (Love 2015, 75). And this borrowing, this building, took a tortured and difficult path as the ideas laid out in *The City* about "social junk" had, and have, staying power. The brief story I am relating out here is by no means a simple one of "old" ideas or "grammars" being replaced by "new" or better ones. It is instead a story of struggle, perseverance, risk, and, all too often, negative material consequences for those outside the charmed circle of the academic–state–social services nexus.

As Heap (2003) notes, the studies that Park and Burgess and their students undertook on the "social organization of sexuality" were quite "remarkable for their day," a day in which medical and psychological models of sexuality prevailed. As already mentioned, though, they were at the same time in tune with "the day" insofar as they propped heterosexuality up as a norm and stigmatized homosexuality. The time did not dictate that they do this, though. In fact they exercised agency, and they advanced a particular politics. Contrast Park and Burgess with another Chicago School sociologist, W. I. Thomas. He studied sexuality, and especially the ways that "changing social conditions inevitably produced shifts in the construction of sexual norms and practices" within what he called "heterosexual communities." He and Florian Znaniecki, in their landmark five-volume text *The Polish Peasant in Europe and America* (1918–1920), looked at the ways that "normal" sex lives for Polish migrants to the United States included nonmarital sexual practices and even polygamy—distinct changes from sexual norms in the "old country." In other words, Thomas looked at shifts in sexual norms within middle-class white communities, in the context of growing social acceptance of divorce and non-monogamy. Further, Thomas rejected the findings of "vice commissions" as stigmatizing different modes of sexual expression while Park and Burgess worked on such commissions consistently, demonstrating "a willingness to participate directly in the regulation of urban sexuality and the maintenance of middle-class social norms" (Heap 2003, 464, fn. 7). Ultimately, Thomas himself was a victim of the vice crusades. After being found in a hotel room in 1918 with a woman who was not his wife, he was fired from the University of Chicago, even though the charges against him were eventually dropped. Later, in the 1930s, during an era of sex panics spurred on by the sorts of vice reports that Park and Burgess participated in producing, two more University of Chicago faculty members were arrested and eventually fired from the university for their "homosexual activities." The arrests were discussed widely on campus, and the "dismissals undoubtedly had a chilling effect on the study of homosexuality and other non-normative sexualities at the University of Chicago" (Heap 2003, 481).

So we see grammars in competition, as a factor of the differential power to produce knowledge that some hold over others. The city is not merely a "laboratory" for the study of "human nature," as Park and Burgess and many of their followers asserted. Not in the way they purport, anyway. In addition to the contrast with W. I. Thomas, consider their relation to Jane Addams, one of the recognized founders of social work as a field of study in the United States and a leader of the settlement house movement. Another contemporary of Park and Burgess's, and likewise associated with the University of Chicago, Addams knew their work well, as they did hers. Park and Burgess dismissed Addams' and the settlement house movement's work more broadly, though, saying it lacked scientific rigor, a dismissal bound up with their well-known antipathy toward female scholars (see Deegan 1988). This dismissal was one with significant repercussions, as it is credited with playing a large role in separating out social work from sociology, as well as the association of greater prestige with the latter field of inquiry. Addams likewise had views on Park and Burgess's work. As Daphne Spain states: "First, she disliked the idea that the settlement was merely an experimental site for the work of scholars: 'I have always objected to the phrase "sociological laboratory" applied to us, because Settlements should be much more human and spontaneous than such a phrase connotes.' Second, she would have asserted that the settlement was a precursor to the university, not the other way around, as Burgess claimed" (Spain 2011, 58; see also Deegan 1988).

As Sampson notes in the foreword to the 2019 edition of *The City*, Park and Burgess's work therefore does indeed exhibit "old ideologies." It exhibits sexism, homophobia, and prudishness, plus an arrogant sense of entitlement over the stories of others as scientific properties. The two sociologists did not merely study the city as a social laboratory, they produced it as such, as a laboratory of "care" for those poor social anomalies whom they cataloged and, interrelatedly, as a laboratory of punishment. And they did this with the weight of the scholarly establishment behind them, an establishment that, like Park and Burgess themselves, saw women, homosexuals, and perverts more as "social junk" than as valuable scholarly voices.

Nonetheless, some of these "underdogs," as Goffman and other deviance studies scholars might instead characterize them, persisted in the academy and finally came to the surface. For studies of sexuality, this personal and scholarly "breakthrough" is evident in the contemporary existence of a large body of queer theory. But, again, this is not simply a "new" grammar that holds potential to displace the "old." Rather, it is a "competing" grammar locked in a differential power relationship and following an overdetermined path. I turn to this point and its repercussions for queer and urban theory now.

The Trouble with Silos

"The time has come to think about sex." Gayle Rubin opens her essay "Thinking Sex" (1984), a widely considered founding text of queer theory, with this sentence. She continues: "To some, sexuality may seem to be an unimportant topic, a frivolous diversion from the more critical problems of poverty, war, disease, racism, famine, or nuclear annihilation. But it is precisely at times such as these, when we live with the possibility of unthinkable destruction, that people are likely to become dangerously crazy about sexuality" (Rubin 1984, 267). This bold statement is a far cry from the unpublished monographs on the oddities of "homosexual" urban communities that Park and Burgess's students undertook in the 1920s and 1930s. Her aim, and the aim of queer theory broadly, is a departure from the aims of the Chicago School sociologists discussed above. Rather than cataloging "social junk" in order to control and correct it for a liberal order, queer theory gives shelter to difference and seeks to enhance it so that we might build a radical future. Following Martin Manalansan, queer seeks to "mess" with the normal. He states: "Queer, as I conceptualize it, is about messing things up, creating disorder and disruptive commotion within the normative arrangements of bodies, things, spaces and institutions" (Manalansan 2015, 567). Rubin does this beautifully in "Thinking Sex." Moving far away from the "social type" approach to sexuality and (urban) space, she castigates homosexual "witch

The charmed circle:
Good, Normal, Natural,
Blessed Sexuality

Heterosexual
Married
Monogamous
Procreative
Non-commercial
In pairs
In a relationship
Same generation
In private
No pornography
Bodies only
Vanilla

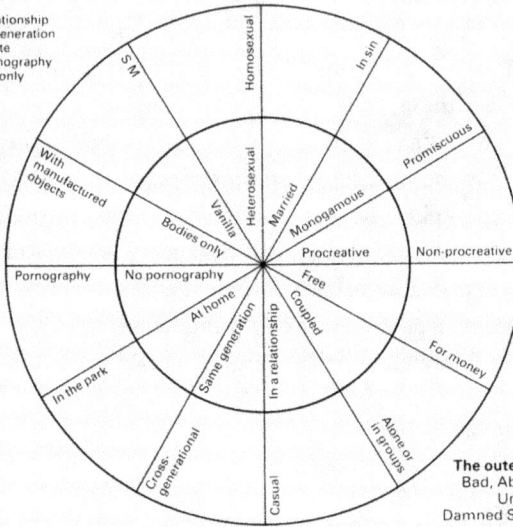

S M
Homosexual
In sin
With manufactured objects
Promiscuous
Vanilla
Heterosexual
Married
Monogamous
Bodies only
Procreative
Non-procreative
Pornography
No pornography
Free
At home
Same generation
In a relationship
Coupled
For money
In the park
Cross-generational
Casual
Alone or in groups

The outer limits:
Bad, Abnormal,
Unnatural,
Damned Sexuality

Homosexual
Unmarried
Promiscuous
Non-procreative
Commercial
Alone or in groups
Casual
Cross-generational
In public
Pornography
With manufactured objects
Sadomasochistic

1.3 "The charmed circle." Source: Gayle Rubin, "Thinking Sex: Notes for a Radical Theory of the Politics of Sexuality" (1984)

hunts," "moral panics," the regulation of prostitution and pornography, and more. Her diagram "The Charmed Circle" (see figure 1.3) pushes past facile descriptions of normal and abnormal sexual subjects to detail a "sex hierarchy" that affects *all* people. The distinction between this image and Park and Burgess's "moral regions" diagram (figure 1.2) is stark, and the contrasting political investments behind both images are clear. There is no "social junk" in Gayle Rubin's formulation, but instead social *systems* that flatten and sort human experiences into valued and devalued, fit and misfit, norm and freak.

Again, though, I cannot label Rubin's take a "new" grammar. As she notes in a reflection some years on from "Thinking Sex": "much of what we now take for granted in the anthropology of sexuality and homosexuality owes a great deal to an odd assortment of urban sociologists, historians of homosexuality, and brave, pioneering ethnographers who went where almost no one had gone before and undertook considerable risks to their careers to do so" (Rubin 2002, 54). She acknowledges the contingencies and curiosities of scholarship, stating: "When I finally did encounter Robert Park and Howard Becker, for example, they were shockingly familiar because their fingerprints were all over other texts I had read" (Rubin 2002, 3). "Old" debates and frames hang on through the canon, as performatives with both intended and unintended effects. Texts that break away from existing, established canons and help form alternate grammars—texts like "Thinking Sex"—are not immune from this gravitational pull. The "Charmed Circle" is an important departure from the "Moral Regions." But the two intellectual projects are nonetheless tethered, with the latter exercising influence on the former.

Park and Burgess's concentric zones obviously do much more than describe or reflect the city. They shape it, through the "real-world" reformist extensions (such as vice commissions) of their ideological underpinnings, most obviously, as well as through the ways they hem in scholarly thought. The zones function as silos of understanding. They flatten lived experiences into "social types" and transmute the segregated city of their authors' observations into segregated social imaginations. I've mentioned above, in separate parts of this essay, that Park and Burgess have been critiqued for their views on gender and normative sexuality, as well as on race. On the latter, Robert Sampson notes in his foreword to the 2019 edition of *The City* that even Andrew Abbott—the scholar whom, again, he describes as "one of the Chicago School's strongest defenders"—found that Park's views on race caused "one to be embarrassed" (2019, x; see Yu 2001 for an extended critique of racism and the Chicago School). But what of how these views on gender, sexuality, and race come together? Is the "Charmed Circle" really only about "sexual" hierarchies?

Roderick Ferguson provides answers in his 2004 book, *Aberrations in Black: Toward a Queer of Color Critique*. In it, he "tells a story of canonical sociology's regulation of people like the transgendered man, the sissy, and the bulldagger as part of its general regulation of African American culture" (Ferguson 2004, ix). Such people—those who "allegedly represent the socially disorganizing effects of capital," he writes—"play a powerful part in past and contemporary interpretations of political economy" (Ferguson 2004, 1). Ferguson shows clearly and powerfully how Park, Burgess, and other Chicago School sociologists deployed notions of depraved sexuality and inappropriate family forms to sort not merely sexualized subjects but also racialized subjects into categories of "junk" and "norm." He states: "The state's regulation of nonwhite gender and sexual practices through Americanization programs, vice commissions, residential segregation, and immigration exclusion attempted to press non-whites into gender and sexual conformity despite the gender and sexual diversity of those racialized groups" (2004, 14). The polymorphous social, sexual, and intimate formations of immigrant communities had to be tamed, in the view of "canonical" sociologists. "For New Dealers," he states, "restoring responsible intimacy meant eradicating the nonheteronormative formations that obstructed gender and sexual ideals held dear by middle-class whites. Restoring responsible intimacy also meant establishing heteropatriarchal households within minority communities" (Ferguson 2004, 37).

Thus, Ferguson and many others in the "queer of color" scholarly lineage (for example, see Muñoz 1999 and Reddy 2011) offer another "competing" grammar, blazing a different interconnected trail and further complicating the relationship between queer theory and urban theory. Sex and gender must be accounted for in the city, and so must race and migration. Holding all the components and categories in the same frame yields profoundly important results. That is, the concentric zones make visible a city and a worldview, simultaneously, and it takes a concerted effort to reveal the extent of its deliberate blind spots, to build connections across its conscious divides. While urban sexuality studies have been around in the United States since the days of Park and Burgess, at least, it took decades for queer theory to gain an institutional foothold, and decades more for a "queer of color" critique to complicate its narrative. This, at root, is why I do not think we actually need a queer urban theory, as consisting of an independent "grammar" in the multi-modal "grammars" of contemporary critical urban theory. There is no end, only auto-critique. There is no reading and writing to get to an answer, but instead to unlearn. Urban studies and queer studies, like everything else, both took shape under and persist within white supremacist heteropatriarchal capitalist conditions. So there is no "queer" savior. There is, instead, "social junk," a capitalist surplus composed of gendered, sexualized, racialized, and classed (and more, always more) waste. That is the grammar that we all, as urban theorists, dwell within, and must collectively work to rewire. As Ferguson argues, "as formations that transgress capitalist political economies, surplus populations become the locations for possible critiques of state and capital" (Ferguson 2004, 15). There is something admittedly "queer" about this argument, but also something anti-racist and anti-capitalist and feminist, and more. So while we need queer theory, we need it to be always already multi-modal, or, better yet, coalitional. We must think not from raced, classed, gendered, or sexualized subject positions, but from an urban undercommons. Then we can hope to seize the story of "social junk."

Note

1. Readers will also find the same paltry attention to LGBTQ+ lives and movements in the contents of virtually any textbook surveying urban studies today.

References

Deegan, Mary Jo. 1988. *Jane Addams and the Men of the Chicago School, 1892–1918*. New York: Routledge.

Deegan, Mary Jo. 2001. "The Chicago School of Ethnography." In *Handbook of Ethnography*, edited by Paul Atkinson, Amanda Coffey, Sara Delamont, John Lofland, and Lyn Lofland, 11–23. London: Sage.

Ferguson, Roderick. 2004. *Aberrations in Black: Toward a Queer of Color Critique*. Minneapolis: University of Minnesota Press.

Foucault, Michel. 1978: *The History of Sexuality: An Introduction, volume 1*. New York: Vintage Books.

Goffman, Ernest. 1963. *Stigma: Notes on the Management of Spoiled Identity*. Englewood Cliffs, NJ: Prentice Hall.

Halley, Janet E. 2000. "'Like Race' Arguments." In *What's Left of Theory? New Works on the Politics of Literary Theory*, edited by Judith Butler, John Guillory, and Kendall Thomas, 40–74. New York: Routledge.

Heap, Chad. 2003. "The City as a Sexual Laboratory: The Queer Heritage of the Chicago School." *Qualitative Sociology* 26, no. 4: 457–487.

Judd, Dennis R. 2001. "Theorizing the City." In *The City, Revisited: Urban Theory from Chicago, Los Angeles, and New York*, edited by Dennis R. Judd and Dick Simpson, 3–20. Minneapolis: University of Minnesota Press.

Love, Heather. 2015. "Doing Being Deviant: Deviance Studies, Description, and the Queer Ordinary." *Differences: A Journal of Feminist Cultural Studies* 26, no. 1: 74–95.

Manalansan, Martin. 2015. "Queer Worldings: The Messy Art of Being Global in Manila and New York." *Antipode* 47, no. 3: 566–579.

Muñoz, José. 1999. *Disidentifications: Queers of Color and the Performance of Politics*. Minneapolis: University of Minnesota Press.

Park, Robert E., and Ernest W. Burgess. 2019 [1925]. *The City*. Chicago: University of Chicago Press.

Reddy, Chandan. 2011. *Freedom with Violence: Race, Sexuality and the US State*. Durham, NC: Duke University Press.

Rubin, Gayle. 1984. "Thinking Sex: Notes for a Radical Theory of the Politics of Sexuality." In *Pleasure and Danger: Exploring Female Sexuality*, edited by Carole S. Vance, 267–319. Boston: Routledge and Kegan Paul.

Rubin, Gayle. 2002. "Studying Sexual Subcultures: Excavating the Ethnography of Gay Communities in Urban North America." In *Out in Theory*, edited by Ellen Lewin and William L. Leap, 17–68. Champaign: University of Illinois Press.

Sampson, Robert. 2019. "Foreword: *The City* for the Twenty-First Century." In Park and Burgess, *The City*, edited by Robert E. Park and Ernest W. Burgess, xii-xiv. Chicago: University of Chicago Press.

Spain, Daphne. 2011. "The Chicago of Jane Addams and Ernest Burgess: Same City, Different Visions." In *The City, Revisited: Urban Theory from Chicago, Los Angeles, and New York*, edited by Dennis R. Judd and Dick Simpson, 51–62. Minneapolis: University of Minnesota Press.

Thomas, W. I., and Florian Znaniecki. (1918–1920). *The Polish Peasant in Europe and America: Monograph of an Immigrant Group*. 5 vols. Chicago: University of Chicago Press.

Warner, Michael. 1991. "Introduction: Fear of a Queer Planet." *Social Text* 29: 3–17.

Yu, Henry. 2001. *Thinking Orientals: Migration, Contact, and Exoticism in Modern America*. New York: Oxford University Press.

ANANYA ROY

GRAMMARS OF DISPOSSESSION

Racial Banishment in the American Metropolis

But how does epistemic decolonization work? What is its grammar (that is, its vocabulary, syntax and semantics)?

WALTER MIGNOLO, "DELINKING," 2007

On an afternoon of still and heavy heat in July 2019, I met with homeless and formerly homeless veterans on the sprawling campus of the Veterans Administration of Greater Los Angeles. VA doctors, concerned about high rates of housing precarity among veterans, especially Black veterans, had invited me to explain what they termed the "structural determinants of homelessness." The veterans themselves had ample knowledge to share. Daniel, an Army veteran, describing his eviction from an apartment building in Los Angeles's Koreatown, stated: "I was banished." I asked, "Where did you go?" He replied: "I was banished to the desert."

AUTHOR'S FIELDNOTES

For a while now, a lively debate has unfolded within urban studies about the limits of dominant epistemologies and methodologies. In response to the call to generate "new geographies of theory" (Roy 2009), there has been a Southern turn in urban studies. In broad brushstrokes, that turn can be characterized as a challenge to a universalizing urban theory that rests on Euro-American provincialism. Thus, this new moment of theorization in urban studies attempts to deploy what Jean and John Comaroff (2012, 7 and 12) have termed "theory from the South," where the South is "a distinctive vantage point" revealing "radically new assemblages of capital and labor."

Yet, this Southern turn requires scrutiny. In particular, I wish to raise two points of concern, the first of which is citationary asymmetry. Despite the Southern turn, the epistemological and methodological foundations of urban studies remain mostly untouched by traditions of thought forged in the crucible of anticolonial struggle and liberation movements, such as post-colonial critique, the Black radical tradition, feminist thought, and queer geographies. These continue to remain on the outside of an ossified regime of critical urban theory, one that Kate Derickson (2017) has pinpointed as "the unbearable whiteness of geography." A key part of this reproduction of knowledge is citationary asymmetry, which reflects the structural logic of epistemic and geopolitical power. Can one dare to write an article on the right to the city in Brazil without reference to David Harvey and Henri Lefebvre? Will it be published even if it ignores the significant writings of Brazilian scholars, especially if these are in Portuguese? One aspect of such asymmetry is what can be understood as citationary alibis: how "other" knowledges are integrated into the canon without challenging epistemic dominance. Citationary alibis perform recognition while leaving untouched the architecture of Theory.

Second, one of the main mechanisms through which knowledge–power relations is reproduced is the repertoire of concepts that lie at the heart of dominant epistemologies and methodologies. As Erin McElroy and Alex Werth (2019, 878) have recently argued, the Southern turn in urban studies has demonstrated the limited applicability of concepts such as gentrification to postcolonial contexts; but, by the same token, it has possibly reified the use of such concepts in the analysis of North Atlantic urbanism. They note that such theorizations obscure historical difference in the West and thus produce "deracinated dispossessions, or accounts of displacement uprooted from grounded histories of racial violence and resistance." Put another way, the reworlding of urban studies, for which many of us have argued (Roy and Ong 2011), is not simply a project of foregrounding colonial relationalities in the global South but also the task of resituating the cities of the Global North in the long history of racial capitalism, including slavery, settler-colonialism, and imperialism. Such work remains incomplete.

With such considerations in mind, I take aim at the lexicon of displacement that is commonplace in both critical urban theory and radical geography. I argue that the conceptual frameworks of displacement, such as gentrification or eviction, or even accumulation by dispossession, are limited in their capacity to address the structuring processes of racial capitalism and the settler logics of spatial settlement and expulsion. I thus propose a new concept—racial banishment—that emphasizes state-instituted violence against racialized bodies and communities. In doing so, I follow the imperative laid out by Adam Bledsoe and William Jamaal Wright (2018, 1) to analyze anti-Blackness "as a necessary precondition for the perpetuation of capitalism" rather than as "the effect of capitalist relations." I also follow the debate and conversation between Michael Dawson (2016) and Nancy Fraser (2016, 163) on the need for "an expanded conception of capitalism," one that is able to explain not only exploitation but also "an ongoing but disavowed moment of expropriation" and the forms of "racialized subjection" on which this rests. It is important to note that my use of the term "racial banishment" coincides with its mobilization by urban social movements, including the LA Community Action Network. The theorization of racial banishment is thus part of a shared terrain of scholarship, one that refuses to acknowledge the divide between valorized academic knowledge and devalorized movement praxis. In keeping with the global imaginations of such movements, I view racial banishment as an articulatory practice with global reach. Be it Cedric Robinson's pathbreaking *Black Marxism* or contemporary scholarship on hemispheric geographies of racialized policing and Black death (Perry 2013), it is important to understand racial banishment in transnational terms. However, for the purposes of this chapter, I will focus on the United States and its specific structures of racial capitalism.

Racial Banishment

Historically, banishment has been a form of punishment that imposes exile, often from the demarcated territory of a city or nation (Bleichmar 1999; Alloy 2002; Borrelli 2003). It often entails "civil death" (Kingston 2005) and indeed even social death. Implicated in banishment are thus notions of security and sovereignty. Banishment is closely related to another concept, deportation, and especially what Park (2019) has recently analyzed as "self-deportation," meaning "the removal strategy of making life so unbearable for a group that its members will leave a place." As Park demonstrates, self-deportation signifies a complex relationship between containment and expulsion that has long been a central organizing logic of state power and racial subordination in the United States, one that enables and legitimizes direct deportation regimes.

I am interested in how banishment structures contemporary urban life. Here, I rely on the scholarship of Katherine Beckett and Steve Herbert (2010, 1) and on their definition of banishment as "legally imposed spatial exclusion." Banishment, they argue, is undergirded by "new social control techniques" that are "punitive in nature" and express the "central role of the state's coercive power." Examples of such control tools include civil-gang injunctions, loitering ordinances and trespass laws, nuisance abatement measures, and even the criminalization of houselessness. Banishment is experienced, they note (p. 6), as "an expulsion from the body politic," a spatial logic that is "expansionary," such that for targeted bodies "subjected to multiple exclusion orders . . . much of the city becomes a 'no go' area for them." Banishment can thus be understood as an "emergent form of regulation by exile" (Mitchell 2009, 255).

I seek to understand racial banishment as being a grammar of dispossession, one that expands understandings of displacement by taking better account of the territorialities of racial capitalism. I thus interpret banishment as the necessary counterpart to what George Lipsitz (1998) has called "the possessive investment in whiteness." He shows that the project of white unity and white power has always operated through possession and explains how such possession, in a settler-colonial country such as the United States, is inevitably expressed in spatialized processes such as housing policy. This is what Brenna Bhandar (2016, 122) means by the "immense significance of possession as a ruling concept." Following Chery Harris (1993), who shows how whiteness itself has evolved into a form of property protected by law, Bhandar (2016, 122) argues that possession rests on the means that is law, including "legal techniques of dispossession." Similarly, Alyosha Goldstein (2008, 836) notes that it is legal reason that has built "proprietary regimes," thereby underpinning settlement as "an entitled and possessive relation to place" while casting Indigenous populations as "supposedly unsettled." Possession, then, as Robert Nichols (in Goldstein 2017) argues, must be understood not as preceding dispossession but rather as its effect. "Differential racialization," Goldstein (2017) emphasizes, is necessary for this colonial capacity to possess. Racial banishment and the possessive investment in whiteness are thus interlocking structures bound together by legal reason. Such expulsions, to use Saskia Sassen's (2014) term, cannot be understood as primarily a manifestation of neoliberalization. Expulsions, along with David Harvey's (2003) conceptual framework of accumulation by dispossession, are instances of what McElroy and Werth (2019) call "deracinated dispossessions," obscuring the long-standing racial and colonial violences through which possession, over both land and people, has been established in the United States.

As a grammar of dispossession, racial banishment is rooted in specific forms of legal authority and reason. In a much-cited article, Matthew Desmond and Nicol Valdez (2012, 117) draw attention to the proliferation of nuisance property ordinances and their role in tenant evictions, describing the process as "coercive third-party policing of the urban poor." But such a description is insufficient to pinpoint the types of state violence and legal reason that constitute racial banishment. Beckett and Herbert (2009, 9 and 12) emphasize that the new social control tools taking hold in cities "fuse civil and criminal legal authority" and have the "cumulative effect of multiple exclusion zones." In my current research with Terra Graziani of the Anti-Eviction Mapping Project (AEMP) and Shayla Myers of the Legal Aid Foundation of Los Angeles (LAFLA) on municipal ordinances in Los Angeles, we find both dimensions to be present. Our preliminary work on the Citywide Nuisance Abatement Program (CNAP) uncovers the central role of the City Attorney's office in filing property abatement lawsuits against individual landlords in South Central Los Angeles. These lawsuits invoke the role of municipal power in securing the "reformation of property," a point to which I will return in the section on property and personhood. But they also entail the banishment of targeted bodies, identified as persons belonging to gangs, from buildings as well as zones. Both practices are part of a national trend to fuse civil and criminal legal authority. Thus, Stephanie Smith (2000, 1462) argues that the "civil banishment of gang members," often done through the declaration of the gang as a public nuisance, is "unconstitutional because it actually administers a criminal penalty through a civil hearing and therefore 'circumvents criminal due process.'" In Los Angeles, Graziani, Myers, and I also find evidence of multiple, overlapping zones of exclusion and exile, including narcotics abatement, gang injunctions, and the city's notorious predictive policing programs, two of which are Operation LASER and the Chronic Offender Bulletin.

Such forms of legal reason and authority have not only a spatial logic but also a temporal one. Ruth Wilson Gilmore (2007, 26) reminds us that racism is the "state-sanctioned . . . production and exploitation of group-differentiated vulnerability to premature death." Premature death haunts our cities. And racial banishment is a key process in the making of such death. As widely reported, the life expectancy for an unhoused woman in Los Angeles is forty-eight years; it is fifty-one years for an unhoused man (Block 2019). It is this disposability of human life, especially Black life, that is a key logic of both racial capitalism and the foreclosing of Black futures throughout the United States. Racial banishment must also be seen as producing criminality rather than as a response to crime. As Katharyne Mitchell (2009, 239) argues, the forceful and justifiable removal of individuals and populations from "commonly held spaces and resources" is a "contemporary liberal form of sovereign dispossession" and rests on the designation, in advance, of those who are risk failures. This, she notes, is the making of "pre-black futures."

Property and Personhood

The shift from the lexicon of displacement to that of racial banishment entails an expanded conception of dispossession. As I have already indicated, it necessitates the critical inquiry of possession as a mode of colonial rule. Such possession consists not only of the expropriation and ownership of land but also of the ownership and control of people. Dispossession, then, has to be understood as the loss of property as well as that of personhood, or of personhood as property. The conceptual framework of racial banishment thus provides new insight into the relationship between property and personhood that lies at the heart of liberal democracy and its regimes of legal reason and authority.

The study of banishment as a historical practice, as for example the work of Rebecca Kingston (2005, 26), reminds us that perpetual exile from a territory of sovereign rule—for example, a kingdom—brought about "civil death," which meant both a "complete suspension of the individual's civil and political rights" and the loss of property, including the state's seizure of all goods "remaining within the relevant jurisdiction." But also at stake in banishment is what Lisa Marie Cacho (2012) has called "social death" and "racialized rightlessness." What does this mean at the contemporary urban moment? Borrowing a term from Nicholas Blomley (2004, xvi), I ask: what are the "enactments of property" at stake in racial banishment? Let me provide two preliminary examples. The first are narcotics abatement lawsuits brought by the Los Angeles City Attorney's office against "nuisance property," mainly in the city's South Central district. Rooted in the "War on Drugs" era, these filings continue the work of civil-gang injunctions and expand the eviction of tenants that "one strike" laws first perfected in public housing. Narcotics abatement is a particularly dense analytical site, one at which various forms of state-organized violence converge, ranging from anti-Blackness to the criminalization of migrants. The second are municipal ordinances that target homeless personhood with cruel precision, such as LAMC 85.02, which prohibits vehicle dwelling, and LAMC 56.11, which enables the destruction of personal property.

As I have already noted, one of the new urban control tools deployed by municipalities in the United States to ensure the twinned spatial logics of containment and removal is nuisance abatement. While nuisance law itself has a long history best understood through a transnational lens, in the United States the activation of "nuisance" as the grounds for tenant evictions gained momentum during the historical conjuncture known as the War on Drugs. As Andrew Waks (2018) shows, starting in 1988, and subsequently deepened through the One Strike policy launched nationwide in 1996, eviction provisions focused on drug charges, targeted public housing residents, and turned public housing authorities into evictors. Indeed, in the first six months after the adoption of the One Strike policy, public housing evictions increased nationally from 9,835 to 19,405, an 84 percent increase (Waks 2018, 198). Waks provides a convincing argument that state and local policies mirrored "the punitive structure and tone of the federal approach" (p. 199). These policies must be understood not only as a termination of the tenant's rights to domicile and residence but also as the loss of possessory rights, including the loss of property. Indeed, in most nuisance lawsuits, tenants have no legal standing. In Los Angeles, the recent nuisance abatement case involving Chesapeake Apartments, a 425-unit apartment complex in South Central Los Angeles, is a notable exception. The Chesapeake Apartments lawsuit is only one of scores of nuisance abatement complaints filed each year by the Los Angeles City Attorney. However, this case is unusual because in an unprecedented turn of events, tenants demanded, and were granted, legal standing in the case proceedings. While the City Attorney labeled the property a "hotbed of terror" and insisted that the nuisance abatement lawsuit was an action to "take back our communities" (Tchekmedyian 2017), tenants rejected such portrayals of criminality and critiqued the security systems as simply being expanded policing and surveillance. In a settlement, filed in September 2018, Chesapeake tenants, as intervening defendants, won a time-bound prohibition of the property's removal from the rental market as part of a set of "tenant and community benefits"—a temporary, yet important, protection from the rapid gentrification surrounding the apartment complex, which is now only a few blocks from a newly built Los Angeles Metro Line transit station and other residential and commercial developments.

The second example comes from the persistent criminalization of houselessness in Los Angeles. In March 2016, four unhoused individuals, along with the Los Angeles Community Action Network and the Legal Aid Foundation of Los Angeles, filed a lawsuit against the city for the illegal seizure and destruction of property belonging to the houseless (Mitchell v. City of Los Angeles). In a preliminary injunction, the city was ordered to stop such seizure and destruction. In April 2016, Los Angeles adopted LAMC 56.11, a municipal ordinance that limits how much property a houseless person is allowed to possess. In particular, this ordinance defines "excess personal property" as "any and all Personal Property that cumulatively exceeds the amount of property that could fit in a 60-gallon container with the lid closed," referencing the trash containers of the city's sanitation department. While the Los Angeles City Council has settled the Mitchell case, LAMC 56.11 is being aggressively deployed by the city to conduct sanitation sweeps. The Legal Aid Foundation of Los Angeles (2016) has argued, on the basis of a Ninth Circuit ruling (Lavan v. City of Los Angeles, 2012), that "violation of a City ordinance does not vitiate the [constitutional] protection of one's property." But city officials insist that this is not about the confiscation of people's belonging or even "moving people along," but rather about making sure that "the streets are clean and the sidewalks are passable." The City of Los Angeles was expected to spend $30 million in 2019 alone on such sweeps (Tinoco 2019). In San Francisco, the Coalition on Homelessness has thus launched a project titled "Stolen Belonging" (https://www .stolenbelonging.org/), making visible the city's theft of houseless possessions through sweeps.

What is at stake here are important questions about property and personhood. If, following Jane Baron (2004), we understand houselessness as "a problem not of poverty but of property" and specifically of "no property," then what are the rights attached to this legal category? In previous work, I have argued that, in the United States, houselessness can only be understood in relation to the norm that is "propertied citizenship" (Roy 2003). If that is true, can the status of "no property" include the rights of liberal democracy, especially the constitutional protections afforded to propertied citizens? Can those without property have the right to possess? In a landmark essay, Jeremy Waldron (1991, 296) argues that houselessness means a loss of human liberty: "Everything that is done has to be done somewhere. No one is free to perform an action unless there is somewhere he is free to perform it." The rule of private property, he (1991, 302) comments, is, at least for the houseless, "a series of fences that stand between them and somewhere to be, somewhere to act." But as Blomley (2009, 577) argues, such an interpretation retains property within a "liberal geography of rights." Put another way, it takes both private property and its literal fences as being an established truth. What if we were to see property differently? What if we were attuned to what Blomley (2009) has called the "delusions of property"? How would this, then, transform the meanings of tenancy and houselessness and of the dispossession enacted by state violence?

Beyond the City

Processes of racial banishment are under way in cities such as Los Angeles. But where do the banished go to? Daniel, the Army veteran quoted at the beginning of this chapter, says he was banished to the desert. Research conducted in the San Francisco Bay Area by advocacy organizations such as Urban Habitat and PolicyLink show that many working-class communities of color are being pushed out of urban cores and relegated to the far margins of urban life. While often described as the suburbanization of poverty, this urban transformation is more appropriately understood as "residential resegregation" (Samara 2016). Indeed, this process of suburbanization is a far cry from the protected white suburbanization of the homeownership boom of the twentieth century. As Alex Schafran and Jake Wegmann (2012) have shown, in metropolitan regions such as the Bay Area, the exurbanization of communities of color coincides with geographies of foreclosure. The spaces to which African-American and Latino households are arriving are those that have been hit the hardest by the foreclosure crisis, thus adding another layer to sedimented histories of race and class exploitation and expropriation. Schafran and Wegmann correctly note that such processes of peripheralization must be understood as the latest iteration of ghettoization. Thus, critical legal scholars such as Norrinda Hayat (2016) and Priscilla Ocen (2012) draw attention to how such peripheralization is accompanied by renewed forms of racialized surveillance, code enforcement, and legal violence, often through municipal ordinances. Drawing on the cases of the city of Antioch in the Greater Bay Area as well as Palmdale and Lancaster in the Los Angeles region, Ocen (2012) likens these ordinances to today's version of racially restrictive covenants. An integral part of such regimes of racial banishment is what Rahim Kurwa (2018) identifies as "participatory policing" and what Ocen (2012, 1555) calls "white collective action," meaning legal actions taken by white residents against nonwhite neighbors with the assistance and encouragement of the city. Kurwa (2019) thus concludes that "policing and punishment not only take advantage of, but also produce racial residential segregation."

The regional geography of racial banishment calls for a new vocabulary of urban movement, exclusion, and settlement. Existing terms such as "suburb" or "periphery" or "edge" are inadequate in capturing the forms of state violence through which such forced mobility takes place. Daniel's use of the term "desert" is not unusual. It is one I hear often in Los Angeles. A desert is both a spatial allegory and a spatial reality. Our more-commonplace theoretical terms perpetuate deracinated dispossessions, obscuring the long histories of racial capitalism through which spaces of and beyond the city have been shaped. For example, sites such as the Antelope Valley, in Southern California, have been shaped not only through contemporary processes of segregation and foreclosure but also through the dispossession of Indigenous people's land. The municipal ordinances proliferating in cities across the United States have deep roots not only in the renewal of urban policing in the era of neoliberalism, for example, through the paradigm of "broken windows," but also in organized white power and the "Black codes" that were imposed in the United States in the postbellum period (Stewart 1998). Meant to contain and control freed slaves (or enslaved persons), these codes deployed vagrancy ordinances to reassert white possession over Black labor, meaning what was perceived to be "former property" (Stewart 1998, 2259). Sites such as South Central Los Angeles are experiencing not merely gentrification but also, as one example, the repeated deportation of Salvadoran youth, targeted and identified as gang members, to El Salvador (Zilberg 2004). Racial banishment is thus a multi-scalar formation through which settler-colonialism and imperialism are articulated with urban transformations. As Elana Zilberg (2004, 762) puts it, "the Central American barrio in Los Angeles is haunted with voices from, and banished to, El Salvador."

Reworlding Urban Theory

In an essay on the "rhetoric of modernity" and the "logic of coloniality," Walter Mignolo (2007, 485) raises the provocation of the "grammar" of decoloniality. Building on Anibal Quijano's arguments about the relationship between the coloniality of power and the coloniality of knowledge, Mignolo insists on the task of decolonizing knowledge. He argues that this is different from the project of postcolonial critique, which he views as "scholarly transformation within the academy" (Mignolo 2007, 451). "The de-colonial shift," he notes, "is a project of de-linking."

As a conceptual grammar, racial banishment is positioned in various traditions of postcolonial and decolonial thought. It seeks to challenge the epistemic dominance of concepts and methodologies that persistently obscure the forms of racialized dispossession through which the American metropolis has been built. Such challenge to the coloniality of knowledge is not necessarily an endeavor centered in the academy. As I have noted before, the theorists of racial banishment are the movement leaders and community lawyers who work on the frontlines of struggle in cities such as Los Angeles. Thus, Pete White (2016), founder and executive director of the LA Community Action Network (LA CAN), explains why he uses the term "banishment" rather than "displacement": "Banishment is when there is no place for you to go. Places for you to go are jails or death."

One of the important lessons I have learned from White and the decades of organizing by his network in Skid Row and across Los Angeles is that the antonym of "banishment" is neither "inclusion" nor "integration"; it is *liberation*. Racial banishment is a concept embedded in the Black radical tradition and the unfinished work of freedom in the United States. In keeping with the rich transnational imagination of the Black radical tradition, this emphasis on freedom knits together anticolonial and anti-imperial struggles in various parts of the world. Referencing the work of Enrique Dussel, Mignolo (2007, 454) explains that the concept of emancipation maintains the discourses of European enlightenment, whether liberal or Marxist. Liberation is different. It emerges from the many fronts of political, economic, and epistemological decolonization. Liberation, for Mignolo (2007, 462), is the grammar of decoloniality, a body politics and geopolitics of knowledge that is possible when the "geography of reason shifts." This, too, is the Southern turn in urban studies, one where the geography of reason shifts not only from Los Angeles and Oakland, California, to Kolkata, India, but also from the visible and knowable city to the bodies and communities that have faced death and disappearance.

Such a shift in the geography of reason also requires a challenge to our citationary structures and alibis. It requires rethinking the devalorization of knowledge produced outside academic terrains such as radical geography. It requires recognizing that a decolonial architecture of urban Theory already exists, but that this is rarely in our elite academic departments and disciplines. In my role as founding director of the Institute on Inequality and Democracy at the University of California, Los Angeles, I have had the opportunity to journey with a number of radical social movements as they mobilize the concept of racial banishment and enact liberation. Their work—on both the intellectual and the social frontlines—of urban struggle shifts the geographies of reason, transforming territories of death and disappearance into places of life and memory. Their work also creates grammars of dispossession that build a decolonial, rather than deracinated, architecture of urban Theory.

As the COVID-19 pandemic exposes and deepens the lived inequalities of racial capitalism, so the life-generating tactics of community organizations become apparent. While Los Angeles's unhoused communities remain abandoned by the state, without access to housing, sanitation services, or food, movements such as LA CAN have expanded infrastructures of care and have built mutual aid networks. Working at the frontlines of crisis, they have devised handwashing stations, created food supply nodes, and protected houseless encampments. Following Michele Lancione and AbdouMaliq Simone (2020), these modes of social reproduction can be seen as a refusal of "bioterity," a neologism meaning "biologically-structured austerity." They constitute an improvisational practice of collective life interrupting the logics of disposability and banishment. What is at stake, I argue, is actually the politics of liberation.

Like other pandemics before it, the COVID-19 crisis marks the limits of European enlightenment, exposing the lie of techno-scientific emancipation as well as that of liberal democracy. It deepens the urgency of a politics of liberation. As a concluding note, let me share one example of such politics from Los Angeles, and that is about the resignification of tenancy and its possessory rights. Well before the onset of the COVID-19 crisis, the Los Angeles Tenants Union was framing "tenancy" not as a relationship of rent but rather as the lack of control of the means of housing. The Los Angeles Tenants Union, while an emergent force, is rooted in long-standing militant movements such as Union de Vecinos that have insisted on the decommodification of housing and noncollaboration with processes of urban development. Thus, in her chapter titled "101 Notes on the LA Tenants Union (You Can't Do Politics Alone)," Tracy Jeanne Rosenthal (2019), writes: "A tenant is anyone who doesn't control their own housing." When framed in this way, eviction is no longer an individual case of distress but instead part of a political economy of dispossession. Rosenthal goes on to write: "When we re-envision the housing crisis as a tenants' rights crisis, we understand why the crisis seems to be permanent." Racial banishment is the latest iteration of this permanent crisis, the vector of death and disappearance cutting through and connecting Los Angeles's rent-burdened neighborhoods, homeless encampments, and peripheralized communities. The permanent crisis of houseless impermanence sits in stark contrast with the propertied permanence of "landlordism," signifying the inviolable rights to collect rent, protect property values, and banish "nuisance." Yet, the grammars of dispossession being crafted by movements such as the Los Angeles Tenants Union, especially in the context of the deepening social crisis precipitated by the COVID-19 pandemic, resignify not only tenancy but also landlordism. As each Los Angeles City Council meeting becomes a terrain of bitter struggle over tenant protections, eviction moratoria, and rent suspension, housing-justice movements steadily reframe landlordism. For example, when it refuses arguments that landlords are a protected class with protected income, Knock-LA, the journalism and public commentary arm of the grassroots organizing group called Ground Game LA, insists that landlordism must be seen as a risky investment (Knock-LA, tweet, April 22, 2020). Thus, a letter sent by public interest attorneys to the San Jose (California) City Council making the case for a temporary rent suspension, in order to address the COVID-19 crisis, reminds city government of "a wide range of regulations on property rights that have been upheld as legitimate exercises of a government's police power" and argues that rent suspension must thus be seen as "emergency price control." The letter goes on to emphasize that the authority of a city to restrict property rights expands during a public health emergency when the protection of life becomes paramount. Such grammars of dispossession shift the relationship between property and personhood. They also shift the relationship between tenancy, as the lack of ownership of property, and possessory rights. We thus return, in a different manner, to a question I posed earlier in this chapter: can those without property have the right to possess?

As I have argued in previous work (Roy 2017), such resignifications of property and personhood disrupt liberal enactments of ownership and must instead be understood as articulations of "dispossessive collectivism" (see also Masuda et al. 2019). In Los Angeles, such a practice of collective life is increasingly about claims to the public and the social. Thus, Rosenthal (2019) insists that "tenant justice is public control over all housing." Such public control is being asserted in many ways, ranging from the push to use eminent domain to appropriate private property in order to maintain the affordability of housing, to the commandeering of hotel and motel rooms to house the unhoused during the COVID-19 crisis, to reclaiming public-agency-owned vacant homes by poor people's movements such as Moms4Housing and Reclaiming LA. Especially crucial is how the permanent crisis of tenancy, imagined as permanent houselessness, is being linked to a bold imagination about urban vacancy. Not surprisingly, urban social movements, ranging widely from the Chicago Anti-Eviction Campaign to OccupySF, have long conceptualized building occupations as home liberations. Liberation, like the desert, is both spatial allegory and spatial reality. It is a rearticulation of the relationship between property and personhood that is foundational to racial capitalism. It is the antonym of racial banishment. It is the very insistence on forms of possession outside the grid of liberal ontologies and enlightenment epistemologies.

References

Alloy, Jason S. 2002. "158-County Banishment in Georgia: Constitutional Implications under the State Constitution and the Federal Right to Travel." *Georgia Law Review* 36: 1083–1108.

Baron, Jane. 2004. "Homelessness as a Property Problem." *The Urban Lawyer* 36, no. 2: 271–288.

Beckett, Katherine, and Steve Herbert. 2009. "Penal Boundaries: Banishment and the Expansion of Punishment." *Law and Social Inquiry* 35, no. 1: 1–38.

Bhandar, Brenna. 2016. "Possession, Occupation and Registration: Recombinant Ownership in the Settler Colony." *Settler Colonial Studies* 6, no. 2: 119–132.

Bledsoe, Adam, and William Jamaal Wright. 2018. "The Anti-Blackness of Global Capital." *Environment and Planning D: Society and Space*: 37, no. 1: 1–19.

Bleichmar, Javier. 1999. "Deportation as Punishment: A Historical Analysis of the British Practice of Banishment and Its Impact on Modern Constitutional Law." *Georgetown Immigration Law Journal* 14: 115–162.

Block, Cassidy. 2019. "In Los Angeles, Homelessness Means Death." https://knock-la.com/in-los-angeles-homelessness-means-death -25a884ef595e.

Blomley, Nicholas. 2004. *Unsettling the City: Urban Land and the Politics of Property*. New York: Routledge.

Blomley, Nicholas. 2009. "Homelessness, Rights, and the Delusions of Property." *Urban Geography* 30, no. 6: 577–590.

Borrelli, Matthew D. 2003. "Banishment: The Constitutional and Public Policy Arguments against This Revived Ancient Punishment." *Suffolk University Law Review* 36: 469–486.

Cacho, Lisa Marie. 2012. *Social Death: Racialized Rightlessness and the Criminalization of the Unprotected*. New York: New York University Press.

Comaroff, Jean, and John Comaroff. 2012. *Theory from the South: Or, How Euro-America Is Evolving Toward Africa*. Boulder, CO : Paradigm Publishers.

Dawson, Michael C. 2016. "Hidden in Plain Sight: A Note on Legitimation Crises and the Racial Order." *Critical Historical Studies* 3, no. 1: 143–161.

Derickson, Kate. 2017. "Urban Geography II: Urban Geography in the Age of Ferguson." *Progress in Human Geography* 41, no. 2: 230–244.

Desmond, Matthew, and Nicol Valdez. 2012. "Unpolicing the Urban Poor: Consequences of Third-Party Policing for Women." *American Sociological Review* 78, no. 1: 117–141.

Fraser, Nancy. 2016. "Expropriation and Exploitation in Racialized Capitalism: A Reply to Michael Dawson." *Critical Historical Studies* 3, no. 1: 163–179.

Gilmore, Ruth Wilson. 2007. *Golden Gulag: Prisons, Surplus, Crisis, and Opposition in Globalizing California*. Berkeley: University of California Press.

Goldstein, Alyosha. 2008. "Where the Nation Takes Place: Proprietary Regimes, Antistatism, and U.S. Settler Colonialism." *South Atlantic Quarterly* 107, no. 4: 833–861.

Goldstein, Alyosha. 2017. "The Ground Not Given: Colonial Dispositions of Land, Race, and Hunger." Unpublished paper presented at the "Race and Capitalism: Global Territories, Transnational Histories" conference, Institute on Inequality and Democracy, UCLA.

Harris, Chery I. 1993. "Whiteness as Property." *Harvard Law Review* 106: 8.

Harvey, David. 2003. *The New Imperialism*. New York: Oxford University Press.

Hayat, Norrinda Brown. 2016. "Section 8 Is the New N-Word: Policing Integration in the Age of Black Mobility." *Journal of Law and Policy* 51: 61–93.

Kingston, Rebecca. 2005. "The Unmaking of Citizens: Banishment and the Modern Citizenship Regime in France." *Citizenship Studies* 9, no. 1: 23–40.

Knock-LA. Twitter. April 22, 2020. https://static1.squarespace.com/static/577c8338bebafbe36dfc1691/t/5e8cf17666eab44d4580b5a2/1586295159097/LoS+RE+Item+8.3_COVID-19+Rent+Suspension_LF-PC-PILP_0406 2020.pdf.

Kurwa, Rahim. 2018. "Grounds for Eviction: Race, Mobility, and Policing in the Antelope Valley." PhD diss., UCLA Sociology. https://escholarship.org/uc/item/9fm0c3z2.

Kurwa, Rahim. 2019. "Segregatory Consequences of the Carceral State." In *Housing Justice in Unequal Cities*, edited by Ananya Roy and Hilary Malson, 127–134. Los Angeles: Institute on Inequality and Democracy at UCLA Luskin.

Lancione, Michele, and AbdouMaliq Simone. 2020. "Bio-Austerity and Solidarity in the Covid-19 Space of Emergency." *Society and Space.* https://www.societyandspace.org/articles/bio-austerity-and-solidarity-in-the-covid-19-space-of-emergency.

Legal Aid Foundation of Los Angeles. 2016. *Memo to Councilmember Herb Wesson and the Los Angeles City Council.* http://clkrep.lacity.org/onlinedocs/2014/14-1656-S1_pc_3-18-16f.pdf.

Lipsitz, George. 1998. *The Possessive Investment in Whiteness: How White People Profit from Identity Politics.* Philadelphia: Temple University Press.

Masuda, Jeffrey R., Aaron Franks, Audrey Kobayashi, and Trevor Wideman. 2019. "After Dispossession: An Urban Rights Praxis of *Remaining* in Vancouver's Downtown Eastside." *Environment and Planning D: Society and Space*; 1–19, Online First.

McElroy, Erin, and Alex Werth. 2019. "Deracinated Dispossessions: On the Foreclosures of 'Gentrification' in Oakland, CA." *Antipode* 51, no. 3: 878–898.

Mignolo, Walter D. 2007. "Delinking: The Rhetoric of Modernity, the Logic of Coloniality and the Grammar of De-Coloniality." *Cultural Studies* 21, no. 2–3: 449–514.

Mitchell, Katharyne. 2009. "Pre-Black Futures." *Antipode* 41, no. S1: 239–261.

Ocen, Priscilla. 2012. "The New Racially Restrictive Covenant: Race, Welfare, and the Policing of Black Women in Subsidized Housing." *UCLA Law Review* 59: 1540–1581.

Park, K-Sue. 2019. "Self-Deportation Nation." *Harvard Law Review* 132, no. 1878: 1880–1941.

Perry, Keisha-Khan Y. 2013. *Black Women Against the Land Grab: The Fight for Racial Justice in Brazil.* Minneapolis: University of Minnesota Press.

Rosenthal, Tracy Jeanne. 2019. "101 Notes on the LA Tenants Union (You Can't Do Politics Alone)." In *Housing Justice in Unequal Cities*, edited by Ananya Roy and Hilary Malson, 51–57. Los Angeles: Institute on Inequality and Democracy. https://escholarship.org/uc/item/4kq1j0df.

Roy, Ananya. 2003. "Paradigms of Propertied Citizenship: Transnational Techniques of Analysis." *Urban Affairs Review* 38, no. 4: 463–491.

Roy, Ananya. 2009. "The 21st Century Metropolis: New Geographies of Theory." *Regional Studies* 43, no. 6: 819–830.

Roy, Ananya. 2017. "Dis/possessive Collectivism: On Property and Personhood at City's End." *Geoforum* 80: A1–A11.

Roy, Ananya, and Aihwa Ong. 2011. *Worlding Cities: Asian Experiments and the Art of Being Global.* Chichester: Wiley-Blackwell.

Samara, Tony Roshan. 2016. *Race, Inequality, and the Resegregation of the Bay Area.* Oakland: Urban Habitat. http://urbanhabitat.org/sites/default/files/UH%20Policy%20Brief2016.pdf.

Sassen, Saskia. 2014. *Expulsions: Brutality and Complexity in the Global Economy*. Cambridge, MA: Belknap Press.

Schafran, Alex, and Jake Wegmann. 2012. "Restructuring, Race, and Real Estate: Changing Home Values and the New California Metropolis, 1989–2010." *Urban Geography* 33, no. 5: 630–654.

Smith, Stephanie. 2000. "Civil Banishment of Gang Members: Circumventing Criminal Due Process Requirements?" *University of Chicago Law Review* 67: 1461–1487.

Stewart, Gary. 1998. "Black Codes and Broken Windows: The Legacy of Racial Hegemony in Anti-Gang Civil Injunctions." *Yale Law Journal* 107, no. 7: 2249–2279.

Tchekmedyian, Alene. 2017. "Prosecutors Say That This Property Is a Hotbed of Crime." http://www.latimes.com/local/lanow/la-me-ln-baldwin-village-lawsuit-20171127-story.html.

Tinoco, Matt. 2019. "LA Will Spend $30M This Year on Homeless Sweeps: Do They Even Work?" https://laist.com/2019/04/10/homeless_sweeps_los_angeles_public_health.php.

Waks, Andrew. 2018. "Eviction and Exclusion: An Argument for Extending the Exclusionary Rule to Evictions Stemming from a Tenant's Alleged Criminal Activity." *Georgetown Journal on Poverty Law and Policy* XXVI, no. 1: 185–210.

Waldron, Jeremy. 1991. "Homelessness and the Issue of Freedom." *UCLA Law Review* 39: 295–324.

White, Pete. 2016. "Black Banishment and Real Community at Skid Row." Interview conducted by Kenton Card on behalf of the Institute on Inequality and Democracy at UCLA Luskin. https://challengeinequality.luskin.ucla.edu/2016/03/02/luskin-school-students-interview-urban-color-lines-activists/.

Zilberg, Elana. 2004. "Fools Banished from the Kingdom: Remapping Geographies of Gang Violence Between the Americas." *American Quarterly* 56, no. 3: 759–779.

COLIN MCFARLANE

FUTURE DENSITIES

Knowledge, Politics, and Remaking the City

Introduction

Density has always been fundamental to the idea of what a city is, but in recent decades it has become increasingly central to a spatial grammar of the city and urban life. From environmental sustainability and economic growth to building socially vibrant neighborhoods, density is increasingly reached for as a solution to different questions in the city. Policymakers and planners have pushed for "walkable" and "compact" cities, and economists have argued that the serendipities of dense urban spaces can mobilize new urban economies and cultural possibilities. In the face of a general decrease in urban density globally, sprawl has become the dominant form. "Densification," "compactness," and "intensification" have, partly in response, been positioned as vital for our global urban future.

A mainstream consensus has arisen around building denser as being pivotal to our urban present and future. Meanwhile, urban theorists and researchers have examined how intensive compressions of people and things become vital to urban sociality, struggle, and politics. Density has been shown to be a social or political resource, an engine, a background from which to draw new connections and avoid others, as well as an energy that can enliven or even overwhelm situations. If we think about cities as a kind of gathering, in and through which residents attempt to weave different relations, combinations, and possibilities, then density comes into view as a relational force for political, economic, and social change (Simone 2016 and 2018).

At the same time, a growing body of work has been critically examining the politics of density. Partly in response to the prevalence of pro-density positions in mainstream urban and economic policy and practice, this work has shown that while density and densification are often presented as both good and generative, the formation of densities can be exclusive, dominated by higher-income groups, and often organized around lines of class, race, ethnicity, and gender. Some have questioned the claim that denser developments are necessarily environmental wins, while others have critically reflected on the extent to which density might foster urban creativity and innovation. In short, a disparate and growing critical body of work has reminded us that density is not, and never was, simply a question of number and abstraction, but instead a set of profoundly political knowledge claims about how urban space ought to be organized.

Given the reemergence of density in all kinds of scholarly, policy, and practice contexts, I want to make an argument for how we might approach density and its futures. Two closely related steps are pertinent to my argument here. First, I argue that density can be usefully understood as a *knowledge politics*. The current focus on density as an urban good in all kinds of mainstream urban fora needs critical engagement, but more important still is the task of developing *an alternative archive of knowledge about urban density*. I argue for a wider urban project of uncovering the lived experiential worlds of urban density, which are both vital to the collective life of the city and yet increasingly at risk. Too often, these are the "forgotten densities," as Jay Pitter (2020) has put it, of the urban world, often detached from the dominant aesthetics and forms of premium densities.[1] My aim is not to romanticize those lived densities—they carry with them all kinds of exclusions, power relations, and exploitations—but rather to position them as being at once vital for remaking the city, and increasingly at risk all over the urban world.

Second, and to develop this alternative archive of knowledge politics further, I argue for greater attention to the relationship between density and acts of politicization. Here, I draw on a range of examples to foreground the ways in which density is enrolled in the staging of political claims, and which proceed from what I call the *force of density*. My suggestion is not so much that density has a force in and of itself, but that it can relationally become a vital constitutive part of progressive political interventions as well as a provocation for developing an alternative archive of density's knowledge politics.

This focus on the knowledge politics of urban density helps us to track changing forms and valuations of density, to articulate alternatives, and to foreground more-progressive density futures. In the conclusion to this chapter, I briefly go through four steps that, as a minimum, are important for generating the much-needed traffic between the conceptual—an alternative knowledge politics of urban density—and practice.

Density as Knowledge Politics

How do we come to know urban density? We can approach this question from lots of directions. Most obviously, a wide body of work exists that explores how to define density, from people per hectare to dynamic population density that measures population numbers over square miles over time. There is no consensus here (Dovey and Pafka 2016). Some approaches use thematic definitions (population, jobs, buildings, and the like), others spatial (administrative boundaries, postcode areas, districts, and so on), all with their strengths and omissions. Spatial science has produced more-refined measures, including the number of people living in a square miles over twenty-four hours—the so-called "ambient population density"—usually presented alongside other relevant data, such as journeys to work, residential location, and places of employment (Cohen and Gutman 2007; Batty 2008; Taubenböck et al. 2016). A great deal of debate has also occurred, which in part comes out of this concern with definition and measurement, about how best to optimize density, from regulations on building height or congestion charging, to calculations of distributions and infrastructural "carrying capacities."

These debates approach density as a quantitative, abstract question, and they bypass or ignore the political and cultural drivers at work. A quite different history of knowing density is a more-critical social science tradition that has examined why and how some forms of density are celebrated, while others are portrayed as a problem (McGuirk 2011; Tonkiss 2014; McFarlane 2016). This work has considered, for example, why dense low-income neighborhoods are sometimes demolished in the name of building dense, higher-income developments, increasingly sold as "green," "sustainable," and even "vibrant." Other work in this tradition has critically countered boosterist city discourses of generating "urban laboratories," considered to be "incubators" and entrepreneurial urban ecosystems formed through "collision density" innovation, on the grounds that they pay little attention to the social and physical diversities of the city and urban inequalities (Cohen et al. 2016; Blanco and Leon 2017).

These more-critical approaches have given us an important eye on today's mainstream pro-density discourses. What is striking about those mainstream discourses is not only their pervasiveness, but also their repeated presentation of density and densification as apolitical urban goods. Density is indexed to progress in environmental, social, and economic realms in the city. Federico Pérez (2020, 18) is surely right to argue that "as densification becomes a centerpiece of urban agendas across the globe—from upzoning in San Francisco to property readjustment in Mumbai—it is critical to develop situated analyses that shed light on the limitations and contradictions of *density as an urban epistemology.*" What this calls for is a critical urbanism of density as an urban knowledge politics: a critical and expanding dialogue around how density, knowledge, urban space, and the political are differently enrolled, and might be altered.

The more-prominent narratives of urban density today are often put forward by economists. Different versions of the density argument are at work here, however. For the influential economist Ed Glaeser (2012, 47), the aim is to build up into tower blocks through policies and incentives that combat sprawl, and that will mean, he argues, not only less carbon footprint but more-fulfilled people who benefit from what he calls the "magical consequences" of concentration that can "make us more human." Others feel more reticent about the trend to building tall. For Richard Florida (2012 and 2017), the focus ought to be on getting density "right" for economic creativity and social vibrancy, and for him it's about mid-rise densities. For David Sim (2019), an architect, the question is how to turn mid-rise densities into places that balance the "common good" and "personal fulfilment," and here all kinds of material design devices are key—corners, medians, curb extensions, active frontages, setbacks, walking paths, cycle lanes, and so forth.

Despite the differences in these claims for density as a powerful part of tackling urban crises of different sorts, they very often return to the legacy of Jane Jacobs. What's particularly powerful here is the connection Jacobs made not only between density and social texture, or density and economic dynamism, but between density and citylife. As Jacobs (1961, 233) argued in *The Death and Life of Great American Cities*, density for her was part of what allowed human life to "flourish." Density, especially in its connection to social and building diversity, was a source of both "immense vitality" and the richness, differences, and unpredictability of life. The "in-between densities" of places like Greenwich Village, in New York City, were illustrative of these potentials. Her arguments that dense spaces were more inclusive and lively because they catered to a variety of people, ranging from those working in corporate buildings to those performing "basic activities," while also offering the potential for surprises and intimacy, have continued to show remarkable traction—even if that traction has also been made to serve less-progressive ends, including exclusionary forms of gentrification.

This connection between density and citylife has been enormously influential in pro-density mainstream urban thought (for an account of density and citylife, see Chowdhury and McFarlane 2021). We see it, too, for example in another text by an economist, in Charles Montgomery's (2013) *Happy City*, in which he argues that "intermediate zones" that can be found in-between "hyperdensity" and "sprawl"—what he calls "density's sweet spot"—play vital roles in forming a citylife that is not only more connected and proximate, but even healthier, happier, and more environmentally sustainable. If density is portrayed as vital to such central questions—to being human, to citylife, to tackling the climate crisis, to forging new urban creative economies, to building affordable housing—then it is no surprise that it has become so prevalent in urban policy and practice, as well as in cities across the Global North–South divide.

Many of these interventions and forms, as Jamie Peck (2015) and Brendan Gleeson's (2012 and 2013) evaluations of "celebrity urbanology" have shown, are often influential in mainstream urban thought and policy approaches. Taken together, they form part of what Peck calls "a sustained effort to rationalize and normalize lean or limited modes of neoliberal urban governance." There tends to be only a limited role for the state and urban policy along with a critique of state subsidy and redistribution, coupled with an argument for pro-market urbanism, and sometimes even an explicit acceptance of poverty and inequality (Peck 2015). Consider, for example, the powerful and globally influential arguments for Vancouverism, a mixture of tower blocks, mid-rises, and green urbanism. As Jim Russell (2013) argues, Vancouverism has become a global vehicle for what he calls the "cult of density," a "boutique urbanism" that in the end not only sits at ease with neoliberal urbanism and inequalities, but also risks actively entrenching them.

Yet, many of the claims for density are increasingly contested in critical scholarship. Some have questioned the extent to which high-density developments are resource-saving, given their forms of production, consumption, and lifestyle, together with the global networks that sustain them and the work required to make them more adaptive or more resilient to climate change (Wachsmuth et al. 2016). Research shows that higher-density developments tend to be good for higher-income groups, though they price out lower-income groups (Ahlfedt and Pietrostefani 2019). New upmarket apartment blocks in central Mumbai, for example, may intensify vertical densities in some areas while pushing lower-income residents into poorer areas, including often already highly dense and underserviced neighborhoods (Doshi 2013; Weinstein 2013). This shuffling of densities is masked by a particular kind of "density fetish" that provides "greenwashed" densities for the relatively well-off but leaves the poor in dense peripheries of often-fragmented homes and infrastructures (McFarlane 2021).

A growing literature is revealing how plans to build hip, dense neighborhoods that are both green and creative also become caught up with gentrification along racial and class lines, in which predominantly white residents push out predominantly Black residents. James Connolly and Mateus Lira have made this argument in relation to efforts to densify East Austin, Texas, efforts supported not just by the municipality but also by some of that city's strands of activism. As Ananya Roy (2017) has shown in her work in Los Angeles and Chicago on the demolition of public housing, tenant eviction, and the foreclosure of homes that sometimes end up remaining empty, urban transformation in the United States remains a process not just of gentrification but of actual "racial banishment." Groups like the Chicago Anti-Eviction Campaign and the Los Angeles Community Action Network (LACAN) that Roy examines pursue a different kind of urban density knowledge that critiques displacement, banishment, and racial power, and instead seeks community empowerment, voice, and rights. These cases point to a long history of "forgotten densities" that disclose an alternative archive of urban density, and that can enable more-inclusive visions and practices of city-making (Pitter 2020).

Activism has earned a long history across the urban world around urban densities and low-income neighborhoods, in which residents and activists produce their own knowledge of density and seek to take that into negotiations with governing authorities. We might think here, for example, of groups like Slum/Shack Dwellers International or the Asian Coalition for Housing Rights, which form maps, charts, and categories of density in poor neighborhoods, illustrating housing, infrastructure, and services, among other categories. Groups like the Austin [Texas] Justice Coalition (2020), which critique forms of densification that have led to classed and racialized displacement, seek to learn about housing and land regulations and codes, and then aim to develop community youth activities and suggestions for how community policing might take shape. These initiatives articulate other stories about how density might connect to citylife in inclusive, progressive ways.

A long, scholarly tradition on urban density has emphasized the experience and perception of residents themselves, having been influenced in part by the kind of thinking associated with Jane Jacobs's work on social diversity and stretching through—to name just two influential thinkers here—scholars like Richard Sennett or AbdouMaliq Simone's work on the "social thickness" of dense urban markets and neighborhoods (Jacobs 1958 and 1961). What this work has shown is that urbanites do not simply "deal with" density. They form and change it, live and contest it, and do so in ways that include but also take us beyond density merely as an instrumental "problem" (such as congestion or pollution) or "solution" (better housing, carbon reduction, economic innovation, and many others).

Consider, for example, how we might come to know urban density from the context of the economic margins of the urban world, where the relationship between dense urban life, fragmented provisions, and social improvisations become critical and often deeply political (Klinenberg 2018). At the margins, and in the absence of adequate material infrastructure, residents often depend on social infrastructure—a practice of connecting people and things in relations that sustain urban life, and that vary in form and content across the urban world (Silver 2014; De Boeck and Baloji 2016). If the urban environment is "full of machines," as Simone (2018, 18) argues, the machinic is as much peopled as it is material, "anticipated and parsed into varying measures and used by different constellations and densities of actors and things." Social infrastructure is a necessarily flexible resource that responds to and anticipates the contingencies of everyday life, forming a vital but indeterminate relation to densities.

These social infrastructures might be relations of reciprocity, care, coordination, and consolidation, vital for getting by and getting on in the city (McFarlane and Silver 2017a). They support and make use of local densities, and can form particular configurations of people and things within urban densities. Friends, family, and neighbors come together to secure essential needs, to share and support each other during heightened moments of crisis, or to advise on and identify new opportunities. Social infrastructures are not without their exclusions and power relations, of course, and it would not help to romanticize the ways in which their configurations are woven through urban densities. Nonetheless, they can, and routinely do, act as resources of urban survival, support, and opportunity. They also feed into local community initiatives and organizations that enhance fragmented material infrastructures, thereby improving the connective tissues of urban density. Think, for example, of the high-profile case of the Orangi Pilot Project (OPP). For decades, the nongovernmental and community groups linked to OPP have designed and built low-cost simplified sewerage systems in highly dense communities in Karachi, Pakistan, connecting social infrastructures, formal civil society organizations, and new material systems.

In materially fragmented neighborhoods, the very reproduction of everyday life in the city often demands that people be able to connect with and use densities, whether in the form of social connections, rumors of threats and opportunities, or ways to make a little extra money or develop new networks, and so on (Simone 2016 and 2018). Then there are also the everyday, small calibrations and negotiations through which dense urban constellations slowly proceed. Writing about Mumbai, Vyjayanthi Rao (2015) argues that the high densities we often see across urban Asia demand constant forms of "adjustment." Adjustment, she shows, may seem trivial and happenstance, but is in practice an important feature of urban life in Mumbai, ranging from efforts negotiating energy or water to making room on overcrowded trains (on water in Mumbai, see Björkman 2015; Anand 2017). Adjustment is also the locus of a kind of density archive, a form of urban knowhow and the infrastructure of navigation.

Social infrastructure draws from and shapes these patterns of adjustment as part of the ebb and flow of densities. For Jonathan Shapiro Anjaria, writing about street densities in Mumbai, this includes all kinds of comings and goings and the intersecting temporalities that compose everyday socialities, economies, and provisioning—not merely around infrastructure but including the wider repertoire of tea and newspaper sellers, fruit and *paan* vendors, vegetable sellers pushing carts, mobile barbers, stalls fixing shoes or cooking food, and more. Anjaria's (2012) examination of the Mumbai street, as detailed in his compelling book *The Slow Boil*, is no romantic treatise, however (and see Appadurai 1987). He is alert to how urban densities are always already political, shot through with their own exclusions and identities even as they are themselves subjected to all kinds of violences. Yet, at the same time, it is through the sometimes loose, sometimes strong relations between people, things, rhythms, and adjustments that density can be fashioned as a lived tissue of urbanism into progressive and vital social infrastructure. Density can be and is shaped and reshaped in all kinds of ways, from efforts to augment fragmented material infra-structures to forms of urban sociality, economy, and politics (Simone 2018).

Too often in Mumbai, however, as in so many other cities, this form of density—a diverse and changing resource that seems to spill over into various kinds of urban spaces and practices—is portrayed as a congested mess that needs to be removed, regulated, or escaped from. A variety of tactics have been deployed by numerous levels of the state to these ends, ranging from increased efforts to zone hawkers into particular areas, or to demolish their shacks, or to just escape the street through the mass con-struction of elevated "skywalks" (Harris 2013). These kinds of street densi-ties are increasingly at stake, then, and often are intended to make way for the dominant aesthetics of density that facilitate urban land speculation and economic expropriation. In the process, the city loses all kinds of thick social infrastructures, economic substrate, and urban liveliness.

Even in the face of the COVID-19 pandemic, which has generated such intense debate and anxiety around density and its futures, mainstream pro-density accounts tend to portray "density" as an inevitable and apoliti-cal urban good. But the variegated archive of urban density I am pointing to here suggests an urbanism that is not only too often marginal and for-gotten in those discourses and proposals, but one that points to a different knowledge-politics of density. It would be too simple to describe this as a "mainstream Density 1" and an "alternative Density 2"—the knowledge forms, valuations, and politics are too differentiated for that—but it is important to recognize and grow this alternative archive as a source for rethinking densities and making more-inclusive urban futures. From this perspective density cannot possibly be portrayed as a singular process to be achieved and celebrated, but instead as a politics of intimately weaving knowledge, urban space, and claims to the city.

It is, above all, a profoundly political and challenging prospect—this question of bringing the historically marginalized forms of knowledge and ways of knowing density more squarely and meaningfully into the planning and making of the city. It demands of the powers that be—municipalities, surely, but the plethora of other urban operators too, ranging from architects and designers to campaigning groups and researchers—an urban literacy, an ear to the ground, a willingness to listen and then to listen again. It demands a new politics of urban value, the formation of genuinely inclusive plan-ning fora, and an accountability over density management of many kinds.

However challenging that task is, it is increasingly urgent globally. The very right of certain kinds of urban density to exist is now increasingly at stake. The densification of a city through elite apartments and attached commercial activity fits the dominant script set by powerful urban actors in real estate, development, and policy areas. Others fit less well, and are often met with violence (Ghertner 2015; Bhan 2016). Simply occupying certain spaces is increasingly a political act, whether the residents would wish that politics or not. For more-progressive voices in policy and practice, part of their challenge is to learn from and support a wider archive of density knowledges and then to embark on a density pedagogy. The risk, of course, is that alternative knowledges become incorporated within dominant ways of seeing and doing, and here it is vital that urban scholars insist that density and its future be understood first and foremost as a politics of remaking the city. In the next section, I develop this politics further by turning to the force of density as a vital strand in the knowledge claims made through densities.

The Force of Density

Temporary political gatherings in a city are a vital means through which to call into question its urban inequalities or to demand political change and transformation. While they may appear to be isolated expressions of urban protest, solidarity, or even anger, the gatherings also constitute an important part of building an alternative archive of urban density. As Andy Merrifield has argued, over the past decade or so the massing of people in streets and squares in many places around the globe has been vital for urban politicization, ranging from the "Arab Spring" to the Occupy and Indignados movements; to forms of urban presencing, protest, and occupation in Hong Kong; and often connecting through a politics of online as well as off-line encounters (Corsín Jimenez 2014; Dikeç 2018) (see figure 3.1). If anything, the importance of this political massing has only intensified during the present COVID-19 pandemic, as people took to the streets amid lockdowns to protest everything from racial inequality—the Black Lives Matter demonstrations in 2020, for instance—to the very right to protest itself.

"A crowd," writes Deyan Sudjic (2017, 207), is as "unstable, unpredictable and as volatile as the city itself." While the political Right has historically portrayed the crowd in the city as a form of unruly danger, being both destructive and thoughtless, crowds, we know, can perform important progressive political purposes (Wilson and Swyngedouw 2015). They can

3.1 Politicized densities: protest in June 2019 in Hong Kong against the Extradition Bill. Source: author photograph

bear witness, demand rights, or—as we saw, for example, in 2011 through Cairo's massive Tahrir Square demonstrations—help to bring down governments. For Merrifield, the action of a crowd in place—or, as is often the case, both *in* place and connected translocally *beyond* place, especially through social media—provides a powerful example of how urban form is produced. Merrifield (2014, 915) argues that urban form becomes defined contingently when it "is filled by a certain notion of proximity, by people and activity, by events coming together in this proximity." Here too, in the history of the crowd, reposes an archive of urban density and its political potentials, shaped by and generating knowledges typically shunted to the economic or political margins of the city (Borch 2012).

Consider, for example, how the 2019 protests in Hong Kong used crowds to make political statements, or to shift their presence in the city in real time as circumstances changed, or even to move to other sites in response to wider political developments throughout the city. Protesters were keen to avoid being hemmed in, as they were during the 2014 Umbrella movement in that city, to one particular place. Partly to evade the police, partly to keep momentum and action, they shifted the geographies of the crowd. At times, they would rush into particular sites, especially around govern-

3.2 Hong Kong's "stargazing assembly" (Flickr/Studio Incendo). Source: https://search
.creativecommons.org/photos/cb148f9b-38ae-4610-8030-10c19793b381

ment buildings, while at other times they would flow more slowly into other places, informed for example through digital updates via Telegram or other sources, attempting to evade police or to move around resources that supported the protests, or simply to conserve energy as plans shifted in rhythms of rest and action. The crowd was modulated as part of a political strategy, as protesters sought to remain both visible and elusive over time and space.

Simultaneously, an unpredictability usually comes with political crowds. As situations unfold, all kinds of surprises occur, whether they emerge from the actions of activists, the state, or other actors in the city. The protesters then need to decide how to respond, sometimes in ways that do not disclose a sovereign "decision" by a leadership group or individual, but that emerge in the experimentation with various kinds of responses going on at the same time, some of which catch momentum, others that do not. For example, a graduate student, Chit Wai John Mok, has written eloquently of the Hong Kong protests (see figure 3.2):

> Sometimes a new action can be very random. When the police violently ar-
> rested a student for buying laser pointers, and accused him of possessing

"offensive weapons," people were outraged. Some angry protesters surrounded the police station and were later dispersed by tear gas. On another night, protesters held a "stargazing assembly" outside the Space Museum. All the participants brought laser pointers along. It turned into "a symphony of lights" and, eventually, a dance party.

As Henri Lefebvre (2003 [1970], 130) argued, urban centrality has no necessary pre-given geography, and while it can be shaped by all kinds of powerful historical processes, it can also be a spontaneous force: "A crowd can gather, objects can pile up, a festival unfold, an event—terrifying or pleasant—can occur. This is why urban space is so fascinating: centrality is always possible." As cities continue to grow and inequality deepens, it is likely that the politics of the crowd will become a more-common form of urban centrality, and that in turn states and police authorities will continue to combine brutal force in response—as we've seen in places as different as Hong Kong and Chile—alongside ever-more-sophisticated technology and algorithms to anticipate, track, and target activists (Amoore 2013). In other words, the relations between knowledge, density, politics, and urban space are likely to become increasingly intense, contested, and dynamic.

As part of the wider archive of alternative urban densities, the political crowd of urban protest is not quite the same thing, of course, as high density. High density is a proximity of people in a site, often over long periods if we are thinking of residential densities. A political crowd is a particular expression of density: a collective act that people enter into with particular aims in mind, and with a sense of its short-lived temporality (for an excellent discussion of the history of "crowding studies" and the relationships between "density" and "crowds," see Roskamm 2017). A crowd is conscious of itself as a political entity, unlike, say, a crowd in a shopping area or train station (Sudjic 2017). If "density" has been historically linked to the realm of modernist urban governance, management, and regulation, the "crowd" is a less-controlled historical urban phenomenon being more likely to carry with it qualities of improvisation, elasticity, and excess (and here Elias Canetti's *Crowds and Power*, six decades old, remains a key statement). In this sense, the difference between "density" and "crowd" maps onto the distinction between "the people" as a sociological or demographic category and "the people" as a political category (Swyngedouw 2016).

The relationships between high-density urbanisms and the political crowd, however, are multiple and open. Consider for example, in Mumbai, the so-called Right to Pee movement. The movement works with communities and activists across the city to improve sanitation provisions, particularly access to public and private toilets. It works closely to support high-density neighborhoods lacking the most basic facilities. For example, activists help inspect and monitor public and community toilet blocks in low-income neighborhoods, and work to raise resources to address material problems with toilet blocks or to intervene when social or political disputes occur. This is a politics that, following Elizabeth Grosz (2005, 2), is not so much "mapped out in advance" as it is linked to negotiation and experimentation around ways of doing—a kind of immersion in the trajectories, powers, and actors, formal as well as informal, that compose dense sites.

At the same time, Right to Pee is locked into negotiations with the municipality. Negotiations are being held around policy, budgets, and process, using data that Right to Pee itself generates from conditions on the street. This element of Right to Pee's work turns on a politics of density as number: counting people, counting toilet provisions, documenting conditions, and holding the state accountable by speaking in the grammars of urban liberal governance. There are, then, two means through which Right to Pee performs a politics of density: one, a politics of density linked to monitoring sanitation conditions, and two, a politics of density that speaks to a liberal modernist tradition of number, data, policy, infrastructural and budgetary distributions, basic human rights, and so on.

Yet there is a third politics that I want to draw attention to here, which is linked to these two forms and which points to the generative connections between high-density urbanism and the politics of the crowd. In 2015, one of the community groups inspecting Mumbai's toilet blocks became frustrated by the pace of change and the unfulfilled promises of the municipality. As a protest, a group of women announced that they planned to go to the state government building in south Mumbai and, in the area around the outside of the building, stage a "pee protest." This was a political protest and provocation that could only work in a crowd—a massing of people in space performing a particular and controversial political act in which people would shield, protect, and spur on one another. The idea circulated online and off-line, as one activist put it, "like wildfire." "People thought it was exciting," recalled one of the activists. It was picked up on social media, and also by the *Asian Age* newspaper. The paper reported that on the twenty-fifth of the month, the women would go to the building and stage the protest. The very next day, the state government requested to meet with the protesters.

And so the protest didn't happen. Nonetheless, the point here is that in the crowd, even the crowd that didn't happen, density can play its part as a political force. It is important to see that this kind of force is not simply a moment in time. It is that moment, for sure, but it is also part of an alternative archive of density knowledge. Indeed, precisely the form of political action that members of Right to Pee were planning and then abandoned has, at times, served as a political strategy historically in India and beyond. There is a long history of people using their bodies as political weapons, connecting a politics of proximate and concentrated presencing to the metabolic as well as the municipal. Around the same time of the Mumbai protests, for instance, a group of women in the low-income neighborhood of Rafiq Nagar, near where Right to Pee does much of its work, embarked on a similar politicization (Desai et al. 2014). We can note a history here of what Sudipta Kaviraj (1997) has called "small rebelliousness"—a quite-particular politics of density that emerges from the links among density, fragmented provisions, and urban inequalities, and that itself translates density as a force of shock and surprise by instantiating it through the politics of the crowd (McFarlane and Silver 2017b). These relations are part of an alternative archive of density's knowledge politics.

The relations between high-density urbanisms and the political crowd constitute an important lens through which to view the urban political. It is the potential for high densities to be connected to all kinds of political instantiations that marks out density as being a resource of radical possibility in the city. A quality of surprise and possibility is at work here. This is why the politics of density cannot only be a liberal politics contained within, for example, the slow negotiation with the state over provisions, rights, and distributions. As the Right to Pee protesters well know, it also has to be, at one and the same time, a politics *in the wild*, open to the imaginaries, ideas, and practices that emerge from the combinatory possibilities and the many potential instantiations of political crowding.

Urban space matters here. As these cases from Hong Kong and Mumbai indicate, density, knowledge, space, and politics co-constitute in different ways. The politics of density emerge in part from the conditions of urban space, including the sociospatial production of fragmented and unequal urbanism, as in the case of Mumbai. Density is a bundle of relations found *in* space that can form new political combinations and potentials, and that can, then, become generative *of* space across the city and beyond. We see this, for instance, in the changing urban political forms through the histories of the Hong Kong protests. Density can enter into the making of geographies, even if only temporarily. Density co-constitutes, as Merrifield indicates, urban form. And the ways in which density is politicized and brought into measures of action and organization all make use of space, can reform space, and can produce new spaces altogether.

This does not mean, of course, that deterministic relationships exist between space and politics that we can typologize here, as if certain kinds of politics belonged to particular kinds of spatial density. As Ananya Roy (2011, 235) has rightly cautioned, it is important not to fall into the trap that would "assign unique political agency to the mass of urban subalterns." I am not claiming that certain kinds of spaces on the margins produce particular types of knowledge and politics. Instead, my claim is that density is radically open because of its combinatory possibilities—meaning the multiple and changing relations among people, knowledge, and things that it carries with it, and that change not just over space but even over time, and that can become instantiated in often quite different ways. It is not so much that the margins straightforwardly determine the production of an alternative knowledge politics of density, but instead that the ways in which density has come to be lived, known, and politicized in and through the contingent life conditions, struggles, and aspirations of lives historically shunted to the margins all work to form an expansive and alternative archive.

Density can be made into all kinds of things—a political crowd, or something else—and therefore constitutes a resource of great potential. What might that "something else" be? There is much more to say on this. Partha Chatterjee's (2004) effort to document what he so influentially called "political society" has attempted to name another set of politics connecting density, inequality, and community groups. Another example is Asef Bayat's (2010) attentiveness to the "quiet encroachment of the ordinary," of a politics that moves below the radar of state visibility but that at the same time depends on proximate concentrations of people (such as street vendors) both in place and with the capacity to disperse and reconvene elsewhere. Oren Yiftachel's (2009) rendering of a "grey space" between the legal and illegal, through which the very forms of being present on the land can become a dramatic politics of rights, is another still. I do not want to suggest that these thinkers are writing "about density," but instead to say that their work nonetheless offers conceptual and empirical insight into the form and politics of a larger and often marginalized density archive.

Seeing through density—or should it be "seeing *like* density?"—is to see the urban and the political as open and replete with potential, despite the inequalities in power and resource. The politics of density might well be orderly, predictable, and singular; there is no inevitability that the politics of density is anarchic or unpredictable. The force of density is one of potential. It is a force that can be controlled, policed, structured, and led, but that always and already contains within its relations the possibility of being something radically "other." The political crowd is one historical expression of that, and it itself takes on all kinds of forms and meaning at various times in the history of the urban world.

The force of density is a reminder that the urban political can be more open than we often think it to be. It is a force, as Andy Merrifield reminds us, that is fundamentally urban in the form it takes but only ever in contingent and divergent ways. As a resource of potential through its relational interactions, density does not merely exist *in* space but is productive *of* spaces, both short and longer term. For David Kishik (2015), paying attention to density through the more expansive archive I am gesturing to here is one of the ways we might appreciate what he calls, after Walter Benjamin, the "sheer life" of the city.

This a political realm that is often not written down—that in fact might be planned and coordinated but that is also emergent from the improvisations, happenstance, tensions, and lines of flight nascent in people and things together. Kishik's argument is that listening to and attending to the sheer life of the city might teach us something about the urban political, one sprouting not just from political blueprints but also from an immersive engagement in different kinds of densities. "For far too long," Kishik (2015, 45) argues, "we have busied ourselves with thinking about ways to change the city. It is about time that we let the city change the way we think." That, it seems to me, is an inspiring way to think about how the alternative archive of density's knowledge-politics I am pointing to in this chapter might enliven our understanding of density as well as its future in the city.

Conclusion

We are living in an urban moment when, across the world, city managers are seeking to remake their cities through density. Notwithstanding the damaging and exclusive forms of densification discussed above, the fact that density has had something of a (re)arrival on the urban scene—ranging from policy and think tanks to civil society groups and international organizations—creates an opportunity in which urbanists might populate the agenda and shape the discourse. Given that density's rearrival ran into the wall of the COVID-19 pandemic, which has generated all kinds of debate about density and its futures—from new patterns of working from home to alternative uses of city centers and lingering anxieties around crowds—that opportunity is stronger than it has ever been. Foregrounding an alternative history and present of density is an important part of the task ahead for density's futures. From that commitment, urbanists might be able to bring new perspectives and alliances to the density debate. This is not merely a question of bringing knowledge to power, but rather of generating a knowledge *politics*, and this will mean inevitable clashes, protests, and antagonisms with dominant actors, knowledges, and discourses. There are four steps here that I want to suggest.

The first step is to begin the conversation in any given city with a critique of dominant density knowledges and an insistence that "forgotten densities" be recognized (Pitter 2020). This demands careful excavation of the contemporary and historical experiences, perceptions, and narratives of density of those too often shunted to the economic and political margins of the city, including those knowledges that animate the force of the political crowd. The second step is to struggle to ensure that a genuine participatory conversation occurs that can influence change in how density and its futures are both envisioned and managed in the city. This is, as we know, another moment in which relations can break down when the state perhaps ceases to listen or turns away from alternative paths. At that point, other political routes become important, as the case from Right to Pee reminds us, and as groups like Slum/Shack Dwellers International and the Asian Coalition for Housing Rights have shown.

Provided there is a willingness established in the state to challenge and rethink its understanding and valuations of density, the third step involves implementing more-progressive density directions that maintain a connection to marginalized experiences and aspirations. There is much here for states, and indeed scholars, to learn from practitioners and activists.

To return to Mumbai, for example, the urban group URBZ has earned a rich history of promoting ways of augmenting existing forms of density in poor neighborhoods (see, for example, numerous reports on their website, urbz.net). As URBZ has shown, rather than argue that residents would benefit from densities either increased or reduced in order to meet certain social, economic, and environmental goals (which are usually defined by academic researchers or policymakers or officials, anyway), it is more productive to identify and work with the multiple concerns that many residents themselves attach to density. URBZ looks to improve the material fragments found in poorer neighborhoods and then to document and promote knowledges, social infrastructures, and ways of living most often shunted to the economic and spatial margins of the city. The challenge for policy here is to learn from, in a concerted and ongoing way, the heterogeneity of dense, lived urbanisms that already exist in the city, and then to attempt to augment those.

The fourth step is to address urban regulations on density in a given city, and if necessary to reorient these in directions that support the issues and concerns emerging from alternative knowledges of density. The kind of approach that URBZ and others have put forward is not one of optimal densities. This is important, because as history has shown us, an artificial definition of what constitutes "good" or "bad" density could lead to the demolition of a low-income neighborhood or an informal and inexpensive street market. But this does not mean, of course, that regulations should be abandoned. Globally, certain states have a long history of intervening in low-income neighborhoods to improve standards of living, whether conditions of housing, infrastructure, or services, or indeed other regulations on, for instance, public space or environmental controls as well as practices in and beyond neighborhoods.

To return to Hong Kong, one million of the city's seven million people live under the poverty line, with an estimated 200,000 of them eking out a living in cramped, often overcrowded, partitioned homes. Districts like Sham Shui Po are among the poorest and densest of the eighteen in the city, and here some 3,000 households live in makeshift housing on rooftops, sometimes colorfully if pejoratively referred to as "penthouse slums." Waiting to be allocated public housing—the average is 4.7 years, though for people who are young and single the quota system could mean their waiting for twenty years—people live crammed into homes as small as thirteen square feet that are underserviced and vulnerable to rain, heat, cold, and typhoons. As Chick Kui Wai, a community organizer with the Society for Community Organization (SOCO), put it, people are hemmed in, trapped, and unable to stay clean. It is not uncommon to find cases where areas around ceilings and on stairwells are improvised into sleeping areas.

Clearly, a key part of the challenge here is the lack of regulations on privately rented buildings. There are, for example, insufficient minimum floor space regulations for private buildings, which means homes can be partitioned into smaller and smaller slithers of space. Here, density presses down on the body, whether in the form of heat, noise, poor ventilation, or the spatial compression of struggling to keep a tiny place both clean and safe. Such a condition demands state intervention to regulate minimum requirements on space, yet the state has avoided confronting the issue because of the scale of the challenges and the financial claims it would then open up. At the same time, activist groups like SOCO make clear that the real estate economy, which is geared to expensive apartment blocks, also needs significant reform. SOCO is another example of a group building an alternative knowledge politics of density founded both on critique of the urban status quo and a committed effort to push for more-inclusive, progressive conditions.

The relationship between density and urban knowledge will be increasingly important to the diagnoses of urban problems and aspirations for the future. It is likely to remain a key political frontier of urban transformation. As Saskia Sassen (2011) powerfully argues, there is an important story to be told here about how different kinds of density not only perform political possibilities—whether progressive or conservative—but about how they foreground the political more generally. The relation between high-density urbanisms and the political crowd, for example, is one important lens gazing onto the urban political and to alternative knowledges of the present and future city. This knowledge politics will never be fixed or straightforwardly resolved, because it—like density and the city itself—is always changing. What constitutes the "urban" is always plural and provisional. The densities we see in our cities today may be gone tomorrow, turned to fragments or perhaps eviscerated altogether. If we are truly concerned about the presence and future of ordinary and often neglected densities, then it matters greatly that we work to excavate and form critical dialogue around the multiple knowledge politics of density.

Note

1. I thank Simon Marvin for suggesting the term "premium density" in conversation.

References

Ahlfeldt, Gabriel M., and Elisabetta Pietrostefani. 2019. *The Economic Effects of Density: A Synthesis*. International Trade and Regional Economics (DP13440). Centre for Economic Policy Research, London School of Economics and Political Science.

Amoore, Louise. 2013. *The Politics of Possibility: Risk and Security Beyond Probability*. Durham, NC: Duke University Press.

Anand, Nikhil. 2017. *Hydraulic City: Water and the Infrastructures of Citizenship in Mumbai*. Durham, NC: Duke University Press.

Anjaria, Jonathon Shapiro. 2012. "Is There a Culture of the Indian Street?" *Seminar* 6: 21–27, August. https://www.india-seminar.com/2012/636/636_jonathan_s_anjaria.htm.

Anjaria, Jonathan Shapiro. 2012. *The Slow Boil: Street Food, Rights, and Public Space in Mumbai*. Stanford, CA: Stanford University Press.

Appadurai, Arjun. 1987. "Street Culture." *The India Magazine* 8, no. 1: 12–22, December.

Austin Justice Coalition. 2020. Accessed April 15. https://www.austinjustice.org/betterbeforemore.

Batty, Michael. 2008. "The Size, Scale and Shape of Cities." *Science* 319, no. 5864: 769–771.

Bayat, Asef. 2010. *Life as Politics: How Ordinary People Change the Middle East*. Stanford: Stanford University Press.

Bhan, Gautam. 2016. *In the Public's Interest: Eviction, Citizenship and Inequality in Contemporary Delhi*. Athens: University of Georgia Press.

Björkman, Lisa. 2015. *Pipe Politics, Contested Waters: Embedded Infrastructures of Millennial Mumbai*. Durham, NC: Duke University Press.

Blanco, Ismael, and Margarita Leon. 2017. "Social Innovation, Reciprocity and Contentious Politics: Facing the Socio-urban Crisis in Ciutat Meridiana, Barcelona." *Urban Studies* 54, no. 9: 2172–2188.

Borch, Christian. 2012. *The Politics of Crowds: An Alternative History of Sociology*. Cambridge: Cambridge University Press.

Chatterjee, Partha. 2004. *The Politics of the Governed: Reflections on Popular Politics in Most of the World*. New Delhi: Permanent Black.

Chowdhury, Romit, and Colin McFarlane. 2021. "The Crowd and Citylife: Materiality, Negotiation, and Inclusivity at Tokyo's Train Stations." *Urban Studies*. https://journals.sagepub.com/doi/full/10.1177/00420980211007841.

Cohen, Boyd, Esteve Almirall, and Henry Chesbrough. 2016. "The City as a Lab: Open Innovation Meets the Collaborative Economy." *California Management Review* 59, no. 1: 5–13.

Cohen, Michael, and Margarita Gutman. 2007. "Density: An Overview Essay." *Built Environment* 33, no. 2: 141–144.

Corsín Jimenez, Alberto. 2014. "The Right to Infrastructure: A Prototype for Open-source Urbanism." *Environment and Planning D: Society and Space* 32, no. 2: 342–362.

De Boeck, Filip, and Sammy Baloji. 2016. *Suturing the City: Living Together in Congo's Urban Worlds*. London: Autograph.

Desai, Renu, Colin McFarlane, and Stephen Graham. 2014. "The Politics of Open Defecation: Informality, Body and Infrastructure." *Antipode* 47, no. 1: 98–120.

Dikeç, Mustafa. 2018. *Urban Rage: The Revolt of the Excluded.* New Haven, CT: Yale University Press.

Doshi, Sapana. 2013. "The Politics of the Evicted: Redevelopment, Subjectivity, and Difference in Mumbai's Slum Frontier." *Antipode* 45, no. 4: 844–865.

Dovey, Kim, and Elek Pafka. 2016. "Urban Density Matters—but What Does It Mean?" *The Conversation*, May 20. http://theconversation.com/urban -density-matters-but-what-does-it-mean-58977.

Florida, Richard. 2012. "The Limits of Density." *Citylab.* Accessed April 15, 2020. https://www.citylab.com/design/2012/05/limits-density/2005/.

Florida, Richard. 2017. "Two Takes on the Fate of Future Cities." *Citylab.* Accessed April 15, 2020. https://www.citylab.com/equity/2017/04/two -takes-on-the-fate-of-future-cities/521907/.

Ghertner, Asher. 2015. *Rule by Aesthetics: World-Class City Making in Delhi.* Oxford: Oxford University Press.

Glaeser, Edward. 2012. *The Triumph of the City: How Urban Spaces Make Us Human.* London: MacMillan.

Gleeson, Brendan. 2012. "The Urban Age Paradox and Prospect." *Urban Studies* 49, no. 5: 931–943.

Gleeson, Brendan 2013. "What Role for Social Science in the 'Urban Age'?" *International Journal of Urban and Regional Research* 37, no. 5: 1839–1851.

Grosz, Elizabeth 2005. *Time Travels: Feminism, Nature, Power.* Sydney: Allen and Unwin, Crows Nest.

Harris, Andrew. 2013. "Concrete Geographies: Assembling Global Mumbai through Transport Infrastructure." *City* 17, no. 3: 343–360.

Jacobs, Jane. 1958. "Downtown Is for People." *Fortune.* Accessed September 3, 2018. http://fortune.com/2011/09/18/downtown-is-for-people-fortune -classic-1958/.

Jacobs, Jane. 1961. *The Death and Life of Great American Cities.* London: Jonathan Cape.

Kaviraj, Sudipta. 1997. "Filth and the Public Sphere: Concepts and Practices about Space in Calcutta." *Public Culture* 10, no. 1: 83–113.

Kishik, David. 2015. *The Manhattan Project: A Theory of the City.* Stanford: Stanford University Press.

Klinenberg, Eric. 2018. *Palaces for the People: How to Build a More Equal and United Society.* London: Bodley Head.

Lefebvre, Henri. 2003 [1970]. *The Urban Revolution.* Minneapolis: University of Minnesota Press.

McFarlane, Colin. 2016. "The Geographies of Urban Density: Topography, Topology, and Intensive Heterogeneity." *Progress in Human Geography* 40: 629–648.

McFarlane, Colin. 2021. *Fragments of the City: Making and Remaking Urban Worlds*. Los Angeles: University of California Press.

McFarlane, Colin, and Jonathan Silver. 2017a. "Navigating the City: Dialectics of Everyday Urbanism." *Transactions of the Institute for British Geographers* 42, no. 3: 458–471.

McFarlane, Colin, and Jonathan Silver. 2017b. "The Political City: 'Seeing Sanitation' and Making the Urban Political in Cape Town." *Antipode* 49, no. 1: 125–148.

McGuirk, Justin. 2011. "Understanding the Numbers." In *Living in the Endless City*, edited by Ricky Burdett and Deyan Sudjic, 292–307. London: Phaidon Press.

Merrifield, Andrew. 2014. *The New Urban Question*. London: Pluto Press.

Mok, Chit Wai John. 2019. "What the World Can Learn from Hong Kong's Protests: Index or Censorship." Accessed October 11, 2021. https://www .indexoncensorship.org/2019/09/what-the-world-can-learn-from -hong-kongs-protesters/.

Montgomery, Charles. 2013. *Happy City: Transforming Our Lives Through Urban Design*. London: Penguin Books.

Peck, Jamie. 2015. "Economic Rationality Meets Celebrity Urbanology: Exploring Edward Glaeser's City." *International Journal of Urban and Regional Research* 40, no. 1: 1–30.

Pérez, Federico. 2020. "'The Miracle of Density': The Sociomaterial Epistemics of Urban Densification." *International Journal of Urban and Regional Research* 44, no. 4: 617–635.

Pitter, Jay. 2020. "Urban Density: Confronting the Distance between Desire and Disparity." *Azure*. Accessed April 20, 2020. https://www .azuremagazine.com/article/urban-density-confronting-the-distance -between-desire-and-disparity/.

Rao, Vyjayanthi. 2015. "Infra-City: Speculations on Flux and History in Infrastructure-Making." In *Infrastructural Lives: Urban Infrastructure in Context*, edited by S. Graham and C. McFarlane, 39–58. London: Routledge-Earthscan.

Roskamm, Nikolai. 2017. "Lethal Density: The Research Field of Crowding in the 1960s and '70s." In *Rethinking Density: Culture and Urban Practices*, edited by Anamarija Batista, Szilvia Kovács, and Carina Lesky, 252–263. Berlin: Sternberg Press.

Roy, Ananya. 2011. "Slumdog Cities: Rethinking Subaltern Urbanism." *International Journal of Urban and Regional Research* 35: 223–238.

Roy, Ananya. 2017. "Dis/possessive Collectivism: Property and Personhood at City's End." *Geoforum* 80: A1–11.

Russell, Jim. 2013. "Density Boondoggles." *New Geography*. Accessed April 15, 2020. https://www.newgeography.com/content/003634-density -boondoggles.

Sassen, Saskia. 2011. "The Global Street: *Making* the Political." *Globalizations* 8, no. 5: 573–579.

Silver, Jonathan. 2014. "Incremental Infrastructures: Material Improvisation and Social Collaboration across Post-colonial Accra." *Urban Geography* 35, no. 6: 788–804.

Sim, David. 2019. *Soft City: Building Density for Everyday Life.* London: Island Press.

Simone, AbdouMaliq. 2016. "City of Potentialities: An Introduction." *Theory, Culture and Society* 33, no. 7–8: 5–29.

Simone, AbdouMaliq. 2018. *Improvised Lives: Rhythms of Endurance in an Urban South*. Cambridge: Polity Press.

Sudjic, Deyan. 2017. *The Language of Cities.* London: Penguin.

Swyngedouw, Erik. 2016. "Unlocking the Mind-trap: Politicizing Urban Theory and Practice." *Urban Studies* 54, no. 1: 55–61.

Taubenböck, Hannes, Ines Standfuß, Martin Klotz, and Michael Wurm. 2016. "The Physical Density of the City—Deconstruction of the Delusive Density Measure with Evidence from Two European Megacities." *International Journal of Geo-Information* 5: 206. doi:10.3390/ijgi5110206.

Tonkiss, Fran. 2014. *Cities by Design: The Social Life of Urban Form*. Cambridge: Polity Press.

Wachsmuth, David, Daniel Aldana Cohen, and Hillary Angelo. 2016. "Expand the Frontiers of Urban Sustainability." *Nature* 536: 391–393, August 25. https://www.nature.com/news/expand-the-frontiers-of-urban -sustainability-1.20459.

Weinstein, Lisa. 2013. *The Durable Slum: Dharavi and the Right to Stay Put in Globalizing Mumbai*. Minneapolis: University of Minnesota Press.

Wilson, Japhy, and Erik Swyngedouw. 2015. *The Post-Political and Its Discontents: Spaces of Depoliticisation, Spectres of Radical Politics*. Edinburgh: Edinburgh University Press.

Yiftachel, Oren. 2009. "Critical Theory and 'Grey Space': Mobilization of the Colonized." *City* 13, no. 2–3: 240–256.

BIG

Rethinking the Cultural Imprint
of Mass Urbanization

Bigging It Up

The masses have never been more massive: nearly 7 percent of all those who have ever lived on the planet are living today (Population Reference Bureau 2018). An estimated 360,000 people are born each day and 151,600 people die. Big numbers like these are not phantasms. They cannot be wished away. Denial is not an option (Haraway 2018). Yes, the category of population is linked to a modernizing ideology, but that does not mean, as some are wont to imply, that the numbers have no purchase.

Like the global population, urban populations are increasing all the time, taking in more and more people absolutely and relatively. But many social scientists are unsure of what to make of the social and cultural consequences of this urban population growth. The questions are endless. When cities are the size of countries, do we get even more heterogeneity and even more drive, or do we get larger versions of just a few groups? With the growing scale of longer, increasingly global networks, do we get more complication but much the same level of complexity (in a nutshell, the Latourian view [see Langlitz 2019]) or do we get more complexity too as Beer (1974) argued many years ago? Do we get the illusion of more innovation and originality, or do larger urban populations mean that we get more and more of the real thing—a cavalcade of invention? Do we get a more cosmopolitan urban soup with brighter and more varied cultural kaleidoscopes exploding onto the scene or just a few shakes endlessly repeating themselves with only minor variations? Do we get faster and faster cultural turnover in cities or only what Rosa (2015) calls a "frenetic standstill"? Do we get at least a moiety of what might once have been utterly obscure interests and obsessions reaching a point where they are able to survive and reproduce, or do we just get a scatter-gun effect in which these interests and obsessions flick on and off in an endless parade of irrelevancy?

Even describing the new conflicts and commonalities engendered by the "power of big" is a challenge, not least because what is counted as "writing" has shifted its shape, taking in not merely printed text but all kinds of other media, too. That said, new words are being coined at some rate, perhaps more rapidly than ever before, as vernacular and technical vocabularies increase. Although many often sound forced, a few will sink into common usage, changing perceptions as they do so. After all, words harbor ways of seeing and being that can be limiting but can also produce new dispositions and resources. However slowly, a new urban lexicon is beginning to emerge, one that will supplement and extend the compendium of Topalov et al. (2010). Some of the words in this lexicon simply indicate new technologically induced practices. Others are appropriations from existing urban cultures. Yet others are new by design. These words are perhaps the most difficult to put into circulation, since intent and content are difficult to stabilize, but sometimes they get their day in the sun.

Perhaps the most fruitful efforts to coin a vocabulary by design have been made in the environmental arena where new words are badly needed to describe a planetary disposition in which anxiety and dread mix together in an unholy manner as an incontinent humanity acts big but thinks small (Fuller and Goriunova 2020). A vocabulary that can span the multitude of concerns arising from the gradual euthanizing of the planet, one that can make sense of the rubble and the desecration and the disappearances, is beginning to appear, the result of bending old words and inventing new ones. For example, there is Robert Macfarlane's (2015) desecration and counter-desecration phrasebook and the Bureau of Linguistical Reality's attempt to create a new vocabulary for the Anthropocene (Quante and Escott 2019). Words have been coined like "solastalgia," meaning a malady resulting from places disrupted by ecosystem distress, rendered unrecognizable by corporate action or climate change. It was a malady that was already familiar to that nineteenth-century laboring class poet, John Clare, bemoaning the destruction wrought on the land by mechanized agriculture. But it has now become even more familiar. I think of a colleague of

mine in China who went away for six months and came back to his home-
town to find that the pace of change in the built environment was so great
that the railway station had been moved and many of the original streets
no longer existed, the result being that he had to ask directions to his own
home in the place he thought he knew best.

Most of the time, however, we will probably stick with the old vocabulary, reusing it to mean different things. But it is going to be difficult.
Words can be outpaced. For example, the city has often been called a *palimpsest*, but this word is no longer even vaguely adequate to describe the
sheer weight of the way in which geography past creeps into geography
present and upends geography future. As Ings (2014, 104–105) aptly puts it,
this Gormenghast-like state of affairs means that:

> The city picks and scratches itself like an animal kept in too small a cage,
> pining for its lost reflection. It obsesses over its own archaeology. . . . At
> its centre the city has begun to resemble the root system of a neglected
> houseplant. [It] has packed itself around itself to the point where its surface
> has eroded away entirely. . . . There is something exhilarating about this—
> some atavistic hint of forest canopy.

Keeping that thought in mind, let's obsess over the contemporary urban
canopy.

Size Isn't Incidental

Two things we do know about twenty-first-century cities: generally speaking, they are both growing larger and taking up a larger proportion of the
population of humans—and indeed also of nonhumans, like animals and
plants. It often seems to be assumed as a default option that this growth
will produce more of the same but bigger. Yet being numerous has limits,
real limits. I will briefly mention just four.

Let's take the most obvious first. The growth of mammoth cities, and
of the global urban system more generally, has been and is a major driver
of climate change (see Thrift 2021). The using up of resources at breakneck
speed to build cities has real physical limits, in that it both causes climate
change and produces major shortages of the raw materials on which urban
growth has traditionally depended. For example, China's boom in city
building has depended on the use of ferocious amounts of energy derived
from large amounts of coal and oil, which has driven global carbon emis-

sions upward at some rate, as well as on large amounts of concrete and especially two of its main constituents: cement (China is home to more than 58 percent of global cement production, which alone is driving carbon emissions rapidly upward) and sand used for building. Many other countries display similar tendencies toward what might, if you're feeling kind, be called urban energy profligacy or, if you're feeling unkind, urban energy lunacy. Unless the situation changes, not only will basic resources expire but climate change will also put the brakes on urban growth through a whole set of different threats to life and land: air pollution, water shortages, aquifers drained, cyclones becoming stronger and more intense, greater and greater heat stress, rampaging wildfires, and, of course, the cockamamie food system that threatens urban food supplies by polluting and leaching the soil. In turn, as cities have sprawled over more and more land, so they become more susceptible to climate-change-driven disasters—and indeed to chains of disasters. These facts are all well known, of course, but the political will to solve them is still in short supply, even at this frighteningly late hour.

A second limit to being too numerous is the movement of peoples, either voluntarily or forced, especially by climate change (Vesper 2019). According to the United Nations (2019a and 2019b), about 272 million people—some one person in every 30—were living outside their country of birth in 2019. That is a record high: by way of comparison, there were 153 million people in 1990. However, figures like these fail to capture the full count of those living in places other than that of their patrimony. There were 29 million refugees and asylum seekers in mid-2017. But the registered refugees represent only a fraction of all those forced to leave their homes for a multitude of reasons, ranging from war and economic breakdown to the environmental crises induced by climate change. In total, it is estimated that at least 79.5 million people globally are currently experiencing forced displacement (UNHCR 2020). As for expatriates, estimates vary widely, depending on the definition: the U.S. State Department, for example, reckons that 9 million Americans live overseas; about 5 million Britons are also thought to do so and about 1 million Australians (Hill 2018). Then, last but not least, some 10 to 12 million people are stateless, according to various rough estimates from the UNHCR and other bodies.

Whereas, in the past, masses of humans could move to other places on the planet, now other humans often stand in their way, as does the lack of alternative habitable places to move on to (Chakrabarty 2014). Historically speaking, until the twentieth century, comparatively small numbers of humans would be on the move, often over quite long time periods. But now large numbers of people are moving into areas that already have large numbers of people, and moving there over foreshortened periods of time, which makes adjustment very difficult: integration at this kind of scale over these kinds of foreshortened time periods has only rarely been attempted before, and the frictions that have appeared as a result are only likely to grow. The result is obvious: we are now witnessing some of the highest levels of human movement on record—and some of the strongest attempts to stop it.

A third limit is a more-general increase in movement as people make journeys for all manner of reasons. But this "infinite mobilization" (Sloterdijk 2020) now prompts all kinds of congestion. One of the most prominent examples of what is happening is provided by so-called "overtourism."[1] Tourist arrivals around the world grew to 1.4 billion in 2018, and the World Tourism Organization forecasts that this number will rise to 1.8 billion by 2030 (Glusac 2019). More and more people are turning up at favorite tourist spots, and these inundations are now becoming a real problem. In 2018, some 630 million people visited cities overseas, more than 500 million of them concentrated into just 300 locations, many of them historic towns and cities. The result? Venice now charges admission for short-stay tourists. Prague is so overrun that it has prohibited cycling near its most popular monuments. Barcelona has banned the construction of any more hotels. The Forbidden City in Beijing has cut admissions to 80,000 a day (from peaks on some days of 120,000), made all purchases of tickets online, and forbids guides to use bullhorns to attract customers. And it's not just cities. Mount Everest suffers from queues of climbers trying to reach the summit (some die every year making the attempt). Until Uluru was declared off-limits in 2019, it was besieged by queues of tourists wending their way up and down the sacred mountain. Iceland is visited by Justin Bieber and the like, plus their social media followers, with many adverse effects—not just Bieber—ranging from overcrowding to environmental damage that often results from tourists in search of that one perfect Instagram image:

> Just ask the people of Iceland who, having been "discovered" in 2015 . . . by Bieber, who shot the music video to his single "I'll Show You" at its Fjadrargljufur canyon, have subsequently found their natural wonders, hidden thermal springs and indigenous fauna crawling with Beliebers.
>
> The singer claims 105 million followers on Instagram, a number that dwarfs that country's population of 338,000, and last month the canyon was

closed to the public owing to the overwhelming number of visitors (Ellison 2019, 20).

Fourth, there is the question, yet to be answered, of the limits to governability, a point to which I will return.[2] Some of the world's new supersized cities of more than 20 million people may well have reached these limits. Of course, ways can be found around this issue—such as producing mini-city administrative districts, or loading a city up with information technology that can keep a handle on what is going on at micro-scales, a continuation of the old Chinese Communist Party block systems by digital means, or even building new cities that take up the extra load of population. But none of these options can produce the kind of faux-certainty that many governments cling to. In China, for example, there is a constant fear of breakout events, but now at scales that can rapidly become unmanageable. No wonder that China is limiting the size of cities like Beijing and Shanghai. Yes, it's all to do with environmental limits. But it's also to do with governability. The Party thinks these cities have got quite large enough, thank you.

Big and Urban Cultures

But I want to concentrate most of my attention on the effects of size on the urban cultural realm. Such general cultural tendencies used to be difficult to discern in any detail. Yet the rise of algorithmic technologies of numbering that can cope with and influence the supersized urban sphere has made these tendencies clearer, because these technologies are not only detection and measuring instruments but also formative cultural influences in their own right. For example, whereas once upon a time we would pore over the details of a census every ten years, now the census is effectively a continuous activity of tracking and tracing. Counting urban populations in various ways has become a norm, along with associated activities like storing, indexing, comparing, converting, searching, and, especially, predicting (Lury and Day 2019). These numbering technologies don't just represent what we count as persons through new informational pathways and the new means of relation and participation they reveal (Lury and Day 2019). They don't just act as a feedback infrastructure. They don't just piggyback on our decisions, either—insofar as we interoceptive beings actually make determinate decisions at all, a questionable proposition in its own right. They also influence our decisions, especially since the rise of machine learning. Agrawal, Gans, and Goldfarb (2018, 13) argue that what machine learning allows, above all, is an enhanced (and therefore cheaper) ability to predict or, more accurately, the ability to use "information you have [so as] to generate information you don't have." In turn, as prediction becomes easier, so machines will be asked to do more of it, to address problems that were not traditionally thought of as prediction problems, and to leverage the various complements that will have their value enhanced by the new environment that results. In turn, prediction can become so cheap and so commonplace that it starts to affect the organization and strategies of all kinds of informational objects and institutions. Most particularly, objects and institutions will have acquired better powers of anticipation, for example, of which goods and services people want, and when.

With these evolving capacities, and the consequent tendency to follow an unacknowledged but potent urban "governance by numbers," as enacted by governments and corporations, comes the matter of unacknowledged persuasion (Supiot 2017).[3] Although it may not be the case that governance by numbers represents the wiring into human life of B. F. Skinner's experiments with conditioned behavior, still, as has been pointed out many times, a strain of this thinking definitely connects through Madison Avenue and its Silicon Valley successors (see Samuel 2010) as a means of unmooring preferences so that the hidden persuaders can do their work. As Coyle (2019, 21) puts it:

> If a much-loved pet were subject to a Skinnerian behavioural experiment to make them obsessively spend several hours a day pressing levers for food, most fond owners would be outraged and put a halt to the practice. Yet the vast experiment on us is far worse. It does not rely on natural preferences for necessities but creates new wants, some positive, some harmless, others clearly damaging the fabric of our societies.

Indeed, as if to prove Coyle's point, numerous so-called "dark patterns" are becoming apparent: online interface design choices that work by coercing, steering, or deceiving users into making unintended and potentially harmful decisions. These are surprisingly prevalent (Mathur et al. 2019). Many websites do the digital equivalent of pressure selling—for example, by instilling a false sense of urgency by misdirecting, or misrepresenting, or implying scarcity, as well as a host of other maneuvers.[4] And, this is before we even get to more-general practices like astroturfing, in which companies or political campaign consultants attempt to create the perception of an upswell of support for a product or cause, creating the image of a public consensus where none exists by masking the sponsors of a message or organization to make it appear as though it originates from and is supported by grassroots participants. Such practices have become much easier with the advent of information technology, even though some may be illegal.

Again, information technology has allowed new means of representation to become commonplace, as images glowing from screens. One example from close to home is the redesign of academic papers as "computational notebooks" that is now starting to take place in the many scientific domains where computational puzzles predominate (Somers 2018). Writers like Stephen Wolfram argue that it should be possible to produce an inflection point in the pursuit of science itself. Although most commentators would think that this was an inflated claim, still systems like the cathedral of Mathematica, and the bazaar of open enterprise software like IPython (now called Jupyter), and also the open-source plotting library Matplotlib, are gradually producing a world in which results and methods are revealed at the same moment—an important issue, given the current crisis of replication. Equally, the more-inclusive Jupyter has since been adopted by musicians, teachers, and even AI researchers. It is spreading into all kinds of domains it was never intended to serve.

In turn, numbering and representational technologies like these have begun to shift what is counted as the social as well as what counts as valid personhood, and especially what counts as personal efficacy. The world increasingly looks like it turns up individually and must be solved individually. And corporations then sell that individuality, in a relentless feedback loop. Even though its products are more often than not sold to millions of people at a time, a corporation makes it seem that the individual is actually the focus of its undivided attention. To use a familiar anthropological thema, the gods of the upper air are acting as gods of the pigeonholes.

In other words, growth in population size has been amplified by the growth of information technology. Each person is a node in a larger and larger telecommunications network in a way that would have been inconceivable in past times. For example, the number of mobile phone users in the world reached 5.1 billion in 2019, a worldwide mobile penetration of 67 percent. About half of this usage was smartphones. This enhanced capacity to communicate has obvious cultural effects. For example, many of the issues around overtourism arise from not merely more ease of mobility given by one's smartphone, but also from the fact that it is much easier to use them to both search out and access sites, and from the onward ability to instantaneously demonstrate that you have been to them, rather than having to wait for a postcard to be delivered or a photograph to be developed. With the rise of platforms, this "being in place" effect becomes rather like a continuous show-and-tell, woven into the fabric of everyday life as part of a near-simultaneous conversation that is both at a distance and near to oneself. Conversation and urban places interact in new ways that reflect interaction orders with their own ethnomethodological protocols that take in information technology as an integral part of these orders, as framing devices, as chatbots, as "unprompted prompts," as additional pieces of information, and so on.

The result is that something like a genuinely all-encompassing technosphere is emerging, an interlinked supersized urban environment—what Haff (2014) calls a stratigraphic paradigm—of telecommunications, transport, bureaucratic, and regulatory systems with an estimated mass of 30 trillion tons that, to an extent at least, follows its own dynamics that in turn enable large-scale metabolization of energy resources, permit buildings and infrastructure to outweigh the planet's trees and shrubs, and have produced a mass of plastic double the weight of animals (Elhacham et al. 2020; Syvitski et al. 2020). Without this urban technosphere and its large-scale replumbing of the global environment, it is doubtful that the planet would be able to support such large human populations as now exist. But it is also a likely reason for urban downfall, because the levels of resource extraction and energy use that the technosphere entails are causing not only climate change but also the surplus death of a multitude of living things that form the biosphere we live in (Thrift 2021). Thus, as one example, the rise of information technology has added to energy loads:

> We wanted clean energy; we got cryptocurrencies that use as much electricity as Argentina. We wanted sustainable transport. Instead we got millions of car-hire drivers. Where are the tech products that help us slow global warming and adapt to a warmer world? At this rate, parts of the world will gain access to multiple food-delivery apps just as they lose access to clean water. Alexa, tell me why it's 100 degrees outside (Mance 2019, 10).

One common story is that the rise of information technology is congruent with the rise of more and more detailed state and corporate surveillance. It is. After all, we already have a situation where most people carry a tracking device that can reveal their location twenty-four hours a day. But it is all too easy to turn technological developments like the rise of smartphones and internet platforms into a heavy-handed account of surveillance that substitutes technological determinism for complexity (Smith 2019). Why? Because, clearly, one possible future could be a "swarm city" in which surveillance has become all-pervasive, with all the effects that is likely to have on processes of individuation as mobile subjects become governable through location analytics that calculate probabilities and imagined potentials.[5] Track-and-trace becomes a normal part of everyday life, just like roads and paths. Some of the corporate ambitions currently being manifested in China are an index of this. In a demonstration of the capabilities it expects to have, one company turns the fabric of the city against a recalcitrant. Using a combination of GIS, backbone computing networks, smart cameras, and artificial intelligence software, authorities not only can identify that recalcitrant but, if they need to be apprehended, can turn all kinds of features of the urban landscape against them: escalators can be stopped or run in reverse, cars can be immobilized, aspects of the landscape like streetlights or even fountains can be activated. Each possible escape route is blocked off, giving time for the police to catch up and arrest the wrongdoer.

However, if the world could be boiled down to just surveillance, whether by government or by corporations or by some unholy hybrid of the two, it is doubtful that the practice would be so successful. Consent is also needed, and this comes largely through the fact that the new information technology platforms are also machines for dispensing mass entertainment. If all that was happening was the rise of a grim, Sauron-like, all-seeing eye, there might be more kickback. But people sign up to this kind of world. Much of the time, their surveillance comes mixed up with the attractions and sometimes the joys of entertainment produced in such a way that they are inseparable (Thrift 2011). After all, by one estimate, 15 percent of all the internet bandwidth on Earth is taken up by Netflix (Schlossberg 2019). And that's before we get to the trillions of photographs and shortform videos uploaded to platforms like Facebook, Google, WeChat, and TikTok. Partly because of the rise of information technology, this is now a world in which opportunities for people's entertainment are legion and in which a considerable amount of their free time is taken up engaging with entertainment products enabled by the rise of platforms (Langley and Leyshon 2017), mainly in that very large part of the city that constitutes indoors. Many of the platforms that suck up our data are wholly or partially about entertainment, and they typically allow their users to show a (constrained) form of creativity that can act as a kind of cultural appetizer.

Yet entertainment, understood as marketed convivial experience, is remarkably neglected in much of the literature on modern mass societies, even though, as Johnson (2017) points out, mass entertainment has been and is extraordinarily innovative. Indeed, he makes a good case that many of the most significant innovations that we now enjoy originated in the groves of entertainment out of the search to keep ourselves amused. But these inventions are often regarded as frivolous until they reach other domains. They are not. The human appetite for novel, surprising, and pleasurable sensory experiences is pretty much a constant throughout history, and it is surprising how little attention is paid to it as a source of innovation.

> The guilty pleasures of life often give us a hint of future changes in society. . . . Because play is often about breaking rules and experimenting with new conventions, it turns out to be the seedbed for many innovations that ultimately develop into much sturdier and more significant forms (Johnson 2017, 14).

Therefore, as human beings have gained more free time, they have filled it with numerous distractions and amusements that take in the full range of human endeavor, ranging from displays of physical excellence (such as sport) through to reflections on life manufactured using various symbolic registers, from the written novel and the play through to the TV drama series and the podcast, from the use of drugs and alcohol through to the now-vast activities of online gambling and gaming. This is a veritable history of manufactured delight, culture's own Big Bang.

Consider only the near past. The eighteenth century saw the rise of structured gambling based on racing of various kinds, assembly rooms of several sorts, and so on. The pace of change picked up in the nineteenth century, which welcomed numerous entertainment innovations, including a new kind of public house (the gin palace), the music hall, the dancing room, the palace of varieties, the exhibition, the seaside resort, and even the football field (Jackson 2019). The twentieth century saw film and then television, as well as the incorporation of sport into mass entertainment, the rise of theme parks, and a proliferation of musical genres that could claim to be popular in the broadest sense. But Adorno and the Frankfurt School never envisaged twenty-first-century streaming channels, platforms, and social media, or mass gaming and its offshoots like gamification that have taken some of their insights to new levels and, by the way, have shown that entertainment is now a pivot around which mass populations spin. Audiences (for which read "populations") that in years gone by would have numbered in the thousands sequestered into specifically tailored spaces like theaters or arenas can now easily number in the millions, participating by proxy from their own homes (though arenas have got bigger, too).

Three points follow on. First, informationalized mass entertainment has a practical understanding of life that theory often elides. Specifically, it understands that *originality* is constantly having to be redefined in order to keep ahead of the demand for new entertainments. It is a cliché that, with the advent of information technology, we live in a world where entertainment has become a mass production industry, with its own constantly expanding archives of images and texts and sounds and with its own distribution and supply chains, all of which has produced a kind of extended library and warehouse all-in-one that is increasingly powered by social media and streaming sites. But, as with any industry, entertainment can only survive if it can constantly produce a stream of new products.

Second, what is often missing from many accounts of the contemporary informationalized entertainment industry is any sense of why entertainment is, well, entertaining. Talk of fun, delight, thrill, pleasure, surprise, novelty, excitement, or exaltation is greeted with a severe and, more often than not, disapproving mien or simply dismissed as either superficial or a deception (see Ehrenreich 2006).[6]

Third, many accounts of informationalized mass entertainment are too willing to import back into the explanatory mix all the monolithic and reductionist accounts of media power that great effort was put into questioning, back in the days of debates around television and other twentieth-century media, but that now, under another heading like "surveillance capitalism" (Zuboff 2019), are being reborn. Audiences once again become dupes. But, as Livingstone (2019) points out, audiences are active, diverse, and polysemic. Arguably, the new platforms play to exactly these characteristics, vacuuming up creative audience experiences for their own ends, as Zuboff would have it, and also lowering the bar to participation. Yet audiences do not just sit back and take it.[7] No, they complain. They dissimulate. They spoof. They invent countermeasures. They invent new ways of going on. The audience is not a reliable entity that just rolls over and does what it's told. After all, if the new media power combines are so all-encompassing, why bother to talk to audiences at all? If prediction is so all-powerful, why does it keep breaking down? Because, put very simply, on the cusp of any decision, individuals' thoughts and actions are not always clear, even to themselves (Chater 2018). Because individuals suffer from all manner of unconscious cognitive biases in making decisions, such as availability bias. Because individuals, either alone or in concert with others, can suddenly do totally unexpected things that do not follow on logically from their data histories. Because individuals have longings that may suddenly break cover and that they themselves may only partially understand. Because. . . . Well, the list goes on. In other words, there *will* be originality, come what may.

Standing Out from the Crowd

So, against this general background, what are the main cultural effects of big? In this short piece, I cannot cover all the effects, whether innovations, obsequies, inversions, or eversions. So I will choose just one effect, continuing the themes of surveillance, entertainment, and originality from the previous section.

It has been a long-standing story that Western city dwellers (and, so far as I can tell, city dwellers everywhere) like to tell about themselves—that they live fast, intense, and unpredictable lives (see the latest variant of this story by Rosa 2019) while the rural clodhoppers just do the same thing—slowly, very slowly, every day (Glennie and Thrift 2009). But sometime in the nineteenth century, this story began to be generalized and valorized and not merely spun out of the cloth of myth and magic. One variant, in particular, became dominant.

So now, according to some accounts, urban life is about harvesting intense experiences and avoiding the laudanum of routine (even though it can be argued that cities are, above all, precisely routinized conglomerates of actions). We should go everywhere. We should try everything. Into our short lives, we must cram every kind of experience, till every possible field, aim for each and every one of the peaks of a cultural high, so that we can feel more alive. Social media have only made this move toward a model of an essentially urban intensity masquerading as the norm worse, by allowing people to display their lives as though they were a succession of photographs of extraordinary experiences—even though most of these experiences were necessarily packaged and must have been experienced by others many times before on this crowded planet.

These developments have only been hastened by scale. Greater scale means that it becomes ever more difficult to stand out from the urban crowd in an era in which doing so has become an insistent predicate to action. The flaneur treading the urban streets was one of the first attempts at producing this stand-out-from-the-crowd culture. The pursuit of originality has now become a mass pursuit, as if Baudelaire's fear of bourgeois normalization has been multiplied a million times.

However, when so many are in pursuit of originality in mass urbanized societies, one of the problems becomes how to stand out when standing out has become a norm. In particular, a combination of scale and inequality means that fewer people proportionately can win this pursuit: fewer are winning the competition, relatively speaking, but many more want to be winners, also relatively speaking. It is no wonder that there is such an emphasis on celebrity. This has become one of the only ways in which many people can get any time in the sun. This tendency toward a greater and greater emphasis on standing out has only been strengthened by information technology that has "bettering" built into its soul through its emphasis on comparison (Lury and Day 2019). Increasingly, cultures are built on ranking, on dynamic stratification in numerous different environments in which participation can often feel mandatory even when it isn't.

When we cast around for a way into this phenomenon, the obvious port of embarkation is the French philosopher and novelist Tristan Garcia's (2018) general philosophical account of *intensity*. Garcia is a philosopher of the thing and also of the object (see Garcia 2014; Cogburn 2017), but he has also strayed into more-general cultural commentary. As a philosopher, Garcia tends to take the view from the mountaintop. However, that doesn't mean that his insights are worthless. His thesis may not be quite as original as he would like it to be. It is a kind of mash-up that has been foreshadowed many times (Thrift 2011). Yet it has the benefit of being both pithy and bold— even if at times that means it is clearly an exaggeration—as well as being tied closely to the evolution of entertainment: "the spectacle and consumption of intensities . . . were crystallised in the promise of the entertainment industry, nickelodeon, movies, and theme parks" (Garcia 2018, 84).[8]

For Garcia, making life into a series of peak experiences has become something close to a sacred mission for some people, especially those who can afford it. Intensity has become the "standard by which we measure the value of both our intimate life and the moment in which we live" (Garcia 2018, 13). It is, in large part, what he calls "primaverism": the adoration of first times. It is, perhaps, a secular form of religion, one that worships at the altar of beginnings. But of course, if exceptionally intense experiences become the norm, they are no longer exceptional: "to add them is to subtract them and to increase them is to decrease them" (Garcia 2018, 92). In some sense, primaverism is a cultural originality machine intended to produce impressions of intensity in the same way that a roller coaster gives the impression of speed when in fact it is not going particularly fast.

Indeed, Garcia points to the way that an ideal of intensity in sport rapidly became a regulated and normalized machine to assess performance, helped on by numerical comparisons made at finer and finer levels. Hence also the rise of new extreme-sports that raise the performative ante, like base-jumping, paragliding, ski jumping, skydiving, bungee jumping, whitewater kayaking, downwinding, ultra-running, parkour, and even extreme trainings like CrossFit—all trying to outdo each other in their devotion to giving performers intense experiences outside the norm. Or consider the rise of adventure tourism, often including sports like these as a part of the package, which specializes in sending people on trips to remote and sometimes risky destinations to obtain selfies that also act as bragging rights.

This hunger for primary experiences, like the hunger for other positional goods, appears obvious to us now. But it is an edifice that has had to be built over many decades. We can argue about where it came from—the injection of electricity into thinking categories, later revived by thinkers like Deleuze (Mader 2017), romanticism as a kind of libertinism, the discovery of an experience economy by the cultural circuit of capitalism leading to the now-commonsense idea that all selling is somehow about experiences, the growth of a wealthy class able to indulge its whims and industries able to satisfy them, even the rise of ways of bracketing experience like bucket lists.

Garcia's thesis is exaggerated in that he seems to believe that every value is subjected to the high-octane criterion of intensification and that the main presentiment of value is a slogan along the lines of "I promise more life." It is, he argues, the feeling of living that counts—an experience of liberation. Thus, intense persons feel smothered by repetition and afraid of conformity and what they see as the dead hand of routine. They need change, or the promise of it, to avoid predictability (what Garcia calls variation), they need heightened acceleration, and they need the fix of even more sensation that comes from being first. They have become caught up in the logic of their own ritual. In other words, intensification has become the "immense hidden a priori" (Cogburn 2017, 14) to our actions, crowding out values like salvation and wisdom. Of course, societies are never quite this simple—only a philosopher might think they were. Equally, Garcia (2018, 85) tends to oppose "thought" (reason) to "intensity" (feeling), as if there were a clear dividing line, writing that "the intense person distrusts thought, knowledge and language because they all reduce living variation to stable entities or quantities and end up making the world unliveable."

Such a bipolar viewpoint might be seen as a means of making a cultural diagnosis of the problem of how to live—or as simply snobbery.

But that doesn't mean there is no cause to worry. The irony is that the people who think they are getting closer to the truth of the world by inhabiting a privileged zone of experience that has broken out into the cultural clear air have never been farther away from it. They are actually bound up with a marketable phenomenology that is simultaneously a kind of hierophany and a marketplace existentialism (Thrift 2011). Often, they are users with a habit, not actual explorers of life.[9] But if all that was happening was the indulging in a few bourgeois whims, whereas it might not be entirely harmless, I suppose it could be thought acceptable. Not so! This behavior also produces another group of people who think of themselves as losers or supplicants, with all the negative consequences that produces, adding to the hidden injuries of class. It amplifies the competitive instinct that characterizes capitalist societies that are already quite competitive enough. Further, it has real environmental consequences in a world where population is still growing. Cruise ships go to more and more remote places, like Antarctica and the Galapagos, in search of keynote experiences, cluttering them up in the process. Wild animals are disturbed by tourists on safari desperate to get the best close-to-nature picture. And, in our current resource-hungry world, even when the primaverist ambition is achieved, it is often tarnished: the person who finally reached the seafloor of the Marianas Trench found candy wrappers and a plastic bag.

Actualizing Knowledge

I have made a series of leaps to get to this point—from size to culture to entertainment to intensity—and now I want to make another leap: to the nature of knowledge itself. Very often, we talk and write and address and map the world into existence as though it were an unproblematic object—once we get to know enough of it, we will *know* it. This runs straight into the problem of false definiteness. Size only amplifies this issue. Of course, various economies of problems, and their ways of inventing ideas, exist that offer a solution—some kinds of phenomenology, some sorts of pragmatism, the approaches arising out of various interpretations of Whiteheadian metaphysics, contemporary writings on emergent evolution, and so on. Each of these different forms of a kind of empiricism contains different solutions to this tension, but they share both the notion that all existence is situated some*where* and an insistence that possibilities are "always found . . . in actual relation to what exists at a determinate moment" (Debaise 2017, 36).

As a brief personal interlude, I always felt attracted to the kind of "big" social theory that tries to cover the whole of the slope. To begin with, I was overly impressed by theoretical optimists who seemed to know, with an almost absolute certainty, what was going on in the world even though, from early on (see Thrift 1985), I didn't really think that this was possible in a world where "what really exists is not things made but things in the making" (James 1977, 17). Gradually I realized that I was making neither a mountain nor a molehill. Instead, I had wanted, as Blastland (2019, 26) nicely has it, a "comfort blanket over a mess," a volatile and oftentimes inconclusive mess whose situatedness is part of the point. But the comfort blanket isn't available.

Further, leaning on such theoretical optimism is particularly dangerous when phenomena are big, and therefore can often have more—and more varied—associations. The web of potential causes and effects expands, and then expands again. As Cartwright and Hardie (2012, 52) famously put it, "causes work in teams." Take cities as an example. It is doubtful that we can, or ever will be able to, explain every little rustle of activity that goes to make up a city. Cities will always have ragged edges and inconclusive structures and meanings. They cannot be reduced to the trellis of objects and infrastructures that we know we can easily describe. Cities cannot be fully taken in by conventional theoretical means because they are the result of heavily contingent and contextual interactions, the outcomes of which are often decided only in the moment—in the event itself. They produce what some scientists nowadays call "intangible variation." The goal of time-geography, often dismissed nowadays as a kind of cul-de-sac, was precisely to describe and characterize (rather than explain) this "mess" of contingent and contextual variation, a mess with real effects that cannot be set aside as simply noise or some kind of enigma. Cities amplify this mess—they ramp up the "hidden half," as Blastland calls it: the slippery, vague stuff that we know matters but not how (or sometimes even how to get to it) by producing heightened levels of interaction. Cities' increase in size has only made things even more difficult: the number of potential combinations and outcomes has increased.[10]

Indeed, while we fervently believe that a phenomenon like information technology has made the world more and more knowable, it may even be that the opposite is occurring. Greater order may be paralleled by greater *dis*order. Even though information technology has increased our ability to track and trace each and every interaction—think not just of people but also of animals, plants, objects, and places—still, it is all but impossible to catch the moment when unexpected combinations turn up and get amplified. This is true either because a person or animal or plant (or a virus) does something wholly unexpected, even revolutionary, often with little inkling that they are about to initiate a turn of events, or through forms of transitory local self-organization, or because the flavor of a city acts to modulate events in ways that will always be indefinable, even though we can feel it on our skin, like mist or drizzle or haar. The city is a kind of resonance, not merely a bounded set of quantities, and it now resonates in more and more registers, including informational ones that are closely linked to entertainment.[11] The result is that large parts of its multiple being can never be tied down, only evoked.

The point is that for all the talk of the wonders of information technology as manifested in developments like "big data" and artificial intelligence, we can only get a partial theoretical or empirical grip on this mess, not only because of its extraordinary complexity but also because finding out what is going on in the moment is an all but impossible practical task. This is the case because a moment often passes before it can be registered and because, as I have pointed out, very often people don't know why they make the decisions they do in each moment (often it is the makeup of the web of interactions itself that pushes them one way or another), even though they can often give quite convincing accounts of their actions after the event has occurred. That means that a large part of the world will remain unknowable. There isn't "just" missing data or "just" not the right theory problem.

This insight, such as it is, has practical consequences when we consider urban growth and the larger and larger cities that have resulted from it. It means that we must come to terms with the fact that governing these cities can often only take place through a light touch on the tiller, even though challenges like the combination of scale and climate change seem to demand so much more. Many on the left seem to just assume that a "globalized, crowded (9–10 billion), socially just, and technologically connected post-capitalist world can somehow come into being and avoid the pitfalls of the drive to accumulate" (Chakrabarty 2017, 27). It can't—even if the project is given a boost by the new forms of social collaboration done at a distance and made possible by information technology (Morozov 2019). What Marx wanted in 1867 when *Capital*, volume 1, was first published, at a time when the world population was around 1.3 or 1.4 billion people (of which maybe only 12 percent was urban), and what is possible now with the world population at 7.7 billion (of which easily 56 percent is urban) are two very different things. Climate change shows the rub.

> [It] forces us to face the fact that nobody's driving the car, nobody's in charge, nobody knows how to "fix it." And even if we had a driver, there's a bigger problem: no car. There's no mechanism for uniting the entire human species to move together in one direction. There are more than seven billion humans, and we divide into almost 200 countries, thousands of smaller sub-national states, territories, counties and municipalities, and an unimaginable multitude of corporations, community organizations, neighborhoods, religious sects, ethnic identities, clans, tribes, gangs, clubs and families, each of which faces its own disunion and strife" (Scranton 2016, 6).

"Big" has allowed humanity to become the equivalent of a natural force but, by definition, natural forces stray beyond the powers of humans to control. Indeed, if anything, given the complexity of the mess that a world population this size can generate, pulled together as well as generated by supersized cities and the connectome of the internet, and spurred on by some of the social and cultural developments surging through it that I have noted above, the possibilities for what used to be called rational government may even have declined.

Conclusions

All this doesn't mean that nothing can be done or that the cause is entirely hopeless, which brings me back, finally, to the issue of governability.

In the scaled-up urban world we now inhabit, we need some kind of semblance of government if we aren't going to slip off the cliff-edge. That doesn't always have to mean the state, of course, but one of the difficulties of a lot of work put into devising social theory is the pessimistic view that it too often holds about the state's influence. The state is often regarded as necessarily a negative and inherently oppressive force, tying the populace down with the soulless conformism of unnecessary bureaucratic rules or limitless surveillance or just downright oppression (see Graeber 2015). This was always a problematic stance. Even in the early days of modern states, bodies such as police forces may have been greeted as oppressors by some of the working class, but equally they were just as often welcomed as guardians in urban areas that had partly succumbed to the frightening lawlessness of survival of the fittest. Much of what is good about modern life arises from an intricate web of rules, regulations, and bureaucratic institutions that exist to allow practical management issues to be solved. Many of these rules and regulations are not inherently ideological, though they obviously have biases that may well need to be excised (Lewis 2019). They provide the security that allows everyday life to go forward unimpeded as a set of routines (and thank goodness for that, since a world without routine is all but unthinkable). In other words, the combination of state bureaucracy and regulation—and now including information technology—can be a savior as well as a weight. "Government" is not always a pejorative term.

The problem in a more-populous urban world is not that we always need less government (the conservative solution usually means that we need less government for the rich and powerful and hang the rest) or that we always need more government (the solution that seems to appeal to many left-wing commentators, except those who opt for forms of anarchism or notions of self-organization). In truth, the kind of government operating in many places around the world is simply inadequate to the supersized, urbanized world we now inhabit.

Consider the often unpredictable mess that we encountered in the previous section. We often have little notion of what can happen next. In these circumstances, the mass of rules and regulations and routines that constitute an overhang into the future—not to mention the institutions that enforce them—can be a "good," not just a "bad." Whether it's providing medical care, mending roads, controlling air traffic, preventing financial fraud, or investing in research with no obvious immediate payoff, there are forms of government that we truly need to have so as to maintain what we now call "public goods" into the future. In particular, government is expected to keep people safe, though more than ever that doesn't just mean immediate concerns. It also means managing longer-term, recurring risks that may well be hard to calculate but that can have catastrophic consequences if they suddenly transpire. Government is expected to manage a financial crisis, a terrorist attack, a wildfire, a flood, a hurricane, or a pandemic, and then to clean up and make things right again afterward (Lewis 2019).

Yet as cities have ballooned, we seem to be lacking two kinds of government that are now vital for dealing with the scale of what faces us. One, the most obvious, is government of the short term. Our current forms of government are rarely able to react extremely quickly, though more and more actions can now arrive in milliseconds (hypersonic missiles, high-frequency trading, buying goods and making friends online, identifying persons of interest via video surveillance).[12] Some parts of the short term may have been made more open to ordering and regulation by being managed by information technology, though others have clearly been made much more dangerous. We also need more longer-term government. We are regularly confronted now with projects (like mending the broken environment or cleaning up all kinds of wastes) that will take millennia to accomplish and that depend on notions of intergenerational equity for which we have few regulatory, bureaucratic, or institutional models of care for the much longer-term (universities being one of the few partial exceptions). We need to inhabit a longer "now." But we have left much of the millisecond world to the attentions of a private sector that increasingly subcontracts judgments to computation and waits for much of the future to heal itself while the longer-term world is only prodded and probed by planning documents that usually reach just a few years ahead. In both cases, cities are usually left to the tender mercies of various forms of governance by numbers in which the system becomes the substance (Lash 2010). In particular, that means the cities' movers and shakers suffer from the illusion that they know what is going on because it is countable and therefore able to be represented. But, as I argued in the previous section, there is no cover of a set that can take everything that is happening into account. The result is that cities suffer from over-reach about what can be governed and under-reach about what ought to be governed. To move on from this situation will take, first of all, calm and collected decision-making, combined with a new set of technologies that reveal methods and results, somewhat like IPython and Jupyter, and, second, new long-term institutions somewhat akin to universities or monasteries or pyramid- and cathedral-building, similar to very-long-term versions of the disaster-management agencies we have now. These would be institutions ministering to the future, so to speak (Ialenti 2020; Krznaric 2020; Robinson 2020). At the moment, this may look like a pipe dream—but then so, at one point, did technologies and institutions like these!

So, we return once more to the issue of vocabulary. We need other words for processes, cultural and otherwise, that unfold in cities that will always— *always*—be partially unknowable. Cities are uncertain places by definition. And we will have to learn how to govern them more wisely in the face of a climate crisis that is existential, neither attempting to control what is not controllable nor giving up on the attempt to produce better foresight rather than mere prediction. That means retooling our urban vocabulary with words that relish reaching out into the unknown and exploring the uncertain, rather than allow numbering to become the be-all or the end-all. In other words, if we are to avoid the bleak urban landscapes that can seem like our current destination, we need to coin better words and, however haltingly, to harness them to the production of new and better arts of both understanding the world and understanding how and how not to govern it.

Notes

1. Overtourism has a twin, undertourism, which tries to direct visitors to less crowded places (Glusac 2019).

2. For example, there is a literature that argues that with larger and larger populations there can be a bias toward dictatorship, but this is lessened by population concentration around capital cities (see Doy and Campante 2009).

3. As Supiot points out, in a certain sense these developments revive one of the West's age-old dreams: that of grounding social harmony in calculations. Repudiating the goal of governing by "just" laws, this new discourse advocates in its stead the efficient attainment of measurable objectives.

4. No wonder that Romer (2019) has called for a tax on online advertising!

5. Much has been made of China's (still very patchy) social credit system, though in many ways it is simply the logical outgrowth of what has been happening in the consumer sphere translated into state practices, often using variants of the same software and even being run on the spare capacity of servers that belong to companies like Alibaba and Tencent.

6. Entertainment can also be educational. It may be that as the world plummets into the abyss, we make movies imagining ourselves confronting that abyss rather than actually doing anything about it. In the words of one famous book, we may be entertaining ourselves to death. But that doesn't have to be. Think of the reaction to David Attenborough's British TV series *Blue Planet*.

7. Neither, by the way, do workforces. For example, computer coders can undermine the system in numerous ways, ranging from simple things like inserting "Easter eggs" into software to all kinds of hacking.

8. This explains much of Garcia's work on forms of exhibition (Garcia and Normand 2019).

9. But we also need to be careful not to overstate. It isn't clear that every apparent primaverist is moved by the permanently adolescent consumerist impulses that Garcia imputes to them. Take the activity of climbing, for one example. It is a sport that seems to follow a classic primaverist trajectory,

offering sometimes dangerous and extreme experiences and putting a premium on "firstness." The advent of free climbing (with few ropes or protective gear) has meant that climbing has become an even more dangerous pursuit. Yet for the few who are good enough to attempt these kinds of climbs, I have my doubts that the payoff is simply being among the first. Most of the climbers I know climb for rather different reasons: for one, respect from their fellow climbers, undoubtedly (but from the general public, not so much); maybe a chance to be alone or surrounded by only a few companions; and love of these mountain places, certainly. But if you ask most elite climbers why they climb, they are often not sure themselves. It is a compulsion. They *have* to do it.

10. In his later work, Torsten Hägerstrand, the inventor of time-geography, became quite interested in the effects of size and scale.

11. This might occur, for example, through the intersection between "gamification" and design science.

12. There are, of course, partial answers to many of these issues, like the circuit breakers found in the faster-moving financial markets.

References

Agrawal, Ajay, Joshua Gans, and Avi Goldfarb. 2018. *Prediction Machines: The Simple Economics of Artificial Intelligence*. Cambridge, MA: Harvard Business Review Press.

Beer, Stafford. 1974. *Designing Freedom*. Toronto: University of Toronto Press.

Blastland, Michael. 2019. *The Hidden Half: How the World Conceals Its Secrets*. London: Atlantic Books.

Cartwright, Nancy, and Jeremy Hardie. 2012. *Evidence-Based Policy: A Practical Guide to Doing It Better*. Oxford: Oxford University Press.

Chakrabarty, Dipesh. 2014. "Climate and Capital: On Conjoined Histories." *Critical Inquiry* 35: 1–23.

Chakrabarty, Dipesh. 2017. "The Politics of Climate Change Is More than the Politics of Capitalism." *Theory Culture and Society* 34: 25–37.

Chater, Nick. 2018. *The Mind Is Flat: The Illusion of Depth and the Improvised Mind*. London: Allen Lane.

Cogburn, Jon. 2017. *Garcian Meditations: The Dialectics of Persistence in Form and Object*. Edinburgh: Edinburgh University Press.

Coyle, Diane. 2019. "Online Advertising Exploits Humanity's Malleable Tastes." *Financial Times*, May 13.

Debaise, Didier. 2017. *Speculative Empiricism: Revisiting Whitehead*. Edinburgh: Edinburgh University Press.

Doy, Quoc-Anh, and Filipe R. Campante. 2009. "Keeping Dictators Honest: The Role of Population Concentration." Governance Working Papers 220756, East Asian Bureau of Economic Research.

Ehrenreich, Barbara. 2006. *Dancing in the Streets: A History of Collective Joy*. New York: Metropolitan Books.

Elhacham, Emily, Liad Ben-Uri, Jonathan Grozovski, Yinon M. Bar-On, and R. RonMilo. 2020. "Global Human-Made Mass Exceeds All Living Mass." *Nature*. doi.org/10.1038/s41586-020-3010-5.

Ellison, Jo. 2019. "Trending." *Financial Times*, June 8.

Fuller, Matthew, and Olga Goriunova. 2020. *Bleak Joys: Aesthetics of Ecology and Impossibility*. Minneapolis: University of Minnesota Press.

Garcia, Tristan. 2014. *Form and Object: A Treatise on Things*. Edinburgh: Edinburgh University Press.

Garcia, Tristan. 2018. *The Life Intense: A Modern Obsession*. Edinburgh: Edinburgh University Press.

Garcia, Tristan, and Vincent Normand, eds. 2019. *Theater, Garden, Bestiary: A Materialist Theory of Exhibitions*. Cambridge, MA: MIT Press.

Glennie, Paul, and Nigel Thrift. 2009. *Shaping the Day: A History of Timekeeping in England and Wales, 1300–1800*. Oxford: Oxford University Press.

Glusac, Elaine. 2019. "Cooler, Farther and Less Crowded: The Rise of Undertourism." *New York Times*, August 29.

Graeber, David. 2015. *The Utopia of Rules: On Technology, Stupidity, and the Secret Joys of Bureaucracy*. New York: Melville House.

Haff, Peter. 2014. "Humans and Technology in the Anthropocene: Six Rules." *The Anthropocene Review* 1, no. 2: 126–136.

Haraway, Donna. 2018. "Making Kin in the Chthulucene: Reproducing Multispecies Justice." In *Making Kin Not Population*, edited by Adele Clarke and Donna Haraway, 67–99. Chicago: Prickly Paradigm Press.

Hill, Amelia. 2018. "Migration: How Many People Are on the Move Around the World?" *The Guardian*, September 10.

Ialenti, Vincent. 2020. *Deep Time Reckoning: How Future Thinking Can Help Earth Now*. Cambridge, MA: MIT Press.

Ings, Simon. 2014. *Wolves*. London: Gollancz.

Jackson, Lee. 2019. *Palaces of Pleasure: From Music Halls to the Seaside to Football, How the Victorians Invented Mass Entertainment*. New Haven, CT: Yale University Press.

James, William. 1977. *A Pluralistic Universe*. Cambridge, MA: Harvard University Press.

Johnson, Steven. 2017. *Wonderland: How Play Made the Modern World*. London: Macmillan.

Krznaric, Roman. 2020. *The Good Ancestor: How to Think Long-Term in a Short-Term World*. London: W. H. Allen.

Langley, Paul, and Andrew Leyshon. 2017. "Platform Capitalism: The Intermediation and Capitalization of Digital Economic Circulation." *Finance and Society* 3: 11–31.

Langlitz, Nathan. 2019. "Primatology Science: On the Birth of Actor-Network Theory From Baboon Observations." *Theory Culture and Society* 36: 83–105.

Lash, Scott. 2010. *Intensive Culture: Social Theory, Religion and Contemporary Capitalism*. London: Sage.

Lewis, Michael. 2019. *The Fifth Risk: Undoing Democracy*. London: Allen Lane.

Livingstone, Sonia. 2019. "Audiences in an Age of Datafication: Critical Questions for Media Research." *Television and New Media* 20: 170–183.

Lury, Celia, and Sophie E. Day. 2019. "Algorithmic Personalization as a Mode of Individuation." *Theory Culture and Society* 36: 17–37.

Macfarlane, Robert. 2015. *Landmarks*. London: Penguin.

Mader, Mary Beth. 2017. "Philosophical and Scientific Intensity in the Thought of Gilles Deleuze." *Deleuze and Guattari Studies* 11: 259–277.

Mance, Henry. 2019. "Silicon Valley Falls Short on Climate Change." *Financial Times*, July 26.

Mathur, Arunesh, Gunes Acar, Michael Friedman, Elena Lucherini, Jonathan R. Mayer, Marshini Chetty, and Arvind Narayanan. 2019. "Dark Patterns at Scale: Findings from a Crawl of 11K Shopping Websites." doi: 10.1145/1122445.1122456.

Morozov, Evegeny. 2019. "Digital Socialism? The Calculation Debate in the Age of Big Data." *New Left Review* 116/117: 33–67.

Population Reference Bureau. 2018. "How Many People Have Ever Lived on Earth?" https://www.prb.org/howmanypeoplehaveeverlivedonearth.

Quante, Heidi, and Alicia Escott. 2019. Bureau of Linguistical Reality. https://bureauoflinguisticalreality.com/.

Robinson, Kim Stanley. 2020. *The Ministry for the Future*. London: Orbit.

Romer, Paul. 2019. "A Tax that Could Fix Big Tech." *New York Times*, May 6.

Rosa, Hartmut. 2015. *Social Acceleration: A New Theory of Modernity*. New York: Columbia University Press.

Rosa, Hartmut. 2019. *Resonance: A Sociology of Our Relationship to the World*. Cambridge: Polity.

Samuel, Lawrance R. 2010. *Freud on Madison Avenue: Motivation Research and Subliminal Advertising in America*. Philadelphia: University of Pennsylvania Press.

Schlossberg, Tatiana. 2019. *Inconspicuous Consumption: The Environmental Impact You Don't Know You Have*. New York: Grand Central Publishing.

Scranton, Roy. 2016. "When the Next Hurricane Hits Texas." *New York Times*, October 7.

Sloterdijk, P. 2020. *Infinite Mobilization: Towards a Critique of Political Kinetics*. Cambridge: Polity.

Smith, Harrison. 2019. "The Locative Imaginary: Classification, Context and Relevance in Location Analytics." *Sociological Review* 57: 1–18.

Somers, James. 2018. "The Scientific Paper Is Obsolete." *The Atlantic*, April 5.

Supiot, Alain. 2017. *Governance by Numbers: The Making of a Legal Model of Allegiance*. Oxford: Hart.

Syvitski, Jaia, Colin N. Waters, John Day, and 15 others. 2020. "Extraordinary Human Energy Consumption and Resultant Geological Impacts Beginning Around 1950 CE Initiated the Proposed Anthropocene Epoch." *Communications Earth and Environment*. doi:10.1038/s43247-020-00029-y.

Thrift, Nigel J. 1985. "Flies and Germs: A Geography of Knowledge." In *Social Relations and Spatial Structures*, edited by Derek Gregory and John Urry, 330–373. London: Macmillan.

Thrift, Nigel J. 2011. "Lifeworld, Inc.—And What to Do about It." *Environment and Planning D. Society and Space* 29: 5–26.

Thrift, Nigel J. 2021. *Killer Cities*. London: Sage.

Topalov, Christian, Laurent Coudroy de Lille, Jan-Charles Depaule, and Brigitte Martin, eds. 2010. *L' aventure des mots de et la ville: A travers le temps, les langes, les societies*. Paris: Robert Lafont.

UNHCR. 2020. *Global Trends: Forced Displacement in 2019*. Geneva: UN High Commission for Refugees.

United Nations. 2019a. *International Migration Report 2019*. New York: United Nations.

United Nations. 2019b. *World Migration Report 2020*. Geneva: International Organization for Migration.

Vesper, Inga. 2019. "Climate Now Biggest Driver of Migration, Study Finds." *SciDev.Net*, May 8.

Zuboff, Shoshana. 2019. *The Age of Surveillance Capitalism: The Fight for a Human Future at the New Frontier of Human Power*. London: Profile.

5

MARIANA VALVERDE

URBAN LEGAL FORMS AND PRACTICES OF CITIZENSHIP

Introduction: How Law Matters

For much of the twentieth century, urban life was treated by most scholars as a mere object, an empirical site on which to "apply" concepts developed by discipline-based thinkers. Urban studies today, however, is an intellectually exciting field where theoretical and methodological insights have emerged that have been found useful in other contexts and at other scales. Contemporary urban studies today seems to generate as much theory as it borrows from elsewhere. Taking this phenomenon—which one could call "post-disciplinary" if that word had not become a self-serving cliché—in a seldom explored direction, this chapter will show that urban researchers who eschew grand narratives or abstract Chicago-school models in favor of "assemblage" analysis could benefit from a deeper engagement with legal studies—not so much law "in the books," but rather empirical studies of how legal mechanisms actually work, in this case to shape urban experiences.

For some years now, urban legal studies scholars have shown that using one legal tool rather than another can have significant and sometimes unintended consequences for socioeconomic arrangements. Using nuisance lawsuits against particular instances of "offensiveness," for example, as was done throughout the nineteenth century, is a very different way of governing conflicts than the forward-looking, citywide proactive regulation of smells, noises, and businesses that might cause offense (Valverde 2011 and 2019). And municipal licensing of pornography shops and other sexually oriented businesses is a mode of moral regulation that differs significantly from the use of obscenity or other criminal law tools (Hubbard and Colosi 2009; Hubbard et al. 2009). However, outside of the small subfield of legal geography (Blomley et al. 2001; Braverman et al. 2014) the socio-legal contribution to urban studies has rarely been incorporated into most studies of urban life.

In the space available, it would be impossible to enumerate, much less describe, all the legal and quasi-legal tools that make up the regulatory underpinnings of urban life, especially since regulatory systems differ not only between countries but also from one kind of city to another.[1] Yet a few examples of commonly used legal tools that are cross-nationally allocated to local or municipal authorities will show the fruitfulness of using an approach to studying urban life that pays close attention to the dynamics, the "relative autonomy" if you will, of legal forms, and that shows that local law has its own distinct logics and cannot be understood as state law writ small. In keeping this collection's aim of integrating political subjectivity into the study of urban social phenomena, for each legal tool described, it will be shown that certain forms of urban citizenship, certain forms of political agency or political passivity, are encouraged while others are discouraged.

The relation between legal forms and what Engin Isin has influentially called "practices of citizenship" (Isin 2002) is not hard-wired. Legal forms set up a certain path dependence, but the social, economic, and political effects of particular legal forms are not wholly predictable or inevitable. It is possible, for instance, for people living in a privatized, inward-looking gated community to collectively tax themselves to build an infrastructure (say, a swimming pool) that benefits not only their households but also neighboring, perhaps poorer, communities. In that instance the legal form of the small, by-invitation-only contractual community would be used in an inclusionary manner to produce a good that serves the same purpose as a municipal swimming pool, even if it is privately built and privately owned. But it should be obvious that such a decision would go against the governance grain of contractually based exclusionary urban units. The path of least resistance for families living in privatized communities who want to provide recreational opportunities is to set up a private, enclosed facility that is more like a club and less like a municipal pool and is only available to members. An obvious affinity can be seen between those property law and contract law mechanisms that underpin privatized enclaves, on the one hand, and the restricted character of the "common" facilities provided, on the other. Choosing one legal form over another does not completely determine which social and political relations will emerge, since people can always choose to go against the legal and cultural grain; and yet legal forms—property forms, land tenure forms, contracts, municipal legal tools, even national laws—encourage certain ways of living and acting together, often in invisible or unintended ways, while discouraging others. Socio-legal scholarship has long shown that legal structures and legal tools have a "constitutive effect" on social life, including civic habits of urban citizenship, even if unusual or even surprising ways of using established legal tools are always possible. "Constitutive" here does not indicate inevitability but rather the kind of path dependency that was just illustrated with the case of the imaginary gated-community swimming pool.

In what follows, the constitutive effects of legal tools on practices of urban citizenship will be demonstrated with a few examples. The first is the key legal mechanism of private law: the contract. The second example is a type of contract, but one that is unusual in that its conditions "run with the land" (as English law has it) and live on in a particular space even as the original parties die or move away: and that is the "restrictive covenant." This legal tool is not as common today as it once was, though it clearly demonstrates the social effects of legal tools because numerous scholars of urban racism have shown that it has played a key role in enabling residential racial segregation in the United States; what is less well known is that the mechanism continues to exist and be valid, having various and sometimes deleterious effects when used for purposes that have little to do with racial exclusion. The third example of a legal tool takes us into the heart of local public law: the urban park bylaw. The fourth and last example brings us to the very edge of law. Technical standards (for public utilities, streets, and the like) are not exactly considered "law." However, legal scholars have long shown that computer coding has the power of law (Lessig 1999), and similarly, technical standards, in both the physical world and the digital world, can be said to constrain human conduct more forcefully than legal rules. The question here is not whether technical standards "are" or are not law: that is not a useful question. Interdisciplinary scholarship on legal urban issues is not interested in policing the boundaries of law, but rather focuses on tracing existing governance networks, to see where and how legal processes shade into and are intertwined with quasi-legal, material, economic, and even cultural processes.

Contract-Based Urban Communities

Let us consider a privatized district on the edge of a city, an exclusive or would-be exclusive collective created through a private contract rather than created as a standard-issue municipality or municipal district. Such an entity is built not only with bricks and mortar (and not just with bricks and mortar plus cultural assumptions about what counts as a "good" neighborhood), but also by means of overlapping contracts.

This tight little network requires, for its very existence, a condominium contract among property owners. (The same legal form, facilitating a combination of private residential property and certain common property, goes under other names, depending on the jurisdiction, but for the sake of simplicity I use the word "condominium.") The founding agreement may be imagined by the signers to be a horizontal John Locke–style contract in which the amount of liberty each member gives up to the "commonwealth" is negotiated. However, in practice, the all-important founding conditions (such as restrictions on renting one's property or on other commercial uses) are usually set out in advance by the developer, specifically the developer's lawyer. Condominium boards—together with their legal equivalents in jurisdictions using different terminology—can then use a democratic process to pass additional bylaws, acting like a mini-city. They can together decide to ban smoking on balconies, say. Importantly, however, the initial setup requires a quasi-constitutional document (in the province of Ontario, Canada's most urbanized jurisdiction, this is known as the "condominium declaration"). The particulars of the condominium declaration are not ordinary bylaws that can be changed at a board meeting with a simple majority of votes. They are more like the constitutional law of the country, and can only be changed with super-majorities of owners. It is those founding conditions, written into the original document, that give birth to the collective entity and that shape the collective life of privatized communities most strongly.

Thus, while condominium unit purchasers might feel they are in a Lockean condition of autonomy and freedom, having escaped the reach of the law of "the big city" into a kind of original state of individualism in which they are free to create a social contract with like-minded individuals, in fact condominium and gated-community contracts often resemble particularly draconian municipal codes.[2] The lawyer who writes (or more likely copies) the "declaration," meaning the founding document, actually works for the developer, not the condo owners. From the point of view of that lawyer's client, it is thought that rigid rules that preserve physical and social homogeneity and prevent any challenge to conventional middle-class nuclear-family norms (no tenants, no small-business uses, no street parking at night, and so on) will protect property prices and hence enhance the developer's profits.

Once constituted in this manner, the collective entity (which usually takes the legal form of a nonprofit corporation) then enters into a series of external contracts—for electricity, perhaps; for policing and fire services (in many places in the United States, at least); for maintenance services such as snow-clearing and lawn-mowing; for internet access; and perhaps even for very basic services such as water and sewerage. The question then becomes: which social and political effects flow from the contractual nature of the community's legal infrastructure?

As a legal form that is absolutely central to private law, the contract is designed to be specific to both the situation and the parties, in contrast to the universalizing logic of public law. Of course, megacompanies that have contracts with millions of customers (such as Apple and Facebook) standardize the "terms and conditions," and thus their customers have even less power to object to that agreement than condominium members have to alter the founding bylaws. Nevertheless, it *does* matter that the legal form of the contract is designed to produce a singular document, not a set of general rules governing all entities of the same type across a large territory. Here's one probable real-world consequence: one contractually based community is likely to pay a lower price for water or electricity than its neighbor, just as a corporation with a better lawyer or more economic power will pay less to its suppliers. Thus, relying on the contract form to create a community and then to provide it with services is a choice of legal tool that has an in-built tendency to increase inequalities across the sub-units of a metropolitan area (which may be smaller than officially recognized neighborhoods).

In a related manner, contracts, unlike state or municipal laws, are not public documents. The founding contract will likely be made available to the members who signed it, but only to them. This lack of transparency will mean that higher-level public authorities—say, at the state level—will not know who is paying how much for which essential services within their territory; they may not even know which provider has been contracted to provide trash removal or private-security guards. In many jurisdictions, the price of some utilities is regulated, and to that extent limits are placed on some contracts, but the regulation usually extends only to certain utilities (electricity and perhaps water). Some essential services, such as internet providers, may not be subject to public regulation. In addition, when a small autonomous community decides to obtain police or fire services not from the private sector but through a contract with a public municipal or supra-municipal entity (as is common in the U.S. West, where small suburban municipalities typically sign contracts with the county fire service), then the price of that contract is unlikely to be regulated at all.

Lack of transparency is an inherent feature of contracts, and this can encourage spatial as well as social inequities by keeping differential pricing hidden from public view. That very feature makes empirical research on contractually based communities difficult, since neither their founding documents nor their external contracts are subject to freedom-of-information requests. However, one can plausibly predict that unless public authorities impose countervailing measures, those who are economically privileged and have spatially withdrawn from large diverse cities—meaning those who could well afford to pay more—in fact pay *less* than their share for "municipal" services. A suburban enclave of expensive houses owned by people who can afford maintenance and modernization will likely pay less for their fire protection than a community with housing stock of lower quality. Wealthier enclaves will be designated by entities such as fire services as well as insurance companies as less "risky" than average, a designation that will magnify their existing economic advantage.

Thus, an inherent feature of the contract as a legal form (a lack of transparency beyond the parties involved) has important social and political effects, largely along the lines of encouraging or at least enabling greater intra-urban inequalities. And the very legal feature in question prevents scholars and even public authorities from gathering information about the "rich pay less" effects of contractual arrangements.

It is important that whether the entity is a gated community or is technically a municipality does not matter as much as whether it is primarily contractual. Research on American "cities by contract" (Miller 1981; see also Frug 2001) shows that reliance on contractual agreements greatly shapes the political life of small municipalities. The contract form encourages a limitation of the scope of the governing entity; the board of the community or the condominium, if thinking of themselves primarily as a corporation, will tend to limit their activities to acting as providers of a few select services to a group, usually only homeowners (tenants, even long-term ones, are not usually considered to be members of the condominium corporation). Such "cities by contract" are characterized by a lack of civic engagement and an avoidance of redistribution (Frug 2001). The desire of middle- and upper-class families to avoid paying taxes for such things as schools for poor racialized children, added to the cultural preference for living in homogeneous and exclusive enclaves, could not on their own create such communities: the machinery of contract is here the essential intangible legal infrastructure.

Urban scholars have long noted that the privatized exclusive community as a form of urban life tends to produce forms of local belonging in which the members are not so much citizens as rational-choice consumers. This is true; but I have shown here that turning gated communities into municipalities would not necessarily solve this set of problems, especially in the U.S. context, where municipalities are often much smaller than actual cities and frequently act as if they were gated communities. The legal form of the contract, therefore, has effects that can cross the dividing line between public bodies and private bodies, if public bodies (municipal corporations) are designed in such a way as to be very similar to condominium developments.

The Restrictive Covenant: Exclusionary Rules That "Run with the Land"

When one buys urban real estate, one does not thereby become the sovereign of a piece of land or a building. Apart from general, publicly proclaimed rules (such as planning rules), some real estate properties come with contractual conditions that "run with the land," as English common law puts it, and hence they override the supposedly all-important free will of the parties to the sale-of-land contract. These rules remain in place even as owners change.

Some of these "restrictive covenants" serve specific corporate interests. For example, a supermarket chain might sell an urban property because the corporation wants to consolidate branches, though to protect its overall market share it may demand that a condition be attached to the sale of the former grocery store preventing competing grocery stores, and *only* grocery stores, from locating there. (This is an example of a legal restrictive covenant from present-day Edmonton, Alberta, Canada.) Depending on the jurisdiction, such conditions might expire after a certain number of years, due to legislation passed in recent times to limit the power of private land owners to "rule the future."

Importantly, restrictive covenants' conditions such as "no grocery stores" are not the same as the "terms and conditions" of ordinary contracts, because conditions that "run with the land" stick to the property quite independent of subsequent contracts of sale. This would be anathema in French-style legal systems, which privilege the will of the living individual who is a party to the contract (except in the case of wills and inheritance, but that need not concern us here). Throughout the common-law world, by contrast, English law and its successors treat land as a very special type of property. All real estate, even flats, has to be stuffed into the procrustean bed of land-law by means of various legal fictions (which is why for many decades, in numerous common-law jurisdictions, high-rise residential towers could only be built as rental properties). This seemingly obscure legal point—the centrality of land in English property law—explains why when selling one's car one cannot impose conditions regarding future owners' use of it, whereas conveyancing law provides mechanisms that allow land owners, in some cases, to restrictively govern the future. The restrictive covenant is one such mechanism.[3]

In the United States, restrictive covenants proliferated in the interwar years and beyond to ensure racial and other forms of spatial exclusiveness after African Americans from the South began a mass migration to northern cities (Brown and Smith 2013). A typical restrictive covenant would state that a small group of neighbors would all agree that none of their properties would *ever* be sold to a "non-Caucasian." Such a covenant countermands the wishes of a white owner who might be happy to later sell to non-whites. (Jews were sometimes excluded by these restrictive covenants as well, but in the United States the main target was Blacks.)

In 1948 the Supreme Court of the United States struck down explicitly racial covenants as unconstitutional, in Shelley v. Kraemer. But as Carol Rose and Richard Brooks show, this only meant that such covenants could not be enforced. The covenants did not disappear. Indeed, notable Democratic figures over the years, including President John F. Kennedy and then-Vice-President Joe Biden, found, perhaps to their dismay, that properties that they had bought had racial covenants as part of the "chain of title." Real estate agents and lawyers, according to Rose and Brooks, continued to insist, decades after the 1948 decision, that striking out unwanted racial exclusions by hand when buying a property would make the property title "cloudy" and put their mortgage at risk (Rose and Brooks 2016).

Some states, such as California, passed laws that forced racial exclusions to be removed from neighborhood and condominium covenants, with those laws then making it unnecessary for those seeking to fight racism to go through the cumbersome process of challenging the racial covenant in court. However, some other states have failed to do so. Thus, while racially exclusive covenants are unenforceable, being incompatible with the Fair Housing Act and other federal laws and Supreme Court decisions, nevertheless they remain in the title documents of numerous properties across the United States. They are the ghostly persistent presence of a long history of legally enforceable racial exclusion, and they show the remarkable flexibility of "minor" legal tools.

To fill out the picture of urban residential segregation would require exploring all manner of legal and quasi-legal techniques, from mortgage lending rules to zoning regulations. (Both of these have been studied for the United States, but mainly in regard to racial effects; for countries other than the United States, very little information is accessible about how mortgage markets and other financial tools that were made available through evolving banking regulations—yet another little-studied legal tool—have shaped the fabric of urban life.) One would also have to examine rules governing land uses that correlate with racial and class and morally based prejudices, such as restrictive zoning rules for certain kinds of shops or certain kinds of housing. The racial restrictive covenant is probably no longer a major actor within the broad (and deep) network of legalized American residential racial segregation. But it is worth highlighting here as an example of a legal tool that has refused to die, even when some white owners no longer wished it included in their "contract." Restrictive covenants and other non-enforceable or seldom-enforced exclusionary rules persist in the nooks and crannies of the legal network—and might be reactivated if future courts and legislatures turn a blind eye to racial and other forms of spatial urban exclusion.

The larger point is that in urban legal networks, and in many countries other than the United States, a host of legal and quasi-legal tools continue to exert exclusionary effects, despite the rise of antidiscrimination law, human rights codes, and other public-law instruments whose logic is inclusion rather than exclusion. Rental agreements, landlord/tenant laws, leases, and mortgage rules are some of the mechanisms that can be—and are—used in a discriminatory manner. Human rights and equity measures that have assumed a fairly secure position in the public-law framework of most countries today may well be negated, in particular instances, by seldom-studied minor legal mechanisms found within private law.

While the "minor law" mechanisms discussed in this section all encourage or at least enable spatial and social inequality within cities, it is important to note that alongside these persistent exclusionary mechanisms one can often find inclusionary rules. These are usually found either in court decisions that have precedent value, in state statutes (such as, in the United States, the Fair Housing Act), or in municipal rules such as rent controls and inclusionary zoning (a tool that generally forces developers to provide a certain number of affordable housing units when building for the private ownership or private rental market). Such norms and rules do often take precedence over private contracts, as was seen in the case of the racial covenants struck down by U.S. courts; but, again as shown in the racial covenant example, private law rules and logics do not always disappear completely when public-law tools limiting private choice are imposed. Property and contract law are relatively autonomous from public rules such as constitutional rights protections, and only in limited cases are municipal rules and regulations susceptible to being struck down as unconstitutional or against human rights law. Activists promoting urban inclusion and equity would therefore do well to pay attention to the distinct workings of private law, as well as to the insulation of many municipal rules from "higher"-level legal norms about equality and fairness.

Urban Parks: New York's Central Park Conservancy

At first glance, it might seem that city spaces come already clearly divided: they are either private spaces (homes, shops, factories, clubs, churches) or public spaces (streets, squares, parks). In addition, a casual observer might imagine that she can tell which spaces are public and which are private simply by looking. That is not always the case. For instance, just looking does not reveal whether a school playground is or is not public. In much of the world, even fully public schools use locks and fences to prevent non-students from using the taxpayer-funded space both during school hours and after.

This everyday example shows that legal tools carrying quite different logics of governance can be used on the same space quite easily. The school playground with the locked fence around it is public from the point of view of funding, and the school is probably obliged to accept all students living in the catchment area, which reflects a public logic. And yet the school, or the school board, is a private property owner in regard to the playground space, and can fence it or lock it as they see fit, just like any other property owner.

Similarly, when a private café gets a municipal license to cordon off an outdoor patio, as is being done frequently in the age of a pandemic, the municipal permit to occupy the sidewalk functions as the mechanism enabling a legalized privatization of a defined chunk of public space (often with limits on time as well, such as "only in the summer"' or "not past midnight"). The private-property powers of the café owner are not formally increased: and yet the profit possibilities increase as if the owner had bought more land (assuming, for the sake of simplicity, that the business owner is also the building owner). The most mundane of urban legal networks, therefore—a school playground, or a restaurant sidewalk patio—can exhibit remarkable complexity. Therefore, liberal political-legal theories about the essential differences between "the public" and "the private," theories that undergird much of the critical urban studies literature's denunciations of privatization, are not very useful for purposes of concrete analyses of particular assemblages.

To show how numerous everyday legal assemblages confound liberal theory's commitment to a strict public-private divide, it may be useful to look at the legal underpinnings of a world-famous urban park: New York's Central Park, with worldwide visibility because it is visited by tens of millions each year and appears regularly in television shows and films.

The park has the feel of a public space: there are no security gates, and there is no admission price. Based on the absence of a gate and tickets, and based also on their prior experiences with parks, visitors likely believe that Central Park is a municipal park. The casual visitor will likely assume that the premier urban park in the United States is fully public. However, she would be wrong. Urban parks in areas of New York City that are not visited by tourists are generally fully public. Legally, however, Central Park is a public-private partnership. It is managed by a philanthropic entity called the "Central Park Conservancy," which stands at arm's length to the city. This is not a unique setup. Many high-prestige parks as well as some historic districts in cities around the world are governed by a board of upper-class volunteers instead of by the city proper (though a city official or two might also sit on the board, ex-officio).

The board assumes responsibility for raising funds. Central Park's website (www.centralparknyc.org) tells us that 75 percent of the budget required to maintain its lawns, ponds, walkways, benches, monuments, and trees comes from donations.

The legal mechanism of the arm's-length "conservancy" set up as a nonprofit arm's-length corporation means that wealthy New Yorkers can be sure that their public-spirited donations go to the park they are most likely to frequent, not to the far less attractive urban parks and playgrounds found in New York's poorer communities. Again, this legal setup is not unique. The historic district of Mexico City is governed not by the city as such but by a trust (*fideocomiso*), a kind of public-private partnership with a spatially specific mandate.[4] The legal structure of the trust funnels special "historical conservation" public funds as well as philanthropic donations to that particular space. Nothing similar exists to benefit the run-down public spaces of Mexico City's countless working-class areas.[5]

In some cases, the semiprivate entity that governs the park or district issues its own rules. But in this case the rules and regulations that micromanage conduct in Central Park are those that apply to New York City parks generally. The Conservancy can thus retain its philanthropic institutional identity while not completely rejecting the city's jurisdiction over parks. That jurisdiction is quite intrusive (as is often the case with public parks): no alcohol is allowed, in any form or in any situation (hence, no picnics with a bottle of wine); no smoking is allowed anywhere on park property at any time; and—this is specific to Central Park—cyclists are told that when cycling in the photogenic drives on the outside edges of the park, they must do so in a counterclockwise direction. The latter rule has a safety justification, yet many of the other rules applying to this as to other parks are based on nothing but cultural and moral norms.

In Central Park, therefore, one group (the Conservancy) decides how much to spend on what type of greenery, and probably also which events to allow in the park, while another body (the City Council) passes ordinances that apply to most of the other parks, as well. Here as in other situations mentioned earlier, in privately owned public parks users are subject *both* to public bylaws or ordinances *and* to special rules issued by the private property owner. A fully public park may have no mechanism for excluding a political protest, for example, but a semiprivate park has additional tools to exclude people and activities. The public laws can limit the private entity's power to impose arbitrary or exclusionary rules, but only to some extent—as was also the case in many of the examples given above, such as those concerning condominium rules and restrictive covenants.

Peering, even casually, into the hybrid, public-private legal underpinnings of the park reveals some important facts not visible to the park user—such as that philanthropic donations from New York's elite are funneled into Central Park rather than into the budget of the city parks department. And if not all parks are created equal, the corollary is that not all New Yorkers are created equal, either; Puerto Ricans from the Bronx can access

Central Park, if they have a subway fare, but they would probably prefer their local park to be substantially improved.

Given the prevalence, in today's neoliberal cities, of invisible legal tools that tend to privatize power, including those that operate under the banner of philanthropy rather than private property, it is important for civic activists to continually put pressure on elected local officials to maintain public democratic control over public spaces such as parks, and to ensure that limited public budgets are not used as an excuse for further privatization.

The Technical Standard

Critical urban scholars have long decried exclusionary public-law rules, such as ordinances that penalize homeless people who sleep in doorways and on sidewalks or that impose draconian rules on street vending. Many critical studies exist of the legal systems that allow local governments to tightly regulate conduct on public spaces (such as no skateboarding, no playing ball other than in playing fields, and many other rules) and that simultaneously give private owners the power to eject undesirables from privately owned spaces such as shops and malls. What is perhaps less remarked on is that the legal tools, of both public and private provenance, used by local authorities to order urban space are remarkably similar internationally, despite marked differences in larger-scale legal systems. The same legal and policing strategies are being deployed around the globe for purposes of urban order, whether the country in question is a democracy or not, or uses civil law versus common law.

If local ordinances and other legal tools used to secure urban order are rarely if ever specific to a city or a country, then, the regulatory convergence phenomenon is even more striking if we go "below" law, as it were, into the often literally underground world of technical standards.

What kind of legal form is the "technical standard"? First, it must be noted that technical standards do not produce regulatory convergence across jurisdictions in the same way that top-down state law produces, or rather forces convergence among, cities and regions in the same country. There is no world sovereign or even a world UN for technical standards. The International Standards Organization (ISO) is best known for setting standards for manufacturing processes, and currently the ISO is trying to develop standards not only for particular objects or industrial processes but for far more complex urban assemblages (such as "smart cities'); but the ISO has no coercive enforcement mechanisms. On their part, big-tech companies have for quite some time developed operating systems that have been adopted by cities and other public entities, in another curious public-private regulatory hybrid (Mattern 2015; Marvin and Luque-Ayala 2017).

And yet standards can have the force of law, for practical rather than legal reasons. A traveler can choose to ignore driving laws in another country, but cannot "choose" to use the wrong plug. An example: many Latin American countries adopted the U.S. style of electrical outlet at the beginning of electrification, and hence continue to use the U.S.-style plug for appliances; but some went with one of the early European standards for plugs and outlets. And in Chile, both American and continental European electrical outlets can be found, even in the same city.

In general, because they operate infra-legally and infra-politically, technical standards discourage civic engagement and contestation. Chileans are highly political people but they are unlikely to protest in the streets to demand a single, standardized form of electrical outlets.

Today, with the growing importance of internet-enabled communications, it has become clear that Silicon Valley companies are the most important generators of codes and standards—purchasing an Android phone or an iPhone immerses the owner in a ready-made complex assemblage of rules about what is and is not allowed. That all the big corporations dominating electronic communications are American is not an accident, but because the power of these companies is largely exercised through codes and standards rather than through legislation, that power is not highly visible politically—though the situation is changing, especially in Europe where political support is growing for regulating Silicon Valley data-centered capitalism.

Still, privately generated codes and standards are not completely separate from public rules. In general, both local and supralocal authorities constantly generate standards that are both legal and technical: the height of steps in a residential staircase, the emissions standards for vehicles, and the rules governing animals and vegetables destined for human consumption are just some examples. Bodies such as the Food and Drug Administration in the United States and its EU equivalents similarly combine law and technical regulation.

Critical scholarship has long denounced the exclusionary effects of law, but far less has been written about the political effects of rules that govern objects for apparently "technical" purposes—Nicholas Blomley's study of the technical standards for sidewalks is a rare exception (Blomley 2010). Paying due attention to municipal and state technical standards would have the desirable effect of bringing students of the urban closer to those now querying the private, standard-based power of corporations such as Facebook and Google. In many cases, opposition to Silicon Valley is limited to demanding that these corporations pay taxes in the jurisdictions in which they operate and gather data. These critics, however, could be doing more to educate the general public about the way in which computer code, whether publicly accessible or privatized, acts to impose invisible law-like rules on ordinary people, through their cell phones and laptops. The force of technical standards is rarely visible to the ordinary citizen, and much more could be done to publicize the political and economic effects of different "technical" choices embedded in our computers and indeed our lives (Marvin and Luque-Ayala 2017). Disability-studies scholars have done a great deal to show the able-bodied and average-sized-human bias of technical standards for furniture, automobiles, sidewalks, public transit vehicles, and so on; but much more can be done to critically illuminate the force that standards and codes exercise on virtually all everyday urban activities.

Conclusion: Varieties of Legal Infrastructure

One reason for the neglect of the legal dimension of urban life in critical urban studies is that there can be no general answer to the question of why and how law matters, and so there is no grand theory to be offered or any general prescription to be recommended to activists. The limited examples above show that analyzing the legal and regulatory forms present in the particular environment (not merely looking at which forms predominate, but also examining how various forms interact) can shed much light on the invisible shaping of various practices of urban citizenship. Cultural and economic trends, the bread and butter of critical urban studies, do explain a great deal; but under-the-radar legal tools exercise their own, often unexpected, force. And if the scope of the inquiry is broadened to include issues at the edge of law, such as technical standards, then a fuller picture will emerge of how regulatory assemblages encourage certain forms of civic conduct and discourage others. In tackling issues of privatization, economic inequality, and spatial segregation, it is crucial to remember that "big law" (as in national statutes or Supreme Court decisions) is only the tip of a very large iceberg. The hope of this chapter is that the examples presented here help readers to deepen their understanding of how "minor" legal and technical rules and tools work to shape everyday urban life, often with exclusionary effects.

There is no ready-made legal and regulatory toolbox full of "inclusionary" or justice-seeking tools, unfortunately. In each situation, the progressive alternatives can only become visible through a concrete analysis of the particular regulatory infrastructure that exists, an analysis that can then suggest specific solutions. Disability activists have worked hard to demonstrate the political effects of taken-for-granted urban objects, such as the front steps of a shop, and have exposed the bias of the apparently neutral standards and codes that produced these objects. Once made visible, the exclusionary effects of municipal codes, building codes, and vehicle standards could be—and indeed have been—challenged and changed. But as the examples briefly covered here show, much more needs to be done in exposing the political effects of the regulatory infrastructure of our cities.

Notes

1. In certain countries, national capitals are given not only more resources but more legal autonomy than "everyday" cities; for instance, Mexico City was able to write a constitution for itself, something that would be impossible in the United States, not to mention Britain. Along the same lines, China does not have a general law of municipalities. Its cities are classified, for legal-political purposes, as tier 1, tier 2, tier 3, or tier 4 cities, partly depending on population but also based on less-quantitative political and economic criteria.

2. In Toronto today, new large downtown condominiums often have "declarations" written into their contracts that allow Airbnb or other rentals, despite the fact that many owner-occupiers see such rentals as creating noise, disruption, a lack of neighborliness, and even possibly an aggregate inflationary effect. Condo bylaws (such as no smoking on balconies) can be changed by majority vote, but changing the declaration typically requires 80 or 90 percent majorities. The "hosts" or operators can thus block new rules banning such rentals in a building even if they own less than 25 percent of the units in the building.

3. Easements also "run with the land." It is not impossible to overturn them but it *is* difficult, especially if the easement is for a public use, such as emergency services access through a privately owned lane or alley.

4. In the United Kingdom, many public goods, ranging from parks to bridges, use the legal form of a trust, whether or not they were originally created through a private donation. (For instance, the Brunel-built Clifton Bridge, near Bristol, is actually a trust.) In other English-speaking countries, the same type of governing structure is often called an "authority" or a "commission." Nomenclature differences, however, make it difficult to study philanthropic public-private partnerships comparatively.

5. I thank Antonio Azuela for information on the governance of the historic district of Mexico City.

References

Blomley, Nicholas. 2010. *Rights of Passage: Sidewalks and the Regulation of Public Flow*. New York: Routledge.

Blomley, Nicholas, David Delaney, and Richard T. Ford, eds. 2001. *The Legal Geographies Reader*. Oxford: Blackwell.

Braverman, Irus, Nicholas Blomley, David P. Delaney, and Alexander Kedar, eds. 2014. *The Expanding Spaces of Law: A Timely Legal Geography*. Stanford, CA: Stanford University Press.

Brown, Adrienne, and Valerie Smith, eds. 2013. *Race and Real Estate*. New York: Oxford.

Frug, Gerald. 2001. *Building Communities without Building Walls*. Princeton, NJ: Princeton University Press.

Hubbard, Phil, and Rachela Colosi. 2009. "Sex, Crime and the City: Municipal Law and the Regulation of Sexual Entertainment." *Social and Legal Studies* 22, no. 1: 67–86.

Hubbard, Phil, Roger Matthews, and Jane Scoular. 2009. "Controlling Sexually Oriented Businesses: Law, Licensing and the Geographies of a Controversial Land Use." *Urban Geography* 30, no. 2: 185–205.

Isin, Engin. 2002. *Being Political: Genealogies of Citizenship*. Minneapolis: University of Minnesota Press.

Lessig, Lawrence. 1999. *Code and Other Laws of Cyberspace*. New York: Basic.

Marvin, Simon, and Andres Luque-Ayala. 2017. "Urban Operating Systems: Diagramming the City." *International Journal of Urban and Regional Research* 41, no. 1: 84–103.

Mattern, Sharon. 2015. "Mission Control: A History of the Urban Dashboard." *Places Journal*, March 2015.

Miller, Gary. 1981. *Cities by Contract: The Politics of Municipal Incorporation*. Cambridge, MA: MIT Press.

Rose, Carol, and Richard Brooks. 2016. "Restrictive Covenants." In *Race and Real Estate*, edited by Adrienne Brown and Valerie Smith. New York: Oxford.

Valverde, Mariana. 2011. "Seeing Like a City: The Dialectic of Modern and Premodern Knowledges in Urban Governance." *Law and Society Review* 45, no. 2: 277–313.

Valverde, Mariana. 2019. "The Law of Bad Smells: Adjudicating Knowledges of Offensiveness." *Canadian Journal of Law and Society* 32, no. 2: 327–341.

6

TERESA P. R. CALDEIRA

TRANSITORINESS

Emergent Time/Space Formations
of Urban Collective Life

Analyses of modernity never fail to associate it with notions of temporariness and ephemerality. Instability, improvisation, impermanence, uncertainty—inseparable from poverty and precariousness—have always marked the lives of the majority in cities worldwide. However, the ways in which these conditions are experienced shift over time, as I argue by focusing on practices of the everyday in the peripheries of the city of São Paulo, Brazil, over the last forty years. I use the notion of the *transitory* as a way of accessing important changes in combined practices and conceptions of time and space as well as the new formations of collective life they anchor. On the one hand, the transitory refers to perceptions of time that disconnect from notions of linearity, directionality, progress, ascension, and development that served as organizing parameters in previous modes of perceiving time. The movement in the case of the transitory is horizontal and lateral, not ascendant. The transitory does not imply a direction toward a certain desired and anticipated future that is supposed to be better or more advanced or developed. On the other hand, spatially the transitory points to constant circulation; to not being able or willing to settle down; to not investing in fixed spaces; to dislocation; and to going back and forth. Of course, notions of linearity, progress, and ascension continue to articulate several dimensions of the everyday, and there is still investment in fixed emplacement, but not in the same hegemonic way as in the past.

The normalization of transitoriness as a way of articulating the everyday—ranging from leisure and cultural interventions to labor, housing, organization of households, gender identity, and interactions in digital spaces—is especially clear among young people. I analyze some of these dimensions from the perspective of the peripheries of São Paulo, where I have conducted fieldwork since the late 1970s. This historical-ethnographic archive allows me to juxtapose materials from various periods and to identify emergent processes that are being articulated according to the logic of the transitory.[1]

Transitoriness

Transitory means impermanent. The *Oxford English Dictionary* defines it as "Not lasting; temporary; brief, fleeting; impermanent" and adds: "Of the nature of a passage or transition; transitional." Etymologically, the word relates both to the French *transitoire*, temporary, and the Latin *transitorious*, transient, passing, relating to traffic. Although *transitory* and *temporary* may be used synonymously, I use transitory instead of temporary because of the former's association with transiency and transit, which implies a dislocation, an act of passing through or across a place. Thus, transitory carries a spatial connotation in addition to a temporal one. The focus of my analysis is on a shift in interrelated practices and conceptions of time and space, which cannot be thought of in isolation from each other.

Analyses of the modern and of modernity have always associated them with notions of temporariness, a quality of fleeting, ephemerality, rupture, and fragmentation. Indeed, Marx and Engels's famous (1996 [1848]) account of modern bourgeois society as that in which "all that is solid melts into air" is a synthetic representation of the complex condition of modernity. As Marshall Berman argues, this condition is marked by a "thrill" and a "dread"—the paradox being represented by the thrill of constant change and the will to change, on the one hand, and a "terror of disorientation and disintegration, of life falling apart," on the other (Berman 1988 [1982], 13). The transitory is thus inherent in the condition of modernity. However, I argue that at the present moment it is experienced in a particular way that should be distinguished from that of modernity.

Without rehearsing the lengthy arguments on modernity and the modern, it is necessary to recall that if modernity has always been marked by processes of rupture, fragmentation, and fleeting, the idea of progress was a powerful way of channeling and directing "the transitoriness of things" and producing a sense of historical continuity (Harvey 1989, 11). Obviously, the notion of progress does not resolve the contradictions of the Enlightenment project, but progress and its associated notions of development and modernization have definitively directed perceptions, practices, and policies in powerful ways, shaping the experience of modernity across disparate parts of the globe.

The notions of modernization and development capture both the power and the optimism associated with progress as an organizing narrative. Although obstacles to these processes and reversals have always existed, they did not dislodge this linear narrative from its position of a central organizing feature of modern life all over the world. But current changes indicate that narratives of progress and development are now losing their force. This means that things may not have become more transitory or ephemeral (though this may also happen), but rather that people's perceptions and practices are different, as not all individuals necessarily see progress, growth, social ascension, modernization, and development as being desirable outcomes. The transitory, fragmentary, and non-connecting are coming to the forefront as dominant perceptions, and people no longer think of their practices as ordered in some kind of linear path that would make them add up to produce a better future. There is a sense of lack of directionality, which may be substituted by repeated experimentation. Movement is constant, but it is lateral—a passing through and across, not going somewhere recognized as better.[2] In the practice of residents of cities of the Global South, this means that their efforts to solve their housing needs may not lead to finding the dream house of one's own that was possible under the autoconstruction model; efforts to acquire formal education do not materialize in social mobility; qualifications may not translate into a professional career; experiments with modes of inhabiting do not coalesce in the formation of families; gender identities may shift from essentialist approaches to performative ones, and so on. There are only a series of lateral moves, dislocations, experiments, and transitory arrangements.[3]

The normalization of transitoriness does not mean that other perceptions of time and space cease to exist. In fact, linear and cyclical notions of time, which have been dominant in modern Western societies, continue to orient people's practices and perceptions in many ways. As Koselleck has argued, at each historical moment, there are different sediments of time that result from different experiences. Historical times, he argues, "consist of multiple layers that refer to each other in a reciprocal way, though without being wholly dependent upon each other" (Koselleck 2018, 4). These different layers can be investigated both historically and ethnographically. Anthropological analyses have clearly shown that notions of time and space are culturally specific.[4] Ethnographic research reveals not only the multiplicity of sediments of time operating at a certain time and according to their cultural specificity, but also emerging experiences and configurations that point to new formations. Thus, assuming that in contemporary societies we will find several sediments of time and practices of space, I use the notion of transitoriness to conceptualize simultaneously a mode of perceiving time and of organizing practice accordingly that differs from both the cyclical and the linear (or progressive) notions that have been dominant in industrial societies, *and* a mode of perceiving spatial practices that emphasize mobility and circulation instead of the production of fixed places and attachment to them. Transitoriness is an articulation of time-space that is becoming increasingly prevalent.

From Autoconstruction to Transitory Arrangements

Many metropolises around the world have been largely constructed by their residents according to the mode of city making that I have referred to as peripheral urbanization and that is articulated around autoconstruction (Caldeira 2017). This formation is still prevalent across the Global South, but is undergoing significant transformation. Although this is not the place for a full analysis of autoconstruction, it is important to keep it in mind, for three reasons. First, it is a historical reference in relation to which it is possible to discern change and emergence. Second, it clearly embeds a linear perception of time associated with notions of progress and social mobility and thus contrasts the transitory. Third, this perception of time is embedded in the production of space and thus demonstrates the intertwinement of temporal and spatial dimensions.

Under autoconstruction, city residents are agents of urbanization, not simply consumers of spaces developed and regulated by others. They build their houses and their cities in a complex process that involves a certain temporality. It happens step-by-step, according to the resources that residents are able to put together at each moment and over a significant period of time. Each phase involves a great amount of improvisation and bricolage, complex strategies and calculations, plus constant imagination of what a "nice home" might look like. House transformations demonstrate a slow and continuous process of change and improvement. Over time, houses, streets, infrastructures, and lives end up being substantially modified and improved. Houses and neighborhoods thus become the material embodiment of progress and social ascension.

In interview after interview that I conducted with residents of the peripheries of São Paulo since the late 1970s, and up to several years ago, I invariably heard the same narrative. When people moved to their neighborhood, they reported, it was the bush, and all that existed were dirt roads and a bunch of shacks; but after many years, the city finally arrived. Year after year, people worked on their houses. All their savings and extra time were channeled into the long process of building their houses and making them into better places. Much collective effort was also put into political organizing that forced the state to improve the quality of the infrastructure and the built environment and to provide better services, ranging from schools and clinics to cultural centers. After forty-some years, the results in the areas I worked in are palpable: better, larger, and carefully decorated houses and urbanized neighborhoods. This process fixed people to their spaces in the city's peripheries. Commonly, people who autoconstructed seldom later moved away, but rather circumscribed their everyday lives to their neighborhoods, the place in which their social mobility could be read.

However, this project of materially and spatially embedded social ascension either is becoming more difficult or seems significantly less interesting to a younger generation born in the peripheries but who want to live other lives. The types of housing available to the poor have diversified significantly in the last two decades. This diversification includes options that are both more and less precarious than autoconstruction. If until the 1990s to autoconstruct a house from scratch was the main possibility in São Paulo's peripheries, in recent years several options have emerged: the house became a commodity that can be purchased as a finished good in the market even by low-income residents; a market of low-cost apartments in buildings constructed by large developers has emerged over the last fifteen years and has been growing; the state, in partnership with private developers, has sponsored a substantial program of social housing (*Minha Casa, Minha Vida*, or "My House, My Life"); rental options have increased, especially under the form of subdivisions of enlarged, autoconstructed houses; and land invasions, usually as part of organized movements, have become more common.

In 2018, some residents of São Paulo's peripheries articulated a different narrative. Because they had several options, many young people didn't even contemplate autoconstruction, a process they considered to have high costs in terms of time, energy, and money. They thus ended up transiting among different possibilities. What seemed to be an increasing number of people decided to rent and therefore moved from place to place, both around the peripheries and sometimes also in central areas of the city. Some people move to a unit in a *Minha Casa, Minha Vida* development, but not uncommonly this is a temporary arrangement as many move back to favelas, for example, to avoid the utilities and condominium fees. People renting may consider joining an organized occupation movement, but this is also a demanding option (as people are required to work on the construction). Some try to buy either a finished house or an apartment, if they can make the down payment and mortgage payments. Frequently people move between these options, circulating around several areas of the city. Thus, for young low-income people to inhabit an enormous city such as São Paulo (population some 12 million) is becoming a practice of repeated dislocations instead of one of direct and strong commitment to a place and a house. People invest a significant amount of effort in each move, but these do not necessarily coalesce into something like a permanent home that can be read as progress, improvement, betterment, or ascension—with the exception of those who purchase an apartment or a house. The multiple dislocations are not necessarily articulated by a dominant project, such as one's urge to become the property owner of an autoconstructed house. The moves are both transitory and horizontal. People have greater spatial mobility and circulation than in the period when autoconstruction was the dominant option, but not necessarily more social mobility. These movements are similar to what AbdouMaliq Simone describes as "parking" in Jakarta, Indonesia.

> In Jakarta, the favorite word now is parking. You know, we need a place to park. I need a place to park my 80-year-old mother. I need a place to park my belongings. It's not about home, it's about parking. And if you're parking you are not really investing in the long term. It doesn't mean that you don't end up staying where you are for a long time, but you also act as if you are not fully "there." So inhabiting becomes something different. It's about your itineraries. It's about arranging short-term stays (Simone 2019, 18).

In sum, the ethnographic record, in São Paulo as well as in Jakarta, indicates that practices and experiences of inhabiting the city, especially among the youth in the peripheries, are no longer necessarily directed by a linear project and no longer restrict them to living in a certain location, but rather embody transitoriness, frequent dislocations, and lateral movements.

These lateral movements in arranging shelter do not happen in isolation, as they are intrinsically connected to ways of living together. Autoconstruction has been strongly associated with the nuclear family in São Paulo. The diversification of types of housing correlates not only with the emergence of several housing alternatives and the types of available transit among them, but also with the experiment with various types of household arrangements. The nuclear family, comprising a heterosexual couple and their children—the type of household configuration that was dominant in that city until recently and was associated with autoconstruction—is currently a minority arrangement. In 2015 in Brazil in general, only 42 percent of the families were characterized as nuclear, compared to 57.7 percent twenty years earlier.[5] In Jardim das Camélias, a neighborhood in the periphery of São Paulo where I conducted socioeconomic surveys in 1980 and followed up in 2013, the proportion of households formed by a nuclear family dropped from 59.4 percent to 45.9 percent.[6] During the same period, the proportion of households headed by a woman increased from 11.9 percent to 30.8 percent. A recent study revealed that in peripheral neighborhoods in São Paulo, on average half of the women who have children are "single mothers" (that is, they do not live with the fathers of their children), compared to only 17 percent in wealthier neighborhoods.[7] Young people, in particular, are experimenting with new arrangements for living and with ways of having and raising children. This tendency may have been emerging for a while, but young folks are now explicitly articulating the different arrangements as new alternatives.

New modes of living together is a dimension of social life in relation to which the inadequacy of existing data and categories of analysis is especially stark. How can one refer to a group of people (including children) who are not a family but still live together and want to experiment with possibilities of collective living? Demographic and social economic statistics are collected in ways that preclude the visibility of new modes of living together, as they tend not to account for non-heteronormative arrangements. The established categories predetermine the collection of information, whose specificities are overlooked so that they can fit the categories, even when it becomes clear that they don't actually match. The inadequacy of existing categories and their inability to capture new social phenomena became especially evident to me when I tried to analyze the results of the survey I conducted in Jardim das Camélias in 2013 and found out that I could not classify some 20 percent of the households according to categories usually used by sociodemographic analyses. For example, how should one classify the arrangement formed by two women who are friends and not necessarily a couple and who live together with their children, who are not biologically related but in practice raised as siblings? I ended up grouping all types of nonclassifiable households under the somewhat vague category of "complex arrangements." That became a strong sign of an emerging phenomenon that my current research tries to problematize, document, and understand.

My preliminary analysis indicates that the way in which alternative modes of living have been interpreted is especially problematic. Usually, several of these alternatives and the increase in "single motherhood" are interpreted as signs both of poverty and of the deterioration of the conditions of life in São Paulo's peripheries.[8] They would indicate that people lack the means to live according to desirable heteronormative standards. The ethnographic research I have conducted in those peripheries in 2018, however, directly contradicts this argument. On the one hand, there has not been a deterioration in conditions of life in the peripheries, but rather significant improvement, especially regarding the quality of the housing stock, transportation, and urban infrastructure. On the other hand, what seems to be under way is a profound transformation of the ways in which women are shaping their own lives. They are forging new subjectivities that enhance their autonomy and rejecting established patterns of male dominance and the frequent violence that pervades domestic life.[9] Our preliminary investigations indicate that young women want to live other lives, quite different from the ones of their parents, and especially of their mothers, who worked mostly as domestic servants when they were not housewives. Younger women are educating themselves to participate in a better position in the expanding service sector of the job market. They conceive of motherhood not necessarily as a step into marriage, but rather as a path (even if a difficult one) away from their families of origins. They think of friendship, sisterhood, and participation in organized collectives as new ways of building networks that will allow them more autonomy and engagement in urban life. In our interviews, it also became clear that women are experimenting with their sexuality; several openly discussed their bisexuality. In this sense, these women are reinventing themselves, and their ways of living are changing accordingly. For those women who are reinventing womanhood and motherhood, to autoconstruct or to buy a house is simply out of the question, being not only unaffordable but also undesirable. They require flexible and transitory arrangements as they experiment with various possibilities of living and of conceiving of their subjectivities, and as the composition of their households changes. If for their parents' generation the house was the core of a collective project, for the younger generation, their projects have other foci. The house becomes only a transitory space, subordinated to other projects.

Rearticulating Gender and Sexuality

Needless to say, changes in women's lives affect patterns of gender relations in general both in a country and in working-class neighborhoods where, until the last generation, the authority of men and their roles as the main family providers were not widely contested. Yet much is still unknown about new articulations of gender roles. Where are the fathers of the children raised by solo mothers living? Do they live with their own single mothers, as rap and other artistic interventions produced in the peripheries suggest? Are many young children in the peripheries in fact members of the second (or even third) generation of children raised with absent fathers? What does this mean in terms of a formation of collective life? Although much is to be discovered, it is evident that this kind of transformation lies at the basis of a great deal of anxiety and insecurity articulated during Brazil's 2018 presidential electoral campaign under the form of attacks against something that the elected president and his allies call *ideologia de gênero* (gender ideology). What this means exactly is never made explicit, but the phrase became the right-wing shortcut to demonize anything associated with women's and LGBTQ+ rights and with other modes of life that diverge from a stereotypical, caricaturized heteronormativity. That this theme was determinant in the electoral campaign and the right-wing victory is a clear indication both of the depth of the transformations and of the anxiety they generate.

Significant transformations in women's lives, including a diversification of options in terms of sexuality, are part of broader changes in articulations of gender and sexuality. Central to them is the role of LGBTQ+ people (the term stands for "lesbian, gay, bisexual, transgender, queer, and other people"), often organized in collectives, whose presence in the public sphere has increased dramatically. LGBTQ + activism is everywhere, with the nation's several Pride parades attracting millions and activist demands reaching the national congress, which finally approved same-sex marriage in 2013. If in the past openly LGBTQ+ people in São Paulo were restricted to a few neighborhoods downtown, now they are increasingly present across the city, including throughout the peripheries. But little is known about their daily practices and modes of living together.

Some of the most powerful interviews we conducted in the peripheries in 2018 were with LGBTQ+ people. They explained their living arrangements, but also articulated a performative and malleable conception of gender and sexuality that points to other dimensions of the transitory. Young LGBTQ+ people in the peripheries live in diverse ways, but not necessarily with their partners, who tend to be temporary. A majority live with relatives with whom they have differing types of disclosure about their sexuality and from whom they get different types of support—or opposition. Although they feel that it is becoming possible to disclose their sexuality or gender publicly in the spaces of the peripheries, this is a decision to be made carefully. Thus they consciously perform gender and sexuality differently, depending on the context. They "play" with their gender and sexuality.

Some of the most powerful articulations of this performative approach come from "genderqueer" people we interviewed and who used the expression *bicha cebola* (onion bicha)[10] to characterize themselves.[11] The expression alludes to the ways in which they put themselves together to travel between the peripheries and the central neighborhoods where most of the LGBTQ+ parties and encounters happen. They pay great attention to their looks and spend considerable time, money, and resources to *se montar* (literally "to mount" themselves), that is, to dress up in a feminine register (wigs, nail polishes, makeup, dresses, jewelry, and the like). But they cannot leave peripheral neighborhoods *montadas* (assembled), so they add several layers of clothes to cover up, ranging from hoodies and hats to baggy pants and sweaters. Then, as they move from the peripheries to the center of the city, they peel off the layers and may add others that they carry in their backpacks, so that they arrive at the parties totally *montadas* (assembled). The reverse happens on the way back, when the layers peeled off are put back on. *Bicha cebola* "é a bicha que se desmonta pra se montar" (meaning: "is the *bicha* that disassembles itself in order to assemble itself"), according to Artur Santoro (2019). This expression treats identities as a complex combination of multiple layers and as something people construct in the everyday dynamics of dislocation and circulation around the city. The term reveals both the instability and the flexibility of the construction of gender and sexuality along with people's agency in assembling or disassembling their identities, as well as in constructing them according to the circumstances, especially their relationships to space. It reveals the transitoriness of each assemblage. The people we interviewed talked at length about their multi-dimensional lives and selves, depending on contexts—not only the peripheries and city center, but also spaces of work and within their homes. In sum, *bicha cebola* is the opposite of the fixing of an identity; it is about the possibility of *un*-fixing identities, of constructing and performing them, but also retreating from them. Thus *bichas cebolas'* dislocations and experiments are embodiments of transitoriness. The same is true for people who refuse to label their sexuality in one stable way.

Rolês: Moving around and Resignifying the City

The *bichas cebolas'* movements, as they assemble and then disassemble themselves whenever they traverse various spaces of the city, resignify these spaces. As they appropriate areas of the city for different performances—by closing streets for some of their parties, as done by the cultural group Helipa LGBTQ in Sao Paolo; by marking subway and train stations as appropriate spaces for the peeling off of their layers; by establishing some shopping malls and streets as relatively safe for their encounters—transgender people and members of other LGBTQ+ populations simultaneously elaborate their public identities and change the character of space. This resignification/appropriation of urban spaces is transitory, in that it happens especially as practices of circulation and movement, rather than as marking the boundaries of territories. This type of relationship to space is, in fact, common among diverse youth groups in the city and in their practices.

Moving around the city for fun, to mark it transgressively with painted tags, in search of encounters, to join cultural events, or as a form of sociability, were not among the practices of a past generation. Up to the 1990s, young people in the peripheries would leave these spaces to work, but otherwise would largely restrict their movements, leisure, and sociability to their immediate neighborhoods, if not strictly to their streets of residence. Circulation as a dominant mode of experience among the youth in São Paulo's peripheries began to become evident in the 1990s, when hip-hop started to become the main cultural production of these spaces.[12] Nowadays, young people do not want to be limited to their own neighborhoods, and many want to claim the whole city. "A City only exists for those who can move around it" stated a famous graffiti painted in downtown São Paulo in the late 2000s. The young people who demand to be able to move around the city, who graffiti it and tag its walls and monuments, who skateboard, break dance, practice parkour, motorcycle here and there, go to funk balls and LGBTQ+ events—these folks are transforming their city into a space of mobility, experimentation, pleasure, and also risk (see Caldeira 2012).

It is only fitting, thus, that the argot of young people includes several expressions referring to circulation, the most prominent of them being *rolê*. This term, in Portuguese (not French), is used by various groups of young people in São Paulo with sometimes different meanings, but always to refer to practices of circulation, leisure, and sociability throughout the city. *Rolê* comes from *rolar*, to roll. *Pixadores*, the "Paulista" taggers, say that they will *dar um rolê* (literally, give a roll) when they go out in groups to tag. Rappers use a similar expression to refer to their practice of circulation in search of events and parties. LGBTQ+ people call some of their spaces of sociability, such as parties, events, and balls, "*rolê*." Gatherings of young people hanging out in shopping malls, usually organized via social media, are called *rolezinhos*, meaning small *rolês*. These events, which in fact are typically very large, usually scare both regular consumers of the malls and even the police. Encounters of large numbers of people in street balls or funk balls or sometimes in other types of cultural events are referred to as *fluxos*, or fluxes.

All the *rolê* practices involve movement and minimal attachment to marked territories. Some refer simply to circulation, as in the continuously moving around of skateboarding, motorcycling, and parkour. *Pixadores* also move around intensively not only to imprint all types of spaces with their tags, but also because many of them work as *motoboys*—couriers paid to move all types of goods around the metropolis (Caldeira 2012). Other practices are hosted in temporary spaces, such as the funk balls and some LGBTQ+ gatherings in public spaces: they may happen today in one street or empty lot and tomorrow in another one, or may occur frequently for a while and then vanish. Transitoriness lies at the core of all these practices.

This constant moving around, this non-fixity, has at least two important and sometimes opposite dynamics. One is that it signals a certain relationship to the city: a relationship of exploration, conquest, and possession, even if only temporary. It marks one's refusal to remain restricted to one's neighborhoods in the peripheries and frequently becomes transgressive in its use and marking of spaces in the center. The second dynamic is that the constant dislocation is also a tense response to the stiffening of repression and violence, especially of the police, but also of private security agencies. The more that young people from the peripheries circulate, the greater that some city residents feel anxiety about the presence of their bodies—predominantly male and black—in their own space, and the more intense the violence that can be waged against them. In fact, at the moment when *rolês* of any kind involve large numbers of young people, they are usually treated as dangerous, as a threat to order, and, not rarely, with repression and violence. Thus, if the *rolês* move from place to place and if young people circulate, it is also to evade violent control. Transitoriness and movement are ways of evading this control, of subverting the gaze to prevent being targeted (Simone 2019, 18), and of transgressing and re-creating spaces of freedom. They are the modes under which those who are relegated to segregated spaces claim other spaces as well as the city itself. It is significant that *rolê* has become a common expression to designate not merely several forms of leisure and circulation, but sometimes also tactics of survival.

Digital Spaces and Multiple Time/Space Formations

Digital platforms constitute crucial spaces where we conduct our lives nowadays. These spaces of flows, to use the expression Manuel Castells (2000 [1996]) coined to analyze them, are associated with experiences of time that differ in significant ways from previous conceptions. This digital time/space configuration is a fundamental articulation of the transitory.

The use of digital platforms is very high in Brazil, especially in urban areas, and even among low-income residents.[13] This use has exploded in recent years and not only has molded everyday interactions but also has had significant political consequences, as the presidential elections of 2018 were disputed on the internet, making "old communication technologies" such as the television basically irrelevant. In São Paulo, around 80 percent of the residents had access to the internet in 2017. The access is unequal, but even in the poorest areas of the city some 70 percent of the residents have access, basically due to several policies of digital inclusion put in place by the municipal government (Wissenbach 2019, 118). This access is almost universal—96 percent—among the younger population (18–34 year old) (NIC.br 2019, 136). Although computers are not widespread in the peripheries of São Paulo, cell phones are. It is via such phones that 85 percent of the low-income Brazilians who access the internet do it daily, and intensively.[14] Telephone land lines have never really arrived at the peripheries. They were bypassed by the cell phones that are now in virtually everybody's hands. While one spends countless hours moving around the city for all possible reasons in packed public transportation, while one inhabits the territories of the peripheries, while one works in all types of spaces (from factories and offices to atop motorcycles), one also inhabits the space of flows, articulating the most different types of encounters, engaging with strangers in chat rooms, following one's own work schedule and attending to the next delivery, playing games, listening to music, watching films, scrolling through countless WhatsApp group messages, and thus assembling and moving among transitory worlds.

"Space organizes time in the network society," argues Manuel Castells (2000 [1996], 407). For him, "space is the material support for time-sharing social practices" (441). Physical spaces, such as cities, streets, neighborhoods, homes, and so on, are some of the main supports of social practices and thus constitute the "space of places" where we live our everyday lives. Superimposed on them, or parallel to them, and also part of our everydayness, there is the "space of flows"—the space of the internet, a circuit of electronic exchanges whose form is a network clustered in hubs and nodes, which selectively connects places to one another (Castells 2000 [1996], chap. 6). For Castells, the crucial characteristic of the space of flows is to establish an environment with a different, nonlinear logic. It is a spatial context whose logic is based on real-time interaction, no matter where its elements are physically located.

Digital technologies were, of course, not the first ones to allow instantaneous transmission of information regardless of physical location. The telegraph did exactly that, but these two technologies have different logics and became associated with completely different notions of time. Up to the 1840s and before the spread of the telegraph, there were a proliferation of local times. The telegraph allowed the unification and standardization of time on the basis of a time signal transmitted simultaneously from a central point to vast territories.[15] "In 1880 Greenwich time was adopted as the legally enforceable measurement of time throughout Britain and Ireland. Four years later it became the "world standard time" (Morus 2000, 469). In other words, the telegraph supported a centralized, integrated, and unified project: the standardization of time. It brought together nations and enabled empires, in addition of course to serving the reproduction of capital and exploitation of the labor forces that were brought to the schedule of what E. P. Thompson (1967) famously described as time discipline.

The notion of time that the space of flows and digital technologies articulate is quite different. Instead of unification and standardization, digital technologies support the opposite experience of time—its dispersal and the proliferation of localized and transitory temporal experiences. By design, the internet disperses instead of centering. As is well known, the internet originated in a U.S. Defense Department project during the Cold War as a way of preventing a Soviet takeover or destruction of the American communication system in case of a nuclear war. The internet is not hierarchical, but rather is constituted of dispersed networks of autonomous hubs and nodes that have numerous ways to link up and cannot be controlled by any center (Castells 2000 [1996], 6). The conception of time associated with this techno-spatial architecture represents a radical departure from previous conceptions; Castells coined a nonsensical expression to characterize it—"timeless time."

Castells (2000 [1996], chap. 7) clearly acknowledges that in contemporary societies time is heterogeneous: there is not a single dominant temporality, neither clock time nor biological time (the time of the life cycles), nor the temporality of the space of flows, timeless time (Castells 2000, 499). But he is especially interested in understanding this temporality associated with the space of flows. For this, he anchors the analysis of time in the network society on Leibniz's definition of time and space, according to which "space [is] an order of coexistences as time is an order of successions" (494). Correspondingly, Castells understands time as sequencing, so the perturbation of sequences becomes its denial—timeless time.

> Timeless time . . . occurs when the characteristics of a given context, namely, the informational paradigm and the network society, induce systematic perturbation in the sequential order of phenomena performed in that context. This perturbation may take the form of compressing the occurrence of phenomena, aiming at instantaneity, or else by introducing random discontinuity in the sequence. Elimination of sequencing creates undifferentiated time, which is tantamount to eternity" (Castells 2000, 494).

Virtual reality, hypertext, instantaneous exchanges in global financial transactions—all would come to represent perturbations in the sequential order of phenomena. In this informational society, Castells argues, the space of flows "dissolves time by disordering the sequence of events and making them simultaneous, thus installing society in eternal ephemerality" (497). However, one should ask whether this understanding of time in the network society is the only one possible. It seems clear that contemporary societies are not on their way to dissolve time, but rather to live it in unprecedented ways. Thus, it is important to examine alternative forms of understanding time.

The debate on how to characterize time in the space of flows and in contemporary societies is still unsettled. Several authors have focused on the question of acceleration of time.[16] But Castells's analysis points to other crucial issues that he does not necessarily analyze: simultaneity, lack of synchrony, superimposition of multiple lateral temporalities, dispersal, and the transitory. Sequence and succession are not the only ways to conceive of time. Michel Foucault, whose philosophical work has had as one of its central undertakings the critique of evolutionist and progressivist ways of conceiving time and history, suggests other possibilities, such as the one articulated in "Of Other Spaces," his essay about heterotopia, from 1967: "Time probably appears only as one of the various possible operations of distribution between the elements that are spread out in space" (Foucault 2008 [1967], 15).[17] In *Discipline and Punish* (1977), he develops the notions of distribution and genesis as some of the disciplinary techniques that constitute docile bodies. In sum, though the idea is not to apply Foucault's framework to the study of the network society, his works remind us that time can be conceived in alternative ways—distribution, geneses, laterality—and not necessarily as successions.

But what *are* the experiences of time associated with the space of flows? The internet accustoms us to the possibilities of "real time," the immediate time of interactions online regardless of physical presence or time zone. The space of flows certainly also accustoms us to the transitory. This can happen at different levels. At the most obvious, the space of flows, and especially social media, contains apps in which exchanges and images disappear after a certain time, such as the posts in stories on Instagram and Facebook or the exchanges in SnapChat. At a less-obvious level, most information posted in social media is simply ephemeral: technically, it remains and can be retrieved, but in practice it is displaced as new information gets in and the old is bypassed and moved away from main screens. Additionally, the internet allows not only instantaneous communications, but also juxtapositions. Several things may happen independently or get combined at the same time. Space-time contexts become fragmented and multiplied. One can participate in different chat rooms simultaneously. One can open several tabs or applications on one screen and move from one to the other, shifting conversations, transferring images and sound and other information, and either merging them or simply letting them sit side by side. There are at least two experiences here: one is simultaneity, meaning all that goes on at the same time in one's devices. The other is the superimposition of pieces of information from different sources or contexts. Some of these juxtapositions may resemble avant-garde collages. However, while these collages are often intended to produce shock, on the screens of digital devices all is possible and surrealism is meaningless. Decontextualization guarantees that "everything goes," more like a pastiche. In fact, the spread and acceptance of fake news may actually be understood as part of these routine online practices of assembling decontextualized images. In sum, the space of flows frustrates ideas of continuity and progress and promotes senses of simultaneity, superimposition, transitoriness, and dispersion.

Koselleck's (2018) analysis, mentioned above, indicates that many sediments of time can be seen in contemporary societies. These sediments interact with each other to produce our multiple temporal experiences. Of course, the rhythms of the cyclical time of the life cycle, of seasons, of weeks and months, constitute some of these layers. Of course, we still operate with standard-time and work-time discipline. Even computers and interactions in the space of flows, such as Zoom meetings, for example, are regulated by standard clock time. But the internet adds other layers of time to standard time and to cyclical time, thus provoking significant transformations in experiences of time. I would argue that the dominant experience of time nowadays—in São Paulo and elsewhere, where digital technologies are ubiquitous—is neither standard time, nor cyclical time, nor network time, but rather the experience of operating with and across these different temporalities as they intersect in the everyday.[18] Although the possibilities of articulation are multiple, transitoriness seems to be one of the main products of these intersections.

Think of a woman interacting in a chat room who has to interrupt the chat to breastfeed her baby. Or of a student attending a class via Zoom in the living room of a house in which other household members are busy in the same room with other tasks. Or of someone simultaneously answering email, navigating the web, and performing manual labor. Young people I talked to in the peripheries of São Paulo keep a constant eye on WhatsApp and social media, while they perform all types of tasks, such as delivering documents or merchandise on their motorcycles, cleaning other people's houses, attending classes, sewing clothes in a neighborhood factory, preparing food in a fast-food restaurant, building a wall in a construction site, or riding the bus to work. Thousands of people ride together on buses and trains to different places, each holding a communication device that keeps them plugged to diverse interactions and time/space configurations disconnected from their commuting experiences. Then when they reach their bus or train stop, they close their devices and enter their boring jobs, maybe in a call center, a bank, or a delivery outlet. The previous interactions online have vanished. Other interactions will come whenever possible. People check email, text their mothers, arrange a party, pay a bill, all while eating lunch at the established lunch time at the firm for which they work. In sum, one goes in and out of the space of flows while performing various activities framed by other times and spaces. The resulting experience of time is thus of transience and alternation between various framings of time. As central elements inserted in the most varied moments of the everyday, digital technologies intensify senses of fragmentation and transitoriness, of oscillation and lateral movements, and of displacements between spaces and times.

Transitoriness and a New Political Landscape

I have argued that transitoriness is becoming normalized as an organizing logic of the everyday and is thus an important way of articulating different dimensions of lives in the peripheries of São Paulo and elsewhere. Lateral dislocation and the abandonment of notions of progress and ascension, moving between housing options, experimenting with new ways of living together and shaping family relations, assembling and disassembling performances of gender, circulating and resignifying the city, and inhabiting digital space/time configurations—all are practices marked by transitoriness and lateral dislocations. The same could be said about other crucial aspects of social life that I cannot discuss here, such as the transformations in labor that make temporary jobs and improvised arrangements the norm (Ferguson and Li 2018). Transitoriness also marks transformations in the political landscape.

Large mass demonstrations have framed the political landscape in São Paulo since 2013. Following the footsteps of the Arab Spring, the Indignados in Spain, the Occupy movement in more than nine hundred cities around the world, and the Turkish uprising, protests in São Paulo mushroomed into a series of events that brought to the streets of multiple cities around Brazil millions of people addressing a huge spectrum of issues.[19] The main features of these protests are well known by now and include the following: a symbiotic relationship with the internet and social media; the diffused and spontaneous organization through networks; the capacity of attracting thousands of participants in a short period of time; the heterogeneity of the participants, who may or may not form coalitions; a high participation of young people; and the disregard for established political institutions and their ways of organizing the political, among other features. In so many words, the logic of the transitory shaped deeply the ways in which the protests unfolded. In São Paulo, issues related to the city lay at the core of the protests: their trigger was the proposal of a small increase in the fare for public transportation. But the issues soon became about the right to circulate freely. In fact, "a city only exists for those who can move around it" had been the motto of the movement that started the protests, and of course resonated deeply with all practitioners of *rolês*, primarily cultural producers and young people wishing to move around the city without being the victims of police violence. The protests also resonated deeply with those who for years had been organizing themselves in *coletivos*, or collectives, throughout the city and especially in the peripheries. Collectives are small groups of people who get together around various forms of cultural production, identity-related interests (such as the experiences of Afro-Brazilians, women, and LGBTQ+ people), or anything else, such as creating collective gardens or addressing the needs of a neighborhood.

But the protests also unleashed other forces, equally decentralized and dispersed, but basically reactionary and authoritarian. They coalesced around issues of corruption and so were highly instrumental in the impeachment process of President Dilma Rousseff in 2016 and three years later in the election of Jair Bolsonaro. The political process that brought Bolsonaro to power is exemplary of a new political landscape. Two issues related to the themes discussed in this chapter are central to this political landscape. First, Bolsonaro is a figure from outside the political landscape, regardless of his history as a federal deputy. He was not a member of a relevant political party and had almost no presence in established spaces of political campaign, such as television and debates among candidates, in which he did not participate. The main media for his campaign were WhatsApp and social media, and he relied significantly on the circulation of fake news. Second, the rancors he and previous protests powerfully articulated included a strong backlash against several of the deep transformations reshaping Brazilian society, such as the remaking of the role of women, their new modes of organizing their lives, and the new practices of LGBTQ+ people.

The new political landscape in Brazil is thus marked by a peculiar articulation that exposes the ways in which practices associated with transitoriness have become normalized. On one side, decentered and dispersed formations within networks that sometimes coalesce in public protests and rely heavily on social media became the mode of political intervention across the political spectrum. They may have started in the spaces that articulate rights discourses and that forge new political identities and spaces of freedom, but they ended up being overtaken by the other side of the political spectrum, erasing the differences between right and left political tactics. On the other side, the right-wing articulates a strong backlash against all the new formations associated with transitoriness, especially the transformations associated with gender roles. Yet they do this by using the possibilities of digital platforms. In fact, the reactionary forces became masters in the use of pastiche, superimpositions, and fake news, thus excelling in the transference of possibilities of time/space formations from digital platforms to people in the streets and to the broader political landscape. Jair Bolsonaro continues to explore the possibilities of the manipulation of social media (he tweets daily, as did ex-president Donald Trump), his family and supporters articulate constant campaigns of fake news, and he continues to vociferate against women, LGBTQ+ people, cultural producers, and a range of others. Bolsonaro does all this while openly supporting a military coup, the use of weapons and torture, the utility of other authoritarian initiatives, and displaying what is recognized as one of the worst attitudes worldwide in relation to the coronavirus pandemic. In a perverse way, Bolsonaro embodies both the possibilities and the worst dangers of a political landscape shaped by transitoriness, but also by the absence of any other powerfully articulated alternative able to deconstruct either the pastiches that he constantly produces or the prejudices he expresses without accountability.

Notes

1. Over the last forty years, I have conducted numerous research projects in the peripheries of São Paulo, mostly by myself but sometimes in collaboration with others, such as Cynthia Sarti in the late 1970s and James Holston since the late 1980s. In this article, I rely on materials from previous research, but especially on data generated in 2018, when I worked with a team of six collaborators: Katia Ramalho Gomes, Danielle Regina de Oliveira, Luiz Paulo Ferreira Santiago, Artur Santoro, Mayara Amaral dos Santos, and Renata Adriana de Sousa. In 2018, I was affiliated with the Fundação Getúlio Vargas and NEV-USP, the Center for the Study of Violence at the University of São Paulo, with a visiting professor fellowship from FAPESP. Fieldwork in the peripheries in 2018 was supported by FTAS, the Fundação Tide Setubal. I

express my sincere gratitude to these institutions and collaborators, as well as to Sérgio Adorno (USP) and Ciro Biderman (FGV). I also thank Alli Appelbaum for making me clarify my arguments and improving my text.

2. This lack of directionality is what differentiates the transitory from the provisional. The provisional refers to "Of, belonging to, or of the nature of a temporary provision or arrangement; provided or adopted for the time being; supplying the place of something regular, permanent, or final. Also: accepted or used in default of something better; tentative," according to the OED. The provisional thus assumes a directionality, a more-permanent or better referent that will come to replace the tentative and temporary arrangement. The transitory does not assume this directionality.

3. AbdouMaliq Simone has been elaborating similar arguments (2018; 2019; 2020). Simone is one of the collaborators on a project investigating formations of collective life in which I participate, together with Gautam Bhan and Kelly Gillespie. Our dialogue over the years has been important for the formulation of the arguments I develop here.

4. Classical analyses of the cultural specificity of notions of time and space include Evans-Pritchard (1969 [1940]) and Thompson (1967).

5. http://www.ipea.gov.br/retrato/.

6. I have been doing research in Jardim das Camélias since 1978, when it was located in one of the poorest districts of São Paulo, called São Miguel Paulista. By 2013, it was no longer one of the city's poorest.

7. In several neighborhoods in the peripheries, the percentage of "single mothers" runs as high as 60 percent. Source: 2010 census data analyzed by Ibope/Estado, http://www.estadao.com.br/noticias/impresso,chance-de-ser-mae-solteira-na-periferia-e-ate-35-vezes-maior-,1030951,0.htm. I use "single mother" (*mãe solteira*) with quotation marks because this is a category in dispute. Many women who opt to have children on their own in São Paulo call themselves *mãe solo*, or solo mother.

8. In fact, the percentage of single mothers is frequently used as an indicator of the level of vulnerability and poverty of neighborhoods, together with data of homicide rates. For example, see Cardia et al. 2003.

9. The pervasiveness of domestic violence in Brazil is clear, and its victims are largely women and children. According to data from IPEA analyzed by Cerqueira and Coelho (2014), countrywide approximately 527,000 rapes or attempted rapes take place each year, of which only about 10 percent are reported to the police. Some 70 percent of the victims of rape are either children younger than 13 (50.7 percent of the total of victims) or adolescents from 14 to 17 (19.4 percent). They are usually victimized inside the home and by members of their own households.

10. The literal (and unsatisfactory) translation would be "onion fag." *Cebola* means onion. *Bicha* is an expression hard to translate and thus I will keep it in Portuguese. The most direct translation is "fag." That is a derogatory word that many gay and transgender people have resignified and use to refer to themselves. If used by others to refer to them, it would be offensive.

11. The interview with a group of transgender people who live in the peripheries and organize large LGBTQ+ parties via social media was conducted by Artur Santoro and myself. Artur has been developing the analysis of LGBTQ+ groups and highlighting the importance of the use of the notion of the performative inspired by the work of Judith Butler to analyze their construction of gender.

12. This mobility is also associated with the fact that public transportation has improved significantly in São Paulo over the last two decades. Although moving around is still very time consuming, the expansion of both subway and train lines has allowed for faster movements. In the past, buses were the almost exclusive mode of transportation, and the lines served the peripheries poorly. Buses have also improved and are complemented by networks of van services. Additionally, large numbers of young people, especially men, own motorcycles.

13. In 2018, Brazil had 126.9 million internet users, or 70 percent of the population. While 92 percent of upper-class Brazilians access the internet, only 48 percent of the low-income classes did so in 2018, but this meant an increase from 30 percent in 2015. https://cetic.br/publicacao/pesquisa-sobre-o-uso-das-tecnologias-de-informacao-e-comunicacao-nos-domicilios-brasileiros-tic-domicilios-2018/.

14. https://cetic.br/publicacao/pesquisa-sobre-o-uso-das-tecnologias-de-informacao-e-comunicacao-nos-domicilios-brasileiros-tic-domicilios-2018/.

15. See Stephens (1989) for the American history of the telegraph and Morus (2000) for the British history.

16. For example, Paul Virilio, David Harvey, Judy Wajcman, Stephen Kern, and John Urry.

17. Interestingly, in this 1967 essay, Foucault also argues that "We are at a moment, I believe, when our experience of the world is less that of a great life developing through time than that of a network that connects points and intersects with its own skein" (pg. 14).

18. Robert Hassan (2005; 2007) has written a series of works on what he calls, following Barbara Adam, the timescapes of the network society. He characterizes the time of the network society as "asynchronous," since they are multiple and "not synchronized to or sublimated by, the logic of the clock" (2005,

7). My argument is that in everyday experiences we cannot disentangle these different logics of time, as people operate simultaneously with all of them.

19. I have analyzed the 2013 protests in Caldeira (2013). The literature on the protests around the world is vast.

References

Berman, Marshall. 1988 [1982]. *All That Is Solid Melts into Air: The Experience of Modernity*. New York: Penguin Books.

Caldeira, Teresa P. R. 2012. "Imprinting and Moving Around: New Visibilities and Configurations of Public Space in São Paulo." *Public Culture* 24, no. 2: 385–419.

Caldeira, Teresa. 2013. "São Paulo: The City and Its Protest." https://www.opendemocracy.net/en/opensecurity/sao-paulo-city-and-its-protest/.

Caldeira, Teresa P. R. 2017. "Peripheral Urbanization: Autoconstruction, Transversal Logics, and Politics in Cities of the Global South." *Environment and Planning D—Society and Space* 35, no. 1: 3–20.

Cardia, Nancy, Sergio Adorno, and Frederico Z. Poleto. 2003. "Homicide Rates and Human Rights Violations in São Paulo, Brazil: 1990 to 2000." *Health and Human Rights* 6, no. 2: 15–33.

Castells, Manuel. 2000 [1996]. *The Rise of the Network Society*. New York: Blackwell.

Cerqueira, Daniel, and Danilo de Santa Cruz Coelho. 2014. *Nota Técnica—Estupro no Brasil: Uma radiografia segundo dados de saúde: Nota Técnica n° 11*. Brasília, Brazil: IPEA.

Evans-Pritchard, E. E. 1969 [1940]. *The Nuer*. New York: Oxford University Press.

Ferguson, James, and Tanya Murray Li. 2018. "Beyond the 'Proper Job': Political-Economic Analysis after the Century of Labouring Man." *Working Paper 51*. PLAAS: Cape Town, University of Western Cape.

Foucault, Michel. 1977. *Discipline and Punish: The Birth of the Prison*. New York: Random House.

Foucault, Michel. 2008 [1967]. "Of Other Spaces." In *Heterotopia and the City—Public Space in a Postcivil Society*, edited by Michiel Dehaene and Lieven De Cauter, 13–29. New York: Routledge.

Harvey, David. 1989. *The Condition of Postmodernity—An Enquiry into the Origins of Cultural Change*. Oxford: Basil Blackwell.

Hassan, Robert. 2005. "Timescapes of the Network Society." *Fast Capitalism* 1, no. 1: 1–13.

Hassan, Robert. 2007. "Network Time." In *Time and Temporality in the Network Society*, edited by Robert Hassan and Ronald Purser, 37–61. Stanford, CA: Stanford University Press.

Koselleck, Reinhart. 2018. *Sediments of Time: On Possible Histories*. Stanford, CA: Stanford University Press.

Marx, Karl, and Friedrich Engels. 1996 [1848]. *The Communist Manifesto*. London: Pluto Press.

Morus, Iwan Rhys. 2000. "'The Nervous System of Britain': Space, Time and the Electric Telegraph in the Victorian Age." *BJHS* 33: 455–475.

NIC.br (Núcleo de Informação e Coordenação do Ponto BR). 2019. *Desigualdades digitais no espaço urbano: Um estudo sobre o acesso e uso da internet na cidade de São Paulo*. São Paulo: Comitê Gestor da Internet no Brasil.

Santoro, Artur. 2019. "Bichas cebolas: Construções de masculinidades na dinâmica centro-periferia." In *Relatório final da pesquisa "Periferias de São Paulo: Heterogeneidade e Novas Formas de Vida Coletiva."* Manuscript.

Simone, AbdouMaliq. 2018. *Improvised Lives: Rhythms of Endurance in an Urban South*. Cambridge: Polity.

Simone, AbdouMaliq, interviewed by Asha Best. 2019. "On Improvisation, Southern Urbanism and Rhythms of the Everyday." *Society + Space*. https://societyandspace.org/2019/06/17/on-improvisation-southern -urbanism-and-rhythms-of-the-everyday/.

Simone, AbdouMaliq. 2020. "To Extend: Temporariness in a World of Itineraries." *Urban Studies*. doi: 10.1177/0042098020905442.

Stephens, Carlene E. 1989. "The Impact of the Telegraph on Public Time in the United States, 1844–1893." *IEEE Technology and Society Magazine* 8, no. 1: 4–10.

Thompson, E. P. 1967. "Time, Work-Discipline, and Industrial Capitalism." *Past and Present* 38: 56–97.

Wissenbach, Tomás. 2019. "Dinâmicas intraurbanas e desigualdades territoriais." In NIC.br (Núcleo de Informação e Coordenação do Ponto BR). Pp. 81–130.

SUTURING
THE (W)HOLE

Vitalities of Everyday Urban Living in Congo

Prelude: Pic Sörensen

On February 26, 1921, four years before he would retire from active colonial service, District Commissioner Sören Sörensen sat down at his desk in his outpost overlooking the Kwango River, in what is now Southwest Congo, to write a letter to his old friend Jürgen Jürgensen. As did many Scandinavians in the latter half of the nineteenth century, both young men enlisted in 1898 in the Force Publique, the armed force of the Belgian King Leopold II's Congo Free State. Unlike Jürgensen, who decided to return to his native Denmark in 1906, Sörensen continued a successful career in the colonial administration after King Leopold's Free State was officially handed over to Belgium in 1908. Between 1912 and 1914, and again between 1919 and 1924, Sörensen was appointed as district commissioner and sent to the Kwango region to enforce colonial authority. Gradually "gaining new land," as he called it, he managed to occupy and map out the whole area, "pacifying" autochthonous populations along the way, and defending Belgian interests against Portuguese intrusions along the border with Angola.

In 1913, during one of his expeditions in the Kwango's southernmost zone, Sörensen "discovered" a mountain some 1,500 meters in height. The highest peak of what colonial cartographers subsequently also referred to as the Crystal Mountains was officially baptized "Pic Sörensen." And so, for decades to come, the district commissioner's name was perpetuated on the official maps of Belgian Congo.

Looking back on his career in his letter to Jürgensen, it is the figure of the mountain that comes to his mind to describe the past decades of colonizing efforts. Using it as a *pars pro toto* for the Kwango area, which, in 1921, was increasingly under colonial control, he muses:

> As Erasmus Montanus says: we now have some folk here on the mountain.[1] The big world company "Lever Brothers-Sunlight, Soap, Pears Soap" has established a big oil mill at the confluence of the Kwengo and Kwila rivers. . . . A little over twenty whites are working there, as well as thousands of black people, not including those natives who are collecting the palm nuts. It is a very big business. It is odd for an old Congo hand like me to see smoking chimneys here in our silent jungle, to hear the sound of the machines and see the white light beaming into the night. It is like an adventure.[2]

Sörensen's account of the "civilizing mission," the bringing of "white light," is unmistakably tinged with a feeling of nostalgia for the bygone world of the "silent jungle" in which he himself had felt so comfortable. But in the end it is the topos of the mountain that prevails. It stands out as a powerful image, an ideological figure, emblematic not only of the cultural superiority of Belgian colonialism, poised at the pinnacle of progress and civilization, but also of its political and military supremacy. Sörensen's Peak literally shows the fact that colonial rule came out on top in its confrontation with the "great black children," as he calls the Congolese in one of his other letters.

Shifting the Ground: From Mountain and Tower to Hole

If the colonizer "thought like a mountain" (see Pandian 2014), the topographical framework offered by the mountain also provided the conceptual ground that enabled the birth of the modern colonial city in Central Africa. In the Belgian Congo, the mountain symbolized not merely the panoptical authoritarianism of the colonial state but also its vertical dimension, as it formed the perfect illustration of the ambitious urban dreams of colonialist modernity. For example, after World War II the sky was the limit for Léopoldville, as Kinshasa (Congo's capital city) was then called, and the colonial image of the mountain was reinforced by and translated into the vertical propositions of tropical modernist architecture. As Tim Ingold recently noted: "In the contemporary world the skyscraper model . . . has come to dominate the way in which mountains, particularly of a more iconic or spectacular kind, have come to figure in the popular imagination" (Ingold 2015, 32). In 1946, the Forescom Tower, Central Africa's first skyscraper, was built at the center of Léopoldville and epitomized colonialism's triumph to such an extent that, after independence, the Mobutist state copied this model and constructed another skyscraper, named the Sozacom Tower, alongside the colonial Forescom Tower. Higher and more imposing than its colonial predecessor, it became the city's new landmark and symbolized the triumph of Zairean nationalism.

However, many of the urban dreams engendered by these colonial and post-colonial mountains and skyscrapers have become disappointments today, even though the topos of the skyscraper continues to be recycled by the Congolese government to embody its aspirations of insertion into a more modern and global world. In August 2018, for example, Joseph Kabila, the now ex-president of the Democratic Republic of Congo, inaugurated a new skyscraper in downtown Lubumbashi, the country's second largest city. This building, officially baptized *Hypnose*, was presented by Kabila as his parting gift to Lubumbashi. As its name suggests, the skyscraper here represents the kind of specular modernity and the powerful political the-atricality of "modernization as spectacle" (Bloom, Miescher, and Manuh 2014) that feeds the imaginary of the "neoliberal city," an imaginary on which Kabila's urban renewal plans, the 5 *chantiers*, rebranded as "the revo-lution of modernity" later on came to rely so heavily.[3]

But even if, to some extent, citizens continue to be hypnotized and mesmerized by the skyscraper aesthetics that is now being revived in the somnia of neoliberal spectrality, the raw urgencies of living in the physical and social environments of Congo's cities constantly belie these dreams. There is a large gap between official urban planning projects with their management policies and the reality of everyday lives in the shadow of the colonial and post-colonial towers, a reality that constantly shatters the promises made by the skyscraper model, for the only verticalities that ap-pear on the horizon of these urban worlds consist of the garbage piles that urban authorities ceased to collect a long time ago.[4] Similarly, the sandy mountains on which large parts of Kinshasa are constructed have often quite literally folded back into the earth to become giant erosion holes after each torrential rain: gaping wounds that swallow roads, houses, cars, and even people in the process, and that revert the upward verticality of the modern city into a downward "vertical noir" (Graham 2016), ripping open the covered, asphalted, trypophobic surface of the modern city to reveal a different kind of urban plane. This plane is no longer the steady, stable, impenetrable, and leveled horizontality of the modernist urban ground but instead opens up a much more bumpy and even incoherent landscape in which the underground of the hole literally becomes foreground and surface, the very center of the vortex that the city is, thereby radically redirecting the upward vertical vision embedded in the geography of the colonial-modernist and neoliberal urban gaze.

In Kinshasa, therefore, in their attempts to make sense of the daily struggles imposed on them by the city, urban denizens have long since turned away from the mountain and the tower as aspirational future-oriented figures to refer to an opposite topographical figure instead: the hole, *le trou*, or *libulu* in Lingala (which is the city's lingua franca). The "hole" has become a local conceptual figure, a master trope to express the dismal quality of urban life in the post-colonial city, and to define the wretched, dreary place that the city has become for many. The notion of the "hole" may refer to the city's many physical holes, such as the above-mentioned erosion points and sinkholes (some of which have even received personal names, and therefore agency, as they command and steer the mobility of the urban inhabitants), but *libulu* may also refer to road potholes—for example, as a particular form of generic urban infrastructure that defines "cityness" in this kind of urban landscape. Similarly, the figure of the hole is commonly used to reimagine the social dimensions of urban living. The concept of hole may refer to the meager livelihoods provided by the holes that punctuate the extractive landscapes of artisanal mining or the city's many informal markets (locally referred to as "market holes"—*wenze ya libulu*, see Lusamba Kibayu 2010, 314). It also denotes the unregistered and hastily dug graves in the city's many informal graveyards (see De Boeck 2016) and the city itself as an ultimate death-world, a "cemetery of the living" (Mavinga Tsafunenga 2011) who give an afterlife to the ruined colonial architecture and infrastructure. And then, as Sony Labou Tansi, the celebrated novelist and playwright from Congo-Brazzaville, reminds us, there are all these other holes that constantly erupt and disrupt the course of urban living:

> The hole of life, the hole of the others. The hole of the world. The hole of hopes. The hole of reality—and the hole of dreams. The hole of religions and the hole that your own flesh is making inside yourself. . . . And then there is

the hole that we call TOMORROW: tomorrow is set up as if it were an explosive. But with its foot, "today" traces "tomorrow" in the sand (Labou Tansi 1998, 61–62; *my translation—FDB*).

The concept of the hole thus not only refers to the tangible physical depressions on the city's surface, but also to the black hole of urban living, the dark matter of the urban praxis itself. "Hole" is used as a metaphor to describe all the shady deals that urbanites have to rely on in order to survive in the city's informal economy, as well as all the impromptu movements into often uncharted spatial, social, and mental territory that the city obliges them to make. "Hole" signifies the city's non-teleological time frame, the pitfalls of its religious ideologies and the trap of its treacherous sociabilities, often played out in violent proximity, or the very real and tangible danger that emanates from the specific kind of ludic urban sexuality and nightlife for which Kinshasa has become famous, the oneiric atmosphere of which was so well described by the novelist Fiston Mwanza Mujila in his novel *Tram 83*. The book is set in a frenetic bar/*bidonville* in an unnamed *ville-pays* that is clearly inspired by Kinshasa and the novelist's own native Lubumbashi, where Lucien and Requiem, the novel's two main protagonists, have been stranded in the hope of "making their hole" in this *ville-cloaque*, this cesspit of misery in which, indeed, the dreams and delights generated by corporeal orifices easily turn into "holes inside your own flesh."[5]

As observed by the anthropologist Joshua Walker, in his rich analysis of the artisanal diamond mining city of Mbuji Mayi, in the Democratic Republic of the Congo (DRC) holes have thus become both a symptom of and metaphor "for an experience of loss that is simultaneously material and moral. Erosion itself signifies not only the city's physical decline; it also informs discourses about the corrosion of wealth and values" (Walker 2014, 76). Holes, in other words, are constantly foregrounded as potent local tropes to encapsulate the experience of living in an urban context said to be marked by discontinuity, disintegration, and what Kinois (as the residents of Kinshasa are called) often refer to as "multi-crisis."[6]

In one brief passage of *The Right to the City* Henri Lefebvre also reflects on the metaphor of the hole when he writes (about a totally different kind of urban world but in terms that seem easily—and quite literally—translatable to the kind of urban existence one encounters in Kinshasa and other cities of the African Global South):

. . . the destructuration of the city manifests the depth of phenomena, of social and cultural disintegration. Considered as a whole, this society finds itself *incomplete*. Between the sub-systems and the structures consolidated by various means (compulsion, terror, and ideological persuasion), there are holes and chasms. These voids are not there due to chance. They are the places of the possible. They contain the floating and dispersed elements of the possible, but not the power which could assemble them. Moreover, structuring actions and the power of the social void tend to prohibit action and the very presence of such a power. The conditions of the possible can only be realized in the course of a radical metamorphosis. (Lefebvre 1996, 156).

What Lefebvre touches on here is the danger of understanding hole, chasm, and void solely in terms of incompleteness and "destructuration." Indeed, discourses of holes may become problematic in their suggestion that urban existence is only defined by depletion, as if these holes "were not, themselves, productive in any sense besides the depletive" (Walker 2014, 31). The hole is never just a black hole or negative space; it is never merely hollow or emptied of content. "Dwelling in the space of the gap" (Stewart 1996, 158) always leaves room for maneuver; holes and gaps in the order of things have the capacity to metaphorically elide how life continues through, and despite, decline. And even if living the experience of the hole considerably complicates life and often degrades the quality of living standards, the hole itself also offers an aperture, an opening, or, as Lefebvre notes, a possibility, at least for those who know how to "illuminate the hole" (*illuminer le trou*), as Kinois say, and who possess the sentient experience to both inhabit and negotiate this dynamic, metabolic urban environment and read an alternative meaning into the gravity of its apparent blackness.

But what, then, precisely are the kind of "floating and dispersed elements of the possible" that lie hidden inside the hole, inside this urban site the inhabitants of which often repeat that "the impossible is not Congolese" (*l'impossible n'est pas Congolais*) (see De Boeck and Baloji 2017)? As an illustration of the notion of a literally "bullshit job," David Graeber, in a 2012 Tedx Talk, introduced the analogy of "digging a hole and filling it back" over and over—a method, he stated, used in some Soviet gulags as a form of torture to drive people crazy. In a later interview Graeber explained that his example of "backyard digging" was inspired by a quote from Dostoyevsky who, while in prison camp, said that "if you wanted to destroy someone psychologically, have them move a rock to the one side of the road and move it back again, over and over. Or fill pitchers of water continuously. Have them perform something meaningless forever. They will do anything to make it stop" (Munday 2016). It is doubtful whether many Kinois would agree with either Dostoyevsky or Graeber on this point. Usually, elements such as potholes, for example, are seen as infrastructural failures because we do not tend to think about them as constructive elements. But they represent not only infrastructures "in reverse," or "negative"' infrastructures, they are also "reverse" infrastructures, or negatives whose hidden potentiality becomes visible as soon as one manages to invert the negation and illuminate the hole, as it were. It is only when one starts to think of potholes as "instructure" that they start to reveal their capacity to create publics, for instance by generating the possibility of "thickening" or slowing down the flow of pedestrians, pushing them to the side of the road and thereby converting them into potential customers for the women (and men) who strategically set up their makeshift market stalls close to such potholes. As car drivers in Kinshasa well know, this is the way in which potholes function everywhere in the city. Turning the hole into a resource, police officers will often position themselves alongside a major pothole that causes traffic to slow down, thus facilitating the possibility to stop and harass drivers. Similarly, in many a street, young men are busy with shovels filling up potholes with sand and gravel. Doing so enables them to stop cars and ask drivers for a small contribution in return for their "service," that is, in recognition of the fact that their on-the-spot road repair facilitates those drivers' mobility and thus improves their well-being. It is of utmost importance to be able to claim as one's own a profitable pothole at a particularly busy point in the street (which in itself is not easy because such a claim will always be simultaneous and competitive with identical claims made by multiple others vying for the same spot). It is key to hold on to that pothole and keep it alive and lucrative for as long as possible. Not only does this necessitate these young men's constant presence, but they will also have to make sure that the pothole never gets filled up or ends up being permanently repaired. That is why the same men, at night, can be seen emptying the potholes they had been busy filling the previous day, in order to secure some earnings, however small, during the next day. I know several men who have been filling and emptying the same potholes on the same street corner for over a decade, in what can only be described as a successful politics of presence in and occupation of public space in the highly competitive urban environment of Kinshasa.

Another example of the hole's "ruinous vitalism" (Wilhelm-Solomon 2017) concerns waste management in the city. Unlike the European Commission, whose official directive for waste management considers landfilling as "the least preferable option" in its waste management hierarchy,[7] the practice of landfilling offers a quintessential livelihood strategy for the thousands of *pousse-pousseurs*, Kinshasa's emblematic pushcart workers, who, in the absence of official public collection services, collect and transport household waste that they sell to the inhabitants of riparian areas along the Congo River. The latter use this waste to fill up holes and cavities, drain depressions, and impolder the river, thus landscaping it into (unsteady) ground for the construction of houses (often no more than shacks), vegetable gardens, and paddies (see De Boeck 2011). Through such informal waste management, landfilling as a literal filling of hollowed land becomes a "groundbreaking" infrastructural practice for the occupation of self-made space as well as the engineering of the possibility for urban expansion.

A last "hole" example is that of the *mena* ("hole" in Chokwe, one of the many languages spoken in Southern Congo and Angola). People sometimes use this word to speak about the money changers (also known as *cambistes*) whom one commonly encounters in markets and on busy streets. One has to know how to approach and address them, how to enter these "holes" in order to negotiate a good rate and come out of this encounter, this descent into the "hole," with a little extra money in hand, like an artisanal diamond digger who emerges from his mining pit with some tiny, valuable diamonds.

Holes as Points of Suture

In this way, literally or figuratively, holes provide a livelihood to a multiplicity of urban actors. For all these urban residents, who are often politically and economically disenfranchised while living a "life full of holes," the "hole" is a conceptual tool good for thinking through the many experiences of lack and loss, while also becoming a metaphor for a fissure, an opening, an opportunity.[8] Therefore, if the hole has become the baseline and ground zero of Congo's post-colonial urban worlds, it also presents itself as a suture. Nancy Rose Hunt has used the concept of suture in order to join together different colonial medical histories in Congo in new ways (Hunt 2007; see also Hunt 2018, 135). Suturing, she argues, suggests closing a wound, making an incision, or stitching together parts, locations, and points of view. As such it points to new kinds of creativity with temporalities, sources, evidence, and interactivity. In *Suturing the City* (2016), the photographer Sammy Baloji and I picked up on this idea and extended the notion of suture as closure, as junction, and as a seam, comparing it to the way in which, often against all odds, the inhabitants of Congo's urban landscapes read meaning into the black hole of the city; the way in which they concretize metaphor into matter and vice versa by using not only material, but also mental and moral, holes as suturing points to fill the gaps, overcome the hiatus, design realignments, and thereby redefine the zero—that is, the impossible circumstances of living in the kind of urban environment that Congo's cities offer—into a possibility, a something else, a surplus. Taken like this, the notion of suture remains close to how Jacques-Alain Miller, who first introduced the concept in Lacanian psychoanalysis, originally interpreted it. For him, suture is always between zero as a lack, as something impossible to conceptualize, and zero as a number, as "one." It is in that sense that the hole as suture both represents lack while also placing and "suturing" it:

"Suture names the relation of the subject to the chain of its discourse; we shall see that it figures there as the element which is lacking, in the form of a stand-in (tenant-lieu). For, while there lacking, it is not purely and simply absent. Suture, by extension—the general relation of lack to the structure—of which it is an element, inasmuch as it implies the position of a taking-the-place-of (tenant-lieu)" (Miller 2012, 93).

Differently put, the zero or void of a situation is the suture to its own being: the void itself is "subtractive suture to being" (Badiou 2005, 66), while the zero number is "the suturing stand-in for the lack" (Miller 2012, 99). In a short text accompanying Sammy Baloji's photographic essay on Kolwezi's artisanal miners and post-colonial mining holes (Baloji 2014), Achille Mbembe also refers to the zero's potential to reformulate lack. "In this zero world," he writes, "neither the material nor life come to an absolute end. They do not become nothing. They simply move on towards something else, and in every case the end is deferred and the question of finiteness remains unanswered" (Mbembe 2014, 76).

Moving On from the Hole to Something Else

What is important to capture and understand, it seems to me, is how urban residents do exactly that: how they manage—with varying degrees of success—to "move on towards something else" by turning the zero into a one; how they read potential, promise, and prospect into the blackness of the hole; how they throw themselves—their words and even their own bodies—into this daily struggle to overcome the city's conundrums and to suture its contrarieties; and how it is the gravity of the hole itself, the un-inhabitability of the urban environment (see Simone 2016), that propels them to do that.

Among those who best know how to realize the Lefebvrean "conditions of the possible" that lie dormant in voids and gaps, Lefebvre himself points to artists and the capacity of "*art* to bring to the realization of urban society its long meditation on life as drama and pleasure. . . . As much the science of the city, art and the history of art are part of a meditation on the urban which wants to make efficient the images which proclaim it" (Lefebvre 1996, 156–157). Not unsurprisingly, given the profound relationship between (modernist) photography and the negative space of the hole (see Henning 2018), or between filmmaking and the concept of suture,[9] it is not only writers such as Sony Labou Tansi or Mwanza Munjila but also photographers such as Baloji, and with him many other Congolese filmmakers and visual performance artists, who seem to be especially apt in turning the hole into a point for meditating on the city's pitfalls while revealing its inherent possibilities. This is exactly what happens in the photographic work of Kiripi Katembo, for example. In *Un regard*, a series of 2009 photographs that portray Kinshasa as it is reflected in the mirror of the pools of stagnant water that fill the streets' abundant potholes (see Kiripi Katembo 2015), Kiripi invited Kinois society to take a good look at itself and reflect on the conditions of its own modes of livelihood. For Kiripi this reflective approach not only served to bring out and reveal the poetry that sometimes lies folded away in the pockmarked skin of the city, but it also enabled him to see his art as a way of "campaigning for a healthier environment and denounce through images what Kinshasa's inhabitants see as fate" (Neshvatal 2015).[10] Along similar lines, but in a more openly activist spirit, another Kin-based artist, Pathy Tshindele, created a street performance on one of Kinshasa's dilapidated central avenues in 2017.[11] Sitting in the middle of the avenue on a plastic bucket in front of a giant, water-filled pothole, with cars passing by on all sides, Tshindele picks up a fishing rod and starts to fish in the pothole, much to the surprise and bewilderment of the car drivers and pedestrians, who soon flock around Tshindele's pothole, shouting comments and questions to the artist. Tshindele's performance as a politics of presence in the urban public space reveals the potential for political and environmental criticism that the active absence of the hole carries within itself, while pointing to ways in which absences can yield new opportunities and can be sutured into the "something else" of potentially more inhabitable urban worlds. Even though their artistic practice rarely offers the radical metamorphosis that Lefebvre deems necessary to realize the conditions of the possible (Lefebvre 1996, 156), Congolese artists are especially adept at exploring the negative space of the hole, at teasing out the hole's potential, and at inventing new vocabularies that bypass the tired institutionalized development rhetorics used by the state, highlighting instead the possibility for action and incremental suturing from the ground up that all holes generate.

By thus "curating" and reimagining the city (see Gurney 2015) and its public spaces along novel lines, Congo's newly emerging generation of artists, who increasingly are becoming visible and present through a rapidly multiplying and proliferating network of new cultural initiatives, platforms, biennales, street performance festivals, art centers, and maker spaces in the city of Kinshasa and across the country as a whole,[12] also connects with a broader artistic dynamics that is currently unfolding across the whole of the continent (see, for example, Pensa 2017), thereby signaling a widespread desire to express and give form to a more inclusive notion of urban recognition and transformation away from and radically opposed to the corrupted spaces of institutionalized politics.

Notes

1. This opening sentence is a quote from *Erasmus montanus*, a satirical play about the introduction of civilization in the backward, rural Denmark of the eighteenth century. Written by Ludvig Holberg in 1722, it tells the story of its main protagonist, Rasmus Berg ("Rasmus Mountain"), who has been given a costly education in Copenhagen. When he returns to his village with all his newly acquired knowledge, he has latinized his name to Erasmus Montanus and insists on speaking Latin with his parents, who are simple country folk.

2. Sörensen, letter from February 26, 1921. Danske Utvandrerarkiv LM-1983-255, box 133:2 Jürgen Jürgensen. The translation is mine. For a full account of Sörensen's career see De Boeck and Baloji (2016, chapter 4).

3. President Kabila launched the *5 chantiers* (five public works) program as part of his campaign for the 2006 presidential elections. It presented a recovery plan for Congo, summarizing the president's pledge to modernize education, health care, road infrastructure, housing, and access to electricity throughout the DRC. The term "neoliberal city" usually refers to a particular kind of "modern" urban reality and experience: a city where the policies and development plans are market-driven, where the production of space is based on the logic of increasing profits, with accompanying processes of gentrification and exclusion of the poorer urban masses from the urban core, while the social character and regulating role of the state is downplayed due to an increasing privatization of services (see also Bayat 2012). The neoliberal

city often presents itself as an ideal model to be followed by the rest of the world—a spectacle, a hyperreal city that exists through images that conjure up particular urban imaginaries and forms of urban infrastructure that become visible and globally exchangeable through the workings of capitalism.

4. See newspaper article by Reagan Tshishimbi in Le Potentiel/MCP, April 24, 2019, "Insalubrité à Kinshasa: Une montagne d'immondices surplombe la place du 30 juin," https://www.mediacongo.net/article-actualite-50368 _insalubrite_a_kinshasa_une_montagne_d_immondices_surplombe_la _place_du_30_juin.

5. In the same vein, a well-known dance hall in Kinshasa, currently located on the Boulevard Kimbuta in the municipality of Ndjili, goes by the name Le Grand Libulu, or "The Big Hole" (see also De Boeck and Baloji 2016, 223).

6. On the "hole world" of extractive industrial mining see also Bridge 2015.

7. See http://ec.europa.eu/environment/waste/landfill_index.htm.

8. *Life Full of Holes: The Strait Project (1998–2004)* is the title of a photographic corpus in which the French-Moroccan photographer Yto Barrada addresses young Morrocans' political exclusion and disenfranchisement by focusing on the Strait of Gibraltar as a corridor of migratory imaginations and desires (see Demos 2013, 95ff).

9. Jacques-Alain Miller was also a critic writing for the *Cahiers du Cinéma*, and as for the concept of suture, it was developed further by Deleuze within the framework of his cinematographic theory (see also Del Rio 2008).

10. As quoted by Joseph Neshvatal in the online publication *Hyperallergic* of August 9, 2015: "Photographer Kiripi Katembo, Master of Reflection, Dies at 36," https://hyperallergic.com/228619/photographer-kiripi-katembo-master -of-reflection-dies-at-36/.

11. The whole performance can be watched on the Facebook page of Tshindele's art collective, the Collectif Eza Possible. Video post of November 2, 2017, https://www.facebook.com/1283861987/videos/10213958501138326/.

12. For a good overview of Kinshasa's diversified contemporary art scene, and its capacity to generate public platforms to reflect on the matter of the urban, see Malaquais (2018).

References

Badiou, Alain. 2005. *Being and Event*. New York: Continuum.
Baloji, Sammy. 2014. *Mémoire/Kolwezi*. Brussels: Africalia.
Bayat, Asaf. 2012. "Politics in the City Inside-Out." *City and Society* 24, no. 2: 110–128.

Bloom, Peter J., Stephen Miescher, and Takyiwaa Manuh. 2014. *Modernization as Spectacle in Africa*. Bloomington: Indiana University Press.

Bridge, Gavin. 2015. "The Hole World: Scales and Spaces of Extraction." In *"Extraction"* (special issue 5 of *Scenario Journal*, retrieved from https://scenariojournal.com/article/the-hole-world/), edited by Stephanie Carlisle and Nicholas Pevzner.

De Boeck, Filip. 2011. "Inhabiting Ocular Ground: Kinshasa's Future in the Light of Congo's Spectral Urban Politics." *Cultural Anthropology* 26, no. 2: 263–286.

De Boeck, Filip. 2016. "Corpus Vile: Death and Expendable Youth in Urban Congo." In *Living and Dying in the Contemporary World: A Compendium*, edited by Veena Das and Clara Han, 743–769. Berkeley: University of California Press.

De Boeck, Filip, and Sammy Baloji. 2016. *Suturing the City: Living Together in Congo's Urban Worlds*. London: Autograph ABP.

De Boeck, Filip, and Sammy Baloji, 2017. "The Impossible Is not Congolese: City Life in the DRC. Sammy Baloji and Filip De Boeck in Conversation with Dominique Malaquais." In *[Applied] Foreign Affairs. Investigating Spatial Phenomena in Rural and Urban Sub-Saharan Africa*, edited by Baerbel Mueller, 384–389. Basel: Birkhäuser.

Del Rio, Elena. 2008. *Deleuze and the Cinema of Performance: Powers of Affection*. Edinburgh: Edinburgh University Press.

Demos, T. J. 2013. *The Migrant Image: The Art and Politics of Documentary During Global Crisis*. Durham, NC: Duke University Press.

Graham, Stephen. 2016. "Vertical Noir: Histories of the Future in Urban Science-Fiction." *City: Analysis of Urban Trends, Culture, Theory, Policy, Action* 20, no. 3: 389–406.

Gurney, Kim. 2015. *The Art of Public Space: Curating and Re-imagining the Ephemeral City*. Basingstoke, Hampshire: Palgrave Macmillan.

Henning, Michelle. 2018. "Holes: Colonialism and Negative Space in Modernist Photography." Paper presented at The Left Conference—Photography and Film Criticism, Lisbon, Portugal, November 16–18, 2017 (text retrieved from http://repository.uwl.ac.uk/id/eprint/4205).

Hunt, Nancy Rose. 2007. *Suturing New Medical Histories of Africa*. Berlin: Lit Verlag.

Hunt, Nancy Rose. 2018. "History as Form, with Simmel in Tow." *History and Theory* 56: 126–144.

Ingold, Tim. 2015. *The Life of Lines*. London / New York: Routledge.

Kiripi Katembo. 2015. *Transit-RDC*. Brussels: Africalia/ Stichting Kunstboek.

Labou Tansi, Sony. 1998. *Théatre 3: Monologue d'or et noces d'argent / Le trou*. Carnières-Morlanwelz: Lansman Editions.

Lefebvre, Henri. 1996. *Writings on Cities*. Translated and edited by Eleonore Kofman and Elizabeth Lebas. Oxford: Blackwell.

Lusamba Kibayu, Michel. 2010. *Evolution des pratiques de sécurisation des conditions de vie dans trois quartiers populaires de Kinshasa: Enjeux et consequences de la production spatiale et sociale de la ville.* Louvain-la-Neuve: Presses Universitaires de Louvain.

Malaquais, Dominique, ed. 2018. *Kinshasa Chronicles.* Montreuil: Editions de l'oeil/MIAM.

Mavinga Tsafunenga, Armand. 2011. *Cimetière de vivants: Poèmes.* Paris: L'Harmattan.

Mbembe, Achille. 2014. "The Zero World: Materials and the Machine." In *Mémoire/Kolwezi,* edited by Sammy Baloji, 73–79. Brussels: Africalia.

Miller, Jacques-Alain. 2012 [1966]. "Suture (elements of the logic of the signifier)." In *Concept and Form: Volume One: Key Texts from the Cahiers pour L'Analyse,* edited by P. Hallward and K. Peden, 91–101. London: Verso.

Munday, Austin D. 2016. "Basic Income and Meaningless Jobs: David Graeber interview and Stenography." *Basic Income,* February 1. https://medium .com/basic-income/basic-income-meaningless-jobs-david-graeber -stenography-402e3bddeb45.

Mwanza Mujila, Fiston. 2015. *Tram 83.* Victoria, Australia/London: Scribe Publications.

Pandian, Anand. 2014. "Thinking Like a Mountain." *Hau: Journal of Ethnographic Theory* 4, no. 2: 245–252.

Pensa, Iolanda, ed. 2017. *Public Art in Africa: Art and Urban Transformations in Douala.* Geneva: Métispresses.

Simone, Abdoumaliq. 2016. "The Uninhabitable? In Between Collapsed Yet Still Rigid Distinctions." *Cultural Politics* 12, no. 2: 135–154.

Stewart, Kathleen. 1996. *A Space on the Side of the Road: Cultural Poetics in an "Other" America.* Princeton, NJ: Princeton University Press.

Walker, Joshua. 2014. "The Ends of Extraction: Diamonds, Value, and Reproduction in Democratic Republic of Congo." Unpublished PhD diss., University of Chicago.

Wilhelm-Solomon, Matthew. 2017. "The Ruinous Vitalism of the Urban Form: Ontological Orientations in Inner-city Johannesburg." *Critical African Studies* 9, no. 2: 174–191.

8

INFRASTRUCTURES OF PLUTOCRATIC LONDON

Introduction

From a street-level perspective of walking and encountering wealthy people and the neighborhoods in which they live and work, I explore in this chapter the infrastructures that make London a plutocratic city. In the process, I develop a more granular understanding of what infrastructure might mean. Keeping with traditions of ambulatory research, walking is how I grasp the daily doings of urban worlds on the ground (Knowles 2017). London's stories seep through the soles of my feet as I navigate a neighborhood with one of London's and the United Kingdom's densest concentrations of wealthy people—Notting Hill. I also walk through one of the most significant locations in London's wealth-expanding machine—the financial district—probing human, algorithmic, and material textures of the city for the infrastructures that make it work. Because infrastructures are among the most relevant empirical and analytic puzzles in this chapter, I will only offer some general insights as a starting point. What Ash Amin and Nigel Thrift (2017) call "infrastructural entanglements" are the assemblages (McFarlane 2011) that keep cities in some kind of working order, the tangles of human and nonhuman, social, and technical processes (Graham and McFarlane 2015), dispositions and relationships that cocreate ecologies of plutocratic dwelling in London. In this chapter I piece together some of the entanglements that create spaces in the ecologies of the city for everyday plutocratic life, and I then point to some new orientations in mobilizing a more-equitable politics of the city.

Framing

Research probing infrastructural entanglements of plutocratic dwelling is unusual, not least because plutocrats are incorrectly judged to have tenuous connections with place as a result of hyper-mobile lifestyles (Urry 2014). Plutocrats appear as abstract analytical categories in elite sociology (Savage 2018), in elite geographies (Atkinson et al. 2016; Forrest et al. 2016), and in conceptualizing the relationship between the elite and political power (Davis 2018), but rarely do they appear in flesh-and-concrete motion. These abstract accounts work from macro-structural positions of various kinds rather than by giving close attention to the bodies and buildings of the plutocratic city and the other infrastructural mechanisms that produce it and hold it together.

Although plutocratic dwelling appears in multiple permutations, it is a constant attribute of urban ecology generated in accumulations of excess. Excess is not just a persistent city story. It is the city's very substance. What form cities are uneven accumulations of resources, materials, dispositions, money, technologies, and other constituents of urban life that exceed what is needed for survival and sustain instead ever-new avenues (literally) of consumption. From the Paris Arcades and the glittering baubles of London's early twentieth-century department stores, to today's sophisticated financial and other algorithmic instruments that generate novel forms of excess, while at the same time urging ever-more discernment in consumption, cities have always been machines for producing and consuming abundance. Significant inequalities in distributions of excess are enduring concerns in the social life of cities. In their palaces, the Romanovs of Imperial Russia and France's Bourbons paid with their lives for obscenely unequal distributions of the benefits of urban life at the hands of the masses. The very conception of a plutocrat—someone who has amassed great wealth—embeds fundamentally uneven relationships with the city. And so it is with London, and other cities too.

Extreme accumulations of capital not seen in a century now shape London (Burrows and Knowles 2019). Translocal circulations of capital, people, and things combine with locally calibrated mechanisms of wealth generation, all coinciding with a dramatic growth in the number of stupendously rich people worldwide and the concentration of wealth into fewer hands. Oxfam reports that today 1 percent of the (global) population owns 52 percent of global wealth. In 2010 it was calculated that it would take the combined wealth of the world's richest 388 people to equal the combined wealth of the poorest 50 percent. Today, just eight people own that same proportion of wealth. The financial services industry, which calculates volumes and distributions of global wealth, reports more wealthy people than ever. High Net Worth Individuals (HNWIS) are those with more than a million British pounds in investable assets excluding their main residence, while Ultra High Net Worth Individuals (UHNWIS) are those with more than twenty million pounds in investable assets. In 2008 there were an estimated 8.6 million HNWIS around the globe (Beaverstock and Hay 2016, 5). Only eight years later this figure had doubled, to 16.5 million. Global distribution of plutocrats—a category that enfolds HNWIS and UHNWIS as I describe them here—is skewed, with the United States having the highest number and China and India the fastest increases. The United Kingdom is high on this list, with over half a million (Capgemini 2019) HNIS concentrated into a small number of West London neighborhoods, including Notting Hill, according to geodemographic analysis based on over four hundred data captures (Webber and Burrows 2018). The Sunday Times *Rich List* claims that London alone has ninety-three resident "sterling billionaires": more than New York, San Francisco, Hong Kong, and Moscow.

People with unprecedented wealth live in London, alongside those of modest means—the median gross annual wage in London is £34,073 (ONS)—and the growing ranks of the dispossessed. Homelessness in the city increased sharply from 2010, when a politics of austerity, following massive public investment to forestall financial collapse after the banking crisis in 2008, hit the public finances and the budgets of local authorities. Poverty and unprecedented wealth coexist and connect the lives of the superwealthy with the poor. In the London borough of Kensington and Chelsea alone, home to many of the city's wealthiest residents, more than five thousand people are homeless (Dorling 2018). These shifts in the life of the city risk creating serious social and political unrest. London is an unfolding experiment in the lived consequences of the coexistence of want and wealth, making the substance of wealth and the mechanisms creating it in the fortunes, lives, and habitats of the city's uber-wealthy plutocrats an urgent research and political priority.

Inside the Money Engine

Creating what Kathleen Stewart (2011, 445) calls new spaces for thinking about what might be going on, and then for writing theory through stories and "descriptive detours" that have "bodies' rhythms and ways of being in noise and lights and space," I walk London's financial district around Bank Junction on my way to meet a banker in one of the city's European banks. The financial sector added £58.2 billion to London's economy in 2016: 14 percent of the city's total economic output, 1.1 million jobs, and 25 percent of the nation's service exports.[1] Christophers (2013, 4) argues that employment and tax figures are mobilized in order to show the economic value of finance, but notes that it circulates rather than *produces* wealth. Finance is surely a key infrastructure generating the excesses of the plutocratic city. From the racial topographies plied by slave ships and Lloyds insurance underwriting to today's complex financial architecture of derivatives, bonds, and the rest, the City of London is finance in bricks, stones, bodies, and bones.

Corinthian columns of eighteenth- and nineteenth-century neoclassical buildings form the architectural substance of London's claim to global financial significance. Street names reveal finance's former operations in labyrinths of passages and alleys—such as Change Alley, St. Swithins Lane, the Royal Exchange at Cornhill, and Nicholas Passage—now the refuges of smokers and hasty stand-up lunches eaten by women dressed in ways that suggest not-so-well-paid service roles holding the financial machine together: constituents of financial infrastructure. There are others. Walking from Bank Junction and the looming, windowless grandeur of the Bank of England, to Moorgate, I pass strings of cafés tucked into ancient buildings: Pod, Starbucks, Eat, Pret, Coco, many offering cheap lunches; and stylish Michelin restaurants like Hispania where waiters in white jackets serve men in dark suits. Dispersed among eateries are other kinds of service centers. Lawyers and accountants steer finance on the right side of regulation and minimize the tax liabilities of wealthy clients and corporations with creative accounting in Capital House. Beyond Daiwa Capital Markets, a Japanese investment and brokerage firm, is the Chinese Imperial Bank of Commerce, which channels circulating finance between London and a meshwork of elsewheres. On close inspection the money machine seems less a monolithic infrastructure of accumulation and more like a cluster of micro-operations, orientations, practices, and movements on different scales.

In the spirit of writing a "geography of what happens" I try to find the "atmospheric attunements" (Stewart 2011, 445) of these streets. Formal in dress and demeanor, with movements purposeful and routine, and sometimes intimate secrets and endearments whispered in doorways. Sharp dark suits and pastel shirts, ties no longer obligatory. Sartorial styles of women aping men's, with the exception of impossibly high-heeled shoes.

Subtly securitized and luxurious: an African security guard stands at the entrance of the Royal Exchange. Seemingly insignificant operations hold things in place. Repurposed from its 1571 origins and its 1844 refurbishment, the Royal Exchange houses expensive restaurants, one run by Fortnum and Masons, along with watch and jewelry shops for lunchtime browsing. I stop at Fortnum and tune into the conversation of a mother and her lawyer-daughter over lunch. Their consociations and modulated conversations compose and reveal ephemeral connections, making this place and hinting at the quietly voiced concerns that leak into it. They discuss workplace politics, abilities, rewards for performance and the injustices of their distribution, even classical dressage, the riding academy, competitive horsemanship, international events in Switzerland and Paris, and their appreciation of "beautiful horses," until the women finally retrieve their identical Burberry macs and head off. Two men at a table nearby are discussing leadership, aspiration, challenge, and people who could be "useful to you." "How is family life?" "Not so good. I am trying to spend more time with my family." Different kinds of operations and attachments hold things together.

Walking from Moorgate to Liverpool Street and the southeast edge of the financial district, I pass Spaces, which rents desks to the city's itinerant workforce, then further huddles of smokers, homeless people shrouded in sleeping bags, their situation and a thriving financial district are connected in a politics of austerity, and finally a street sweeper pushing a cart: these things, too, hold this place together. The ancient financial district ends abruptly toward Liverpool Street, and a modern city rises at Broadgate, the entire area dug up for Cross Rail, London's public transport extension, intended to reduce congestion on the underground. A pedestrianized square owned by British Land and shielded by construction hoardings that announce the new commercial lease possibilities of the square is almost finished: the unfinished city breaks out of the ground, a landscape in constant heave through a thousand different channels. New buildings finished in a dull metal—the Union Bank of Switzerland (UBS) and Deutsche Bank among them—mark the seam between the ancient and the new city. At this junction a twenty-first century financial district in glass and steel sweeps down Bishopsgate to London Bridge and eastward down the Thames to Canary Wharf, London's financial annex whose confident towers reach into the sky.

An anonymous Banker operates at this junction. Security personnel who stand all day by the bank's glass revolving door, which leads into a clinical marble hallway, the scale of which suggests that things of importance happen in this building, protect Banker from the doings of the street. A woman at the reception desk lets me through the glass barriers. Another escorts me into the inner workings of the bank, past some famous modern art, to an anonymous meeting room among meeting rooms, each a perfect clone of the last; tables, chairs, bottled water, conversations about expanding money. In his forties, Banker is wearing an immaculately tailored gray suit and shiny black handmade shoes. He says there are rules that prevent his speaking to journalists and researchers; that most financial sector workers think it best to fly "under the radar"; that "there is no upside to being conspicuous," and I conclude that mechanisms of concealment and separation make this place. I assuage his concerns about anonymity by referring to him as Banker.

Banker counts as a plutocrat because he is clearly an HWNI and lives in one of the neighborhoods that house a high concentration of HNIs identified in the spatial calculations of geodemographics. He is also a service worker—he expands the wealth of already wealthy people—a cog in the human-algorithmic workings of the plutocratic city. He is part of a global stock market trading and wealth management enterprise operating in fifty countries and managing the wealth of over half of the world's billionaires. He tells me that this involves "bespoke" services in assessing the needs of wealthy clients and advising on the expansion of their wealth through a spectrum of financial instruments, including investment and stock market trading, as well as the protections offered by taxation and estate planning. His bank alone provides what he describes as "pretty much every type of financial service that you can offer" to a large sections of the global plutocracy, and this makes his bank a significant piece of infrastructure in creating the plutocratic city.

While Banker's colleagues work on wealth management, he advises and trades on behalf of institutional investors, asset managers, and private equity and hedge funds. He reads the markets, assesses their broader financial landscape, and seizes investment opportunities that expand capital, ideally ahead of other traders. Competitive advantage is a crucial mechanism in wealth accumulation. Banks like his trade commodities, buying and selling shares in publicly listed companies and financial instruments like futures, or bets on the future value of commodities. Value, I learn, is imprecise and negotiable. He says: "we service hedge funds and advise them on what to buy and what to sell. Then we ultimately take those orders and buy and sell those things on their behalf. The other thing that we do for hedge funds, they won't want to custody their own assets and they'll essentially have what's called a 'Prime Broker.' So, we'll provide these services to them as well, which means that we will settle their trades for them. We'll provide them with leverage, so that if, say, they've got $1 billion to invest, if they give us that $1 billion we might allow them to take positions worth $2 billion. A little bit like spread-betting, I suppose; it's spread-betting for hedge funds, where, as a spread bet, you don't have to put down the full amount, you put down the margin. Essentially they give us margin and we allow them to take our balance sheet to invest." I understand that hedge funds are the pooled funds of experienced, meaning wealthy, investors who aim to shield investment portfolios from market risks as investments go up or down. High risks yield high returns. Gambling, leveraging, and "skimming"—banks charging fees and percentages of gains—are the operational mechanisms holding this together.

Banker goes on to explain that much trading is done through automatic programs—or algorithms—that track markets and opportunities across shifting landscapes. Algorithms and models are sold to the bank's institutional clients, and the bank uses them to trade for its wealthy clients. Bank employees, he says, must constantly build, maintain, and adjust algorithms to shifting financial circumstances, including unpredictable performance of markets, so these are not fully automated processes. He adds that "It still requires a whole different set of know-how and experience and client coverage, but from a different perspective, so it's just a different type of job. Private equity is a similar concept [to hedge funds], in that they're investing money on behalf of other people, and it is more typically institutional money, but, to some extent, also some private individuals. It's longer term, so instead of investing in listed securities and trading them on the market, what they'll do is, they'll take a private stake in a company that isn't listed." Banker goes on to describe how private equity looks for small, successful businesses that can be scaled up through private investments, which typically earn high returns for investors. The successful sandwich shop chain Pret a Manger began this way. Private equity invisibly shapes the main streets of the city in this and other ways. It invests in failing businesses by taking a controlling interest and then driving reforms or closure, whichever makes the best returns. Finance capital is predatory and lives on other kinds of capital's roadkill.

We don't talk numbers, but Banker's handsome salary is supplemented by bonuses and stock options that reflect his contribution to the bank's profits, which are skimmed from deals. He goes on: "I would say that most people who work in finance are, to some extent, motivated by earning money, or they probably wouldn't do it. Well, there are easier ways to earn a living, just in terms of the hours and in terms of the pressure. I think, that being said, it is enjoyable! I feel fortunate that banking does pay relatively well, given that I actually also find the work quite interesting. But I think most people are motivated, to some extent, by money and the status. There's probably some element of what it affords someone, the nice lifestyle, the house, the holidays."

In my other interviews with finance workers, they were more emphatic about the importance of competition as a personal driver and about money as a measure of individual worth, absorbing the imperatives of finance into their emotional landscape. Robert Frank (2007, 203) notes that finance is a testosterone-fueled competitive sport driven by fear and greed, just some of the affective mechanisms creating an elite finance labor force. Banker says: "People who end up working up in these roles are bright people who have gone to the best universities, who have done well, typically, academically." He himself was recruited from Oxford. I wanted to ask him whether he thinks expanding capital is really the best use of the nation's most privileged and educated talent. And what other avenues with value to the city overall does he think are disregarded in drawing talented, motivated people into piling up money for the already rich. But I have moved on.

Everyday Plutocratic Life in Notting Hill

Understanding how plutocratic finance workers actually live their wealth, or probing the intimate operations of the plutocratic city, involves walking around Notting Hill in North Kensington. The Central Line connects Notting Hill to the Bank–Moorgate–Broadgate–Liverpool Street financial nexus; and a fast connection from Bank via the Docklands Light Railway (DLR) links it to Canary Wharf: stable channels circulating unpredictable and fluctuating processes. My walks and interviews in this neighborhood revealed a cluster of plutocratic finance workers, some of them from aristocratic backgrounds, some even connected with royalty. Notting Hill is also the scene of the 2017 Grenfell Tower fire, which provoked widespread condemnation of the borough's social polarities expressed in housing. A place of horror and awe: in the same day I stood beneath the charred tower and was invited into a £30 million house.

The Notting Hill street vibe is expensive "boho." Casual linen, silk, designer jeans and trainers, discreet expensive watches and jewelry walk the streets, sometimes with a pedigreed dog or a schoolchild in blazer and cricket-whites in tow. The neighborhood's layered Victorian, Georgian, Art Deco, and modern architecture is more varied than its gardens, which have a uniformity replicated street by street as if planted by the same landscape gardener: planters in gray, terracotta, and black; olive trees; summer perennials shaded in blues and pinks; tumbling greenery; rigid box hedges and bay trees. Walking from Queens Park Station, I turn into St. John's Gardens and discover one of the communal gardens much appreciated by local residents. These run between two rows of terraced houses that stand back-to-back. Residents of both streets access the garden that extends from their own. Metal railings fence it off from the street. The lawn is neatly mowed, rosebushes are planted in clusters, mature sycamore and beech trees abound, wooden benches invite loitering, and the swing gestures toward children.

When I ring the doorbell of a house around the corner, there is no answer. I wait a while and then leave. "Physics" texts to say that she had to pick up her ten-year-old daughter from school, but "my housekeeper was supposed to let you in." I call her Physics, because I have guaranteed her anonymity and so need to invent a name for her, and because of a conversation between her and her daughter about exams that went like this: "How was physics?" Daughter: "Easy." Mother: "Don't be ridiculous!" When I return to the house, her mother-in-law, a highly groomed seventy-year-old with an accent like the Queen's, lets me in. She has stepped in, she announces, as the housekeeper has a migraine and someone must look after the daughter, as Physics and her banker-husband are going to an important function. Mother-in-law holds sway in the basement kitchen, the length of the deep Victorian house, that leads on to a back garden and the communal garden beyond it. Above the kitchen is a beautifully decorated lounge with comfortable furniture in soft muted tones, where Physics joins me and we settle down to talk. Blond ponytail, in her forties but looks younger, black leggings and vest, she seems to have just finished yoga, and appears both intelligent and intense. The family dog joins me on the sofa and sticks his well-manicured nails into my leg. The Daughter comes up and down from the kitchen to inquire about various schoolbooks. She is being prepared for the "common entrance" exam through which she will enter one of the private schools that Physics is considering her for. Daughter bounces into the living room to announce that "Dad's on the phone." I try not to listen while they discuss the evening's arrangements: the dog with sharp nails increases the pressure. All four of us want Physics's attention: a linchpin in the domestic operations of plutocratic life.

Physics likes Notting Hill, she says, because it is "quite eclectic and friendly and outgoing and a bit bonkers." She goes on: "Living on a garden square is particularly amazing because when you've got tiny children, everyone can run around and, sort of, have communal living. So, that was really special! And now [since her other daughters are older], you can go to your yoga class, or you can play bridge, or you can go to an AA meeting—I mean, everything is, sort of, on your doorstep." Notting Hill provides the ideal components of plutocratic family life. Other local women I have spoken to enjoy the edginess of Portobello Road, what they call "the social mix," and the celebrities, whom they name with little prompting.

Physics was taking an art history course, but the demands of family life intervened. "Because we've just bought this house, there's a huge amount of work to do. So, we've got builders doing all sorts of things, and I'm having to coordinate all of that. Also, I have to try and work out what school my daughter is going to go to. And, my husband had quite a stress-y year with his work, so actually it works much better when I'm home and not stressed, myself. I think if the two of us were stressed, it'd be worse than a disaster. So, at the moment, my days are doing a yoga class or a Pilates class. I've started to learn to play bridge. I do all this interior design stuff, I pick up my daughter from school, organize her, and I'm sort of around and available, and a bit bored. But, I mean, I'm on one of the acquisitions committees at X." She names one of the nation's most prestigious galleries. "Also, I work with a charity around here, and I do lots of fund-raising for them. So, I'm super-busy. I'm always running around. But that's how I like it." In highly groomed housing and within habitats producing the next generation of plutocrats, a junction of mechanisms, in the purview of plutocratic women, converge to create London's prime cultural spaces and to set all the imperatives of a busy life without formal employment.

There is more. Country life is a persistent mode of wealth developed by old money. Physics continues: "So, our Oxford life is very spoiling. We have a lovely house that we've just bought, and we go there for weekends and holidays and half terms. It's got a garden, so the kids can muck about in the garden. They're really into their horses, so we have horses. Yes, it's just a very nice antidote to London. I have a really lovely girl who helps me here [in London], sort of, half a day every day Monday to Friday. Then, in the country, I have a housekeeper and a cook. So, she's [the housekeeper] there in the week, kind of tidying it after the weekend or preparing for the weekend. Then, she'll be there at the weekend, and she'll help with the laundry and the cooking and just generally keeping the show on the road.

Which, obviously, is very, very lucky, but it just means that everything is a real pleasure. So, you know, you can have people stay for the weekend, you can have people for lunch. You know, you're much freer!" Plutocratic domestic services, it seems, are vital mechanisms in producing elaborate lives and homes without the drudgery of domestic labor. Another woman later shared with me the fifty-entry spreadsheet from which she directs the maintenance of domestic and family life.

When I ask about the location of their country house, Physics prompts me to reiterate my guarantee of anonymity. "So, that's a village, a tiny village. There are probably, like, I don't know, twenty houses there. They are a real mix. We've got some sort of very significant neighbors and, you know, high-profile neighbors [I suspect these include a former Prime Minister]. So, this weekend, I'd pick my daughter up from school and her friend, we'd drive down with another friend's child, as well, because lots of friends from round here have also got houses down there. So, I'll pick up the girls, I'll drive them down. We'll get there about 7 p.m. We've got some friends coming to stay on Friday night, so we'll have a low-key dinner, because we're going to a big party the next day. Saturday morning, we're all riding. Then, Saturday lunch, we've got a friend's birthday party. She's got about five families going over there for a big lunch. Then, we've got two families coming to stay at our house for the weekend; so then they all arrive Saturday afternoon. My elder daughter comes down, comes back from [boarding] school, and then we'll have a kids' dinner and a grown-up dinner. Then, the next day, you know, walk and lunch and hanging out, a bit of tennis. If the pool is working, we'll go in the pool. Then I'll drop my elder daughter back at school on Sunday night and drive up here." The many ways of living the intersections of leisure and social relationships organized by women are significant mechanisms shaping the domestic life of finance capital.

Conclusions

Finance capital and the plutocracy it generates, maintains, and enriches are evidently key infrastructures holding London together as a plutocratic city—one in which wealth is now so spectacularly unevenly distributed that the city is itself a living experiment in the social consequences of the coexistence of wealth and want. The benefit of having a street view, of taking a look inside the money machine and the lives of those who drive it and live its rewards, provides a grainier and more-practical grasp of infrastructure for its human, algorithmic, and material textures, operations, and micro-mechanisms that I have described. What I want to call an *operational approach* to infrastructure thus arises from such a street view, exposing some of its less-obvious compositional mechanisms as they unfold empirically in the everyday heave of city life.

An operational approach to infrastructure reveals the human, lived, underpinning of algorithms' leveraging, expanding, and skimming of money; it exposes a slightly ragged female labor force in cheap clothes eating hasty lunches on the street, and the still-more-ragged bodies of the homeless huddled in sleeping bags on those same streets. It exposes the human and technological security operations that contain, regulate, and exclude; it exposes atmospheres of quiet entitlement exchanged over lavish lunches or practiced in a daytime yoga class. It exposes the elaborate domestic operations supporting wealthy lifestyles and leisure, and it emphatically announces its complex gendered dynamics. An operational approach exposes the bodies, the buildings, the attachments, the thinking, and the implicit normativity that hold together these plutocratic streets and their overt and covert operations that are expanding and consuming ever-greater concentrations of wealth.

Theoretically, taking an operational approach, a view from the streets, provides a route toward a deeper, more elaborated, and situational understanding of urban infrastructure. By identifying some of its micro-operations, it extends what it is conventionally considered to consist in. It is deeper and more elaborate in probing intersections between the fabrics composing the city, in worrying the links among buildings, operations, algorithms, activities, décor, clothes, movements, and dispositions, and among the individual (and often private) conceptions of the city on which they are based. This opens the way toward reaching an elaborated conception of infrastructure that is personal, distributed, institutional, lived, material, ephemeral, solid, and constantly remade, all at the same time. This is not to suggest that everything is infrastructure, for such an extended conception of it would lose all conceptual purchase, but instead to insist on unbundling some of its assemblages in order to see what it is that they hold together and how they do so.

This approach is inevitably situational. In following it, any urban scene or instance can be examined to tease out the micro-operations and intersections that make it work. This is not intended to reduce the conceptual to the empirical, limiting it simply to the specifics of each case, but also to amplify what cities or their neighborhoods have in common. While at one level all cities, all city neighborhoods, are unique, at another level we know from studying urbanism translocally that circumstances travel. The mechanisms of finance capital's expansion and the uneven accumulations of excess that result, along with the ways in which this is lived, are particularly motile, as are the habits of the wealthy themselves. Unseemly concentrations of wealth and poverty are a feature of most contemporary cities, worldwide, from Mumbai, to Johannesburg, to São Paulo, New York, London, and Paris.

This unbundled approach to infrastructure potentially sustains a new politics of the city. In their close-up and grainy operational details, infrastructures of plutocratic life are much less robust and entrenched than they seem at first. From the street, infrastructure's fragilities become less opaque. The secrecy, concealments, and separations that disconnect the wealthy, and the production and consumption of their money from the mainstream of urban life, expose some of this infrastructural fragility. Equally, the emotional complexities revealed in the vignettes above indicate further infrastructural fragilities. Some of these are buried in the intimacies of gendered relationships. Others are deeply embedded in the fear and competition that drive the human algorithms of trading and precarious speculative gains that could easily (again) collapse (as in 2008). Inevitably, such collapses have far-reaching consequences in reconfiguring family lives that depend on excessive speculative gains. Equally fragile too, are the delegated domestic labor and affective dimensions of serving relationships that support overelaborate, luxurious lives, which can easily unravel (Knowles 2022). Maintaining and displaying wealth in socially appropriate dispositions, acquisitions, and activities is fraught with the anxieties that privilege generates alongside a sense of entitlement. Plutocratic life and its underpinning infrastructures are an anxious and fragile way of being in the world, not least because it coexists with the dispossession and poverty it cocreates. An operational approach invites probing infrastructure's *valencies*, its shifting compositional bonds and micro-operations that expose the instabilities, contingencies, and uncertainties that compose the plutocratic city. These unstable qualities open several emerging repertoires in considering a new politics of the city, in a politics of fragility.

Such a politics of fragility suggests the prospect of a collapse and remaking of the city in new terms. Identifying specific infrastructural assemblages supporting urban ecologies of excess de-normalizes them, places their construction in question, exposes them to the public gaze, suggests things could have been otherwise, and shows that particular political decisions and actions, rather than others, were in play and that things need not be as they are but could, in fact, be quite different. The case for change in urban politics is particularly strongly made by the exposure of finance's leveraging and skimming, its excessive profits, its concealments and separations. Why are these tactics necessary? Why are these mechanisms and its beneficiaries concealed behind the opacities of these urban worlds? Is the money-expanding instincts of private equity the best way to shape the high streets, or indeed the back streets, of our cities? What other interests, activities, and shaping mechanisms are occluded? Which seemingly insignificant micro-mechanisms supporting infrastructures of vastly uneven accumulation might turn out to be crucial in shaping the urban landscapes we currently live with? How could things shift toward less-asymmetric distributions? And finally, which social benefits might accrue if human talent were not funneled into piling wealth into ever-fewer hands and into servicing the plutocratic city? A politics of fragility supports posing critical questions and imagining alternative versions of the city.

There are small signs today that a politics of fragility is slowly gaining traction. The rising popularity of the movement called Extinction Rebellion and the extraordinary spat between climate-change protesters and finance capital (on June 20, 2019) when protesters disrupted the Mansion House speech of the UK's Chancellor of the Exchequer—delivered in one of finance capital's most dramatic inner sanctums—and when Minister Mark Field was videotaped manhandling a female protester, captures a shift in the public mood with potentially dramatic implications for London's plutocrats. The excesses and luxuries of plutocrats' lives, surfaced in a compositional approach to infrastructure, are on a clear collision course with the direction in which public sensitivities are moving: toward more sustainable, less-wasteful, and less-extractive approaches to resources and consumption, as the impacts of climate change and pollution are reshaping cities worldwide. The excessive air travel, private planes, yachts lying idle in Mediterranean and Caribbean harbors, multiple homes around the globe, art and wine collections, interiors designed around rare materials and objects, and elaborately expensive though rarely worn clothes of the wealthy—all are potential targets for public censure and direct action by protesters.

There is a groundswell of opinion, even within the U.K. Conservative Party, that recognizes the urgent need for increased public spending to alleviate urban homelessness and poverty and to properly fund health and social care for all citizens. Demands for higher taxes on the wealthy and an end to tax evasion maneuvers through offshore trusts, and particularly by transnational corporations like Google, are gaining credibility, alongside calls to increase local-council tax on prime London real estate. The United Kingdom has committed to establishing a register of beneficial owners of offshore assets, in an effort to trim some of the opacities of the wealthy. This is a good sign, and may signal a direction of travel across a raft of measures designed to rein in the excesses of plutocratic life. Finally, approaches to the city that censure waste and that stress the need to conserve resources call into question the deployment of human resources—as housekeepers, butlers, nannies, and the rest—in easing the overly elaborate lives that plutocrats cannot service by themselves. While such things are difficult to calculate, the opportunity costs to the city of servicing plutocratic lives are surely a target worthy of reform.

Notes

Empirical data in this chapter come from a Major Leverhulme Fellowship (2016–2019), named *Serious Money: A Walk through Plutocratic London* (MRF-2016-001), which built on an earlier ESRC (2013–2016) research award on which I was a co-investigator with Roger Burrows, Rowland Atkinson, Mike Featherstone, and Tim Butler, titled *Life in the Alpha Territories*.

1. Chris Rhodes (April 25, 2018) Financial Services: Contribution to the UK Economy, House of Commons Briefing Paper 6193.

References

Amin, Ash, and Nigel Thrift. 2017. *Seeing Like a City*. Cambridge: Polity.
Atkinson, Rowland, Roger Burrows, Luna Glucksberg, Hang Kei Ho, Caroline Knowles, and David Rhodes. 2016. "'Minimum City'? A Critical Assessment of Some of the Deeper Impacts of Super Rich on Urban Life." In *Cities and the Super-Rich: Real Estate, Elite Practices, and Urban Political Economies*, edited by Ray Forrest, Bart Wissink, and Sin Yee Koh, 253–272. London: Palgrave.
Beaverstock, Jonathan, and Ian Hay. 2016. "They've 'Never Had It So Good': The Rise and Rise of the Super-rich and Wealth Inequality." In *Handbook on Wealth and the Super-Rich*, edited by Ian Hay and Jonathan Beaverstock, 1–17. Cheltenham: Edward Elgar.
Burrows, Roger, and Caroline Knowles. 2019. "The 'Haves' and the 'Have Yachts': Socio-Spatial Struggles in London Between the 'Merely

Wealthy' and the 'Super-Rich.'" *Cultural Politics* 15, no. 1: 72–87. doi: 10.1215/17432197-7289528.

Capgemini. 2019. "World Wealth Report 2017." https://www.worldwealth report.com/.

Christophers, Brett. 2013. *Banking Across Boundaries: Placing Finance in Capitalism*. Oxford: Wiley Blackwell.

Davis, Aeron. 2018. *Reckless Opportunists: Elites and the End of the Establishment*. Manchester: Manchester University Press.

Dorling, Danny. 2018. *Short Cuts: London Review of Books*, December 20: 14–15.

Forrest, Ray, Bart Wissink, and Sin Yee Koh, eds. 2016. *Cities and the Super-Rich, Real Estate, Elite Practices and Urban Political Economies*. Basingstoke: Palgrave Macmillan.

Frank, Robert. 2007. *Richistan*. New York: Piatkus.

Graham, Stephen, and Colin McFarlane. 2015. *Infrastructural Lives: Urban Infrastructure in Context*. London: Routledge.

Knowles, Caroline. 2017. "Walking Plutocratic London: Exploring Erotic, Phantasmagoric Mayfair." *Social Semiotics* 27, no. 3: 299–309. doi: 10.1080/10350330.2017.1301795.

Knowles, Caroline. 2022 (forthcoming). *Serious Money: Walking Plutocratic London*. London: Penguin.

McFarlane, Colin. 2011. *Learning the City: Knowledge and Translocal Assemblage*. Oxford: Wiley-Blackwell.

Savage, Michael. 2018. "Elite Habitus in Cities of Accumulation." In *The Sage Handbook of the 21st Century City*, edited by Suzanne Hall and Ricky Burdett. London: Sage.

Stewart, Kathleen. 2011. "Atmospheric Attunements." *Environment and Planning D: Society and Space* 29: 445–453.

Urry, John. 2014. *Offshoring*. Cambridge: Polity.

Webber, Richard, and Roger Burrows. 2018. *The Predictive Postcode: The Geodemographic Classification of British Society*. London: Sage.

AFFIRMATIVE VOCABULARIES FROM AND FOR THE STREET

Introduction

Economic life and ambition in urban Africa play out on the street and not in industrial factories of large-scale data processing farms. It is therefore un-surprising that street life in most African cities is teeming with contradic-tions, frustrated plans, incomplete ambitions, inconvenience, repetition, and human toil, amidst makeshift infrastructural armatures and uneven regulatory forces. By definition it is very difficult to ever really know what is going on in these streetscapes, let alone to intervene purposively, or to make plans for the long term. Yet these streets are the very spaces that need to address the aspirations and desires of a burgeoning labor force.

To appreciate the implications of this imperative, this chapter first acknowledges some of the conventional data points that relay a scenario where the majority of new entrants into the labor market face diminishing prospects of finding any form of secure work. Second, without wishing to diminish the severity of a future in which securing work is increasingly difficult, we consider that the notions and everyday practices of *work* in African cities have consistently countered ideals of large-scale industrial wage employment imagined by development economists as the logical stepping stone to modernization and advanced economic progress. We argue that the very conception of a "proper job" is rapidly changing, and its archetypal ideal of the "20th century laboring man" (Ferguson and Li 2018) is more than ever a relic of a highly gendered, geographical and historical exception rather than an aspirational norm (Monteith, Vicol, and Williams 2021). We empirically ground this part of our discussion by describing the lifeworlds and *lifework* of youth living in one African city that has featured across the debates in all manner of scholarship and policy debates concerning informal economies: Nairobi. In the third section of this chapter, we link the ethnographically textured account to wider literatures on informality and livelihoods. Our final section offers a way to think about the needed convergence between social justice imperatives and the making of socially equitable work that are already manifesting at local scales across African cities and that merit further attention and conceptualization. We call this Radical Social Enterprise, and propose that it might provide a lever for rethinking the future of work in African cities, where the coupling of street life and youth imaginations generates forms of knowledge and skills that trouble more mainstream conceptions of labor and life in the city.

It is now widely shown that only 34 percent of Africa's workers have regular wage-paying jobs, while 64 percent engage in what is called "vulnerable" employment.[1] Forty years following the earliest International Labour Organisation reports on informal economies (ILO 1972), building on the first anthropological study of an African city's diversified informal economy (see Hart 1973 on Accra), it is now clear that this dynamic is entrenched and intractable, and not, as development economists assumed for years, a transition phase. The disturbing reality is, of course, the disparity between the wealth that many African countries have generated, while the majority of economically active citizens continue to labor under precarious working conditions. Over the course of the last two decades, for example, most African countries have seen relatively strong GDP growth, yet, by 2017 this sustained trend translated into a meager 2 percent drop in the proportion of vulnerable workers (AUC/OECD 2018). This dynamic is disconcerting in light of the projected expansion of the continent's labor force over the next forty years. By 2050, the current labor force of just under 450 million will reach 1.2 billion, and by 2035 Africa will have a larger labor force than either China or India (Mo Ibrahim Foundation 2015). Yet the prospects of reducing vulnerable employment or growing waged industrial jobs are paper thin (AUC/OECD 2018). Young people in particular are today on the frontlines of vulnerable employment, or what the ILO has recently called "non-standard" work (ILO 2016), because they are the majority population in African countries, and will continue to be the most affected demographic: 1 billion youth are estimated to enter the labor market in the next decade, with less than half of them likely to find waged jobs (World Bank Group 2015).

Development economists have argued that the primary driver of this daunting policy/political task is the phenomenon of "premature deindustrialization." This concept denotes an unprecedented historical process whereby workers who start off in primary sectors with informal employment do not later get absorbed into formal jobs in manufacturing or industrial sectors (Lopes 2019). This narrative goes on to argue that instead, they remain trapped in vulnerable jobs characterized as low-end and precariously waged and mainly services-oriented. The "new normal" in Africa is that the vast majority of workers jump directly from informal agricultural employment to *informal* service jobs. Only a small proportion go on to do informal manufacturing jobs, and an even smaller share enter organized manufacturing jobs (OECD, AFDB, and UNDP 2016). This clearly has profound implications on a continent where 50 percent of the population is younger than 19 years of age. Amid a myriad of exogenous pressures related to climate change impacts, asymmetrical trade relations, mounting debt burdens, and uneven regulatory capacity, it is impossible to overstate the risks and complexity when these dynamics coincide in urban spaces. And yet, though this reality is cause for alarm on multiple fronts, it urges a reorientation of our understanding of working futures on the African continent, as well as a greater attunement to the working lives of young people that goes beyond conventional analytical silos.

The conceptual challenge, then, is to escape the conventional teleological (urban and economic) development studies outlook that has persisted in defining African urban environments and modalities of work, exchange, and distribution in terms of negation—in other words, "what they are not" (Roitman 1990). Here we follow James Ferguson and Tania Murray Li's (2018) invitation to think "beyond the proper job" which, especially during the twentieth century, equated labor with waged manufacturing or office-based occupations. Few benefits accrue in remaining fixated on modernization absences and failure, so we would rather pay attention to what is actually going on, to *see* like an African streetscape, through a lens that identifies sources of resourcefulness and coping strategies that may circumvent the purview of the state (Myers 2005), or indeed may be in continuous dialectical tension with it (Hart 2009). We resist pathologizing these as piecemeal, irregular, or palliative, insofar as they are actually part of the mosaic of urban practices that get things done, and therefore they encompass an urban logic and set of knowledges that merit alternative vocabularies and ways of seeing. But equally and crucially, we also resist romanticizing what might be regarded as hand-to-mouth survivalism, and we wish instead to understand the ways in which forms of hustling and deal-making are born out of struggles (Thieme 2017). It is perhaps because "getting things done" and "struggle" are so intertwined that *doing business* to get things done and *tending to matters of social justice* deserve to be considered as a couplet, in theory and in practice. The next section invites readers to stretch their imagination and take a walkabout on the streetscapes of a quintessential African city, Nairobi, and more specifically, a neighborhood of neighborhoods, called Mathare.

Mathare and the Unseen Scenes

To get to Mathare, you take a bumpy but efficient *matatu* ride from the Central Business District (CBD), asking for Number 46. As always, the *matatu* defies traffic rules and any sense of straightness, and eventually that 46 takes you onto Juja Road to cross the infamous informal settlement known as a Mathare. The visual transition from the CBD to Juja Road bombards the senses. Juja Road opens a kaleidoscopic street ballet where the lines between commercial, residential, social, and pedestrian space are embroiled and constantly swerving. Like the corrugated sheet metal that covers most homes and stalls, lines of destination are jagged—the *matatu* route, the foot paths, the walls presuming verticality seem to reach to a diagonal point instead, defying modernist town planning ambitions. Ironically, the fruits and vegetables, fourth-hand shoes, and pieces of coal are neatly arranged in straight lines, displayed on the handcarts or mats carefully set out by street vendors. Look down at the dusty and often muddy ground, and shoes are meticulously polished, every man's shirt is carefully ironed. Glance up and you see the lines bowing at every story of the gray building-blocks in the distance, where brightly colored and bleached white sheets and clothes hang in the sun. Care, craft, and intent have been inserted into every corner, and as you look around, you see the considerable labor involved in the most minute of tasks, all performed with precision and dexterity. A vegetable street vendor cuts *sukuma wiki* (Swahili for "pushing the week," referring to kale) with intense speed but utmost calm, as she looks up at her friend to share the daily gossip. The shoe shiner on the street corner is sitting on an uneven small stool and has an old, tattered briefcase open with his polish, brush, and cloth, yet he manages to make his customer feel comfortable and at ease on a chair placed carefully under a small parasol, and a paper to read as two friends stare over the shoulder of the seated customer to comment on the daily headlines. An animated discussion ensues about the politics of the day, as though it is worth talking about age-old issues that seem to never change, just because it is important to make one's opinion known. Debate makes the morning move, after all, and helps pass the time both for those who have no time to lose and for those who have too much time to spare. Across the diversity of rhythms and people-scapes, the generalized uncertainty associated with how much each person will earn that day creates an affective atmosphere of expectation, contingency, provisionality, and impermanence.

If you ask anyone stationed at any of the streetside businesses if they've seen Kaka from the Mathare Environmental Youth Group (MEYG), they'll point up ahead and confidently assert that he's around, to be found "at the baze." The *baze* in Nairobi argot refers to the landmark where young people of a particular neighborhood can be found. In a city that otherwise tends to exclude, criminalize, or over-police youth from under-resourced communities, the *baze* is where young people cultivate their social capital and sense of place. It is a point of reference, of departure, of assembly, of productive loitering at the interstices of daily graft that shift between domestic chores; the creative labor involved in making a living on that day, and inevitably the moments of waiting while performing nonchalance. It shapes the raw materials of identity and belonging.

"Today there is no water," Kaka remarks, used to the normalized state of one crisis or another. Kaka, like other youth born and raised in underserved neighborhoods of postcolonial Nairobi, knows never to expect things to work, but rather learns how to fix anything and deal with all manner of unforeseen problems. Kaka's youth group is one of many in Mathare who have made their living collecting, sorting, and reselling residential waste, in the absence of municipal services. But they have not only turned "trash into cash" as a source of revenue for so-called underemployed youth, they have also used their role as local waste collectors as a literal and figurative platform to continuously pitch new ideas to their neighborhoods that purport to turn problems into opportunities and fuse community activism with a fierce entrepreneurial audacity. What might to outsiders or mainstream development economists seem like abject poverty and generalized youth unemployment is under another light a resourceful, vibrant, economically active "self-help city" (Hake 1977) *within* the revanchist city of Nairobi, contending with profound legacies of strategic, segregated, colonial-town planning.

As we walk past the butcher at the corner, only to veer off the paved road into the unpaved labyrinth leading to Kaka's *baze*, a young boy is riding a bicycle three sizes too big for him. He can't sit on the seat, but he is agile and able to ride by bopping up and down, keeping his oversized flip-flops stuck to his feet and to the pedals, swerving his bottom side to side, and his sister laughs on the roadside as she watches. Another girl rides a scooter on the same path, her friends watching. "There's a guy here who owns them," says Kaka, bemused, explaining that these toys were probably found half broken and left for trash in a wealthier part of the city. As Kaka and his other peers have often exclaimed, "You can fix anything in the ghetto," and then you make money from it. So now the guy who recovered and fixed the "broken" toys makes a bit extra on the side by charging local children for each ten-minute ride. Ten shillings for ten minutes; the price of a cup of *chai*, or of a *matatu* ride. The other kids wait for their turn, or if they don't have the money they find enjoyment in simply watching their friend have fun, the same way their older siblings find meaning in standing at the job-less corner while their friend *does* work. All forms of labor (and leisure) are consistently adjoined with company—someone to banter with, someone to watch your back, watch your goods, go fetch some change in case you need it for your customers. Sociality and livelihood are inseparable.

When you reach the *baze* of the Mathare Environmental Youth Group, you spot a group of young men draped over a few *boda boda* motorcycles, two of them wearing yellow vests and clearly the drivers, while the others hang out as wingmen. In the social hall, there is a palimpsest of rough graf-fiti art on all the walls; one tag jumps out in particular: "'crazy world' B care-full. None but prayers. One Love." You know that this tag is a reminder of all the young lives lost through police- or gang-related violence. To get to your thirtieth birthday here can be a feat. In contrast to the gritty graffiti, one wall displays a laminated board with a series of NGO and corporate brand logos, including UN-Habitat, Samsung, USAID, and Comic Relief, among others. At first it might seem that these organizations have sponsored the social hall in some way. But the cluster of organizations exhibited on that board are, in effect, more of an archive of those who have come and gone—at best, those whose sponsorship has been fleeting and often more about the photo oppor-tunity for the organization in question, making them then able to qualify their claims to be addressing the "urban youth crisis" with a notable set of anecdotes from the "slum tour." But these names also give a certain credi-bility to the group, whose members as individuals and as a collective have perfected their narrative and perform resilience or dejection, depending on what response they want to elicit. In many ways, the occasional presence of external support or visits is just one of the various income-generating activities of these youth whose hustle economy comprises a portfolio of business operations, each of which has its own specific function and form of redistributing gains and assigning leadership.

For many youth groups in Mathare, residential garbage collection has been foundational to their ties to each other, their community, and even outside forms of support—ranging from the tokenistic one-off sponsors to the more regular "social investors." Youth groups in Mathare (and indeed across Nairobi) tend to average forty members, with some becoming veteran shareholders over the years, while room is made to accommodate new younger members once they have "proven themselves." Vertical blocks, four-to-eight-story walkups, each averaging a dozen apartments per floor, are each managed by a member. Everyone knows which block is managed by whom, and a careful allocation of waste collectors then get paid each month once payment has been collected from each household. The manager of that building then gets his or her cut.

In the early 2000s, youth groups across Mathare started to think about ways they could add value to their waste collection business. Rather than simply charging households for collection, they realized that the materials found in the rubbish had value. Sorting became a crucial part of the post-collection activity, specifically finding what could be resold. Plastics soon became a hot commodity, and MEYG was in a good position because they had space to store the plastic (which allowed them to wait for the right moment to rent a truck to take it to the industrial area for resale). In 2007, the group received a plastic shredder as a "gift" from Pamoja Trust, a social justice organization tied to the Slum/Shack Dwellers alliance. The shredder gave the group an important distinction: adding value to each kilogram of plastic. With the shredder, the group was easily identifiable as "organized," and this drew the attention of the local area MP, who courted youth votes during her election campaigns. In exchange, she would help Kaka and his youth group upgrade their hall, and even provide a water tank on the roof. Over time, the space also allowed the group to organize events, feeding programs for street families, and activities for young mothers, but also opening up the social hall for a fee to various NGOs hoping to run events seeking to "engage community residents." And then, of course, football (soccer) nights were especially popular, and lucrative, given that the social hall benefited from a flat-screen TV!

Not far from Kaka's *baze* is another: Mathare Number 10 Youth Group (MANYGRO). Having grown up playing football with Kaka's group, in 2008 the members of MANYGRO started taking their plastics for shredding to the social hall in Mlango Kubwa where the plastic shredder was based. MANYGRO were also courted by Pamoja Trust in the early 2000s when it seemed clear that youth needed to be included in slum-upgrading schemes, but were not preoccupied with land and housing tenure as much as the claim to a piece of space in their own neighborhood from which to assemble and operate their various micro-enterprises. MANYGRO has over the last two decades established a small but diversified constellation of businesses that benefit from and serve local community interests. Examples of these include the tree that provides shade for three chairs where a few youth-group members sit to manage the public toilet at a distance. The tree stands next to a small M-Pesa (mobile money) kiosk running hourly mobile-banking operations, while taking payment for the water point that is fixed to the outward-facing wall of the kiosk. A cold fridge in the kiosk takes up most of the space but provides a vital additional source of income and respite from the heat, selling a variety of "cold drinks" (soda) to the local youth and workers around. A patch of green vertical farming lies up ahead, which over the years has been turned into a small greenhouse growing kale and spinach for local consumption and resale at a time when food prices have skyrocketed. Wally, who manages both the M-Pesa kiosk and the greenhouse, smiles and says they are thinking of "food security," then points to the chicken coop next the greenhouse where food scraps from garbage collection are taken, so "everything can be reused."

Apprehending Lifeworlds

This stylized vignette of dynamic, makeshift practices can be read in multiple ways. Various literatures offer up a range of emphasis, with several implications for policy practice. How do we assess the diverse economies of Mathare described above? In these popular neighborhoods, industry may be scant, but all manners of repair and maintenance abound. Self-employed workers may not appear to make notable profits, and margins of any business may seem slim at best, but any gains are either reinvested into the running costs of the business or used as seed capital to start another venture. Full-time jobs may be nowhere to be found, but work is made at all hours of the day and night, and the natural leaders who want to maintain their street credibility (and some form of power) make sure that any available work creates multiple (albeit smaller) jobs. To give many people enough for lunch that day is a more-rational and more-sustainable form of leadership, as opposed to enriching the few.

In this section, we briefly rehearse a few of these bodies of thought on alternative economic readings in order to prepare the ground for a more synthetic, practice-oriented conceptual framework that requires deepening and experimentation. Our first entry point is the persuasive intervention of J. K. Gibson-Graham (2008, 615), when they insisted that we have a choice either to see and foreground structural constraints, or to see heterogeneity and diversity that exceed the class-based systems of "producing, appropriating, and distributing surplus." We take up their invitation to "represent economy differently" by reconceptualizing the "economic landscape as a proliferative space of difference" (615). It is in this way that we might find alternative vocabularies for more credible "re-description" (Simone and Pieterse 2017) of economic-scapes, such as those depicted in the Mathare vignette above. Indeed, the forms of labor, productivity, and value in and around these youth-led economic terrains challenge normative classifications. So we draw on Gibson-Graham's call for novel economic representations and "performances" as well as on the recent exploratory reflections of Ferguson and Li (2018), who confront head-on a world and a future where formal work and regular wages are no longer the norm (if they ever were). Ferguson and Li challenge us to move beyond nostalgia for an industrial (predominantly male) working class that never came into being; instead, they wish us to focus our attention on the actual lives and practices of ordinary people navigating tough and complex challenges. These efforts, strategies, and logics reflect what Gibson-Graham (2008, 618) call "the plethora of hidden and alternative economic activities that contribute to social well-being and environmental regeneration."

In calling for more-exploratory and anticipatory ways of theorizing urban economies, Gibson-Graham's writing provides an opening for a more pluralistic way of seeing economies in their performative, affective, and relational registers. So first, we want to revisit some of the conceptual and policy frameworks that have been in circulation to address questions of economic precarity and exclusion. Though it is well beyond the modest scope of this chapter to delve into these in depth, we will briefly review some of the seminal texts that have attempted to render informal economies legible both theoretically and practically. Then, we will offer an experimental typology that makes a case for the conceptual potential of thinking about questions of productive social enterprise and social justice together, despite their divergent genealogies in urban studies.

The two concepts that have been used most extensively to capture and explore the economic lives of urban residents are informality and livelihoods. Both stem, in part, from development studies, and the former can be traced back to studies in the early 1970s to make sense of practices and processes in East Africa (ILO 1972; Hart 1973; King 1996). Since then, there has been an explosion of work on informality, providing by now a reasonably accurate understanding of the scale and scope of the sector. The informal economy is studied in three ways: as a form of labor, as a type of enterprise, and as a set of sectors, for example, waste pickers or street vendors (Heintz and Valodia 2008). The incisive definitional work of Martha Chen (2014) demonstrates the gendered nature of informal work—men are overrepresented as owners of informal enterprises, while women are the lowest paid and the most precarious members of the casual sector and home-based workers.

Another strand of literature has focused on the concept of livelihoods to capture the economic, social, and familial resources, as well as the practices and strategies of poor households to make a living in precarious circumstances (Rakodi 2002; Beall 2004; Moser 2008). A central conceptual aim in this work is to foreground the assets and resources of the urban poor and not merely focus on the material and economic deficits (Friedmann 1992). The rationale is that navigating a difficult and demanding set of circumstances requires formidable resourcefulness, including social capital and various forms of intelligence. Any analytical or policy approach must seek to understand that first, before obsessing with deficits and needs, not least because any intervention that lacks this insight risks displacing or even destroying the very mechanisms of support and ingenuity that underpin local knowledge and place-making (Hamdi 2004). Of course, the livelihoods perspective is not naive about power or predatory institutions, but insists that ordinary people have ways and means of engaging those forces, and even subverting them from time to time. The difference between the informality and the livelihood perspectives is that the former is focused on economic activity, identity, and agency. Livelihoods include informal work or enterprise but also locate these in a relational understanding with other strategies that are deployed to secure a home, access public goods, acquire useful information, and forge collective action to advance both individual and collective interests.

Beyond economic activities and the household, a swathe of other activities and strategies are deployed on a daily basis. Many of these fall within the realm of organized civil society interventions, ranging from those by religious organizations to those by various other cultural and social formations. In contexts of acute infrastructural poverty and limited reliable municipal services, these forms of associational life often play a central role in mediating access to essential services and mutual support. In the literature, this category of social action, having a social purpose, is defined as the *social economy*, or, in more limited expressions, as the third sector—a term that has currency in the anglophone literatures that reference the North American and European experiences. Some of these activities are deemed to be within the realm of solidarity economies, at least in the francophone literatures (Moulaert and Ailenei 2005; Hart et al. 2009). In general, it can be argued that the social economy categorizes the actions of voluntary organizations such as mosques and churches, cooperatives, savings associations, mutual societies, and so forth. Although they do not have a profit motive, they can see the value of adapting business operating practices to achieve greater efficiency and scale for the delivery of (or access to) goods and services in contexts where there is high demand but low supply. Ultimately, social economies and enterprises seek to hybridize market and social-value principles in ways that are typically place-specific and embedded in fine-grained social-cultural webs that demand incessant engagement and reciprocity, rather than pure financial returns on investment.

In the last decade, there has been an interesting shift and extension of these literatures as a new economic imperative became inextricably linked to the widening calls for ecological transitions. Here we see how a concept championed by industrial ecologists in the 1970s such as E. F. Schumacher (1973) has become more recognized and promoted: *circular economies*. On the back of the mainstreaming of sustainable development as a dominant discourse to frame macroeconomic policies, industrial and trade policies, and environmental frameworks, the importance of dematerializing economic growth from materials consumption and carbon emissions has become a major goal. This consensus is reflected in the Sustainable Development Goals (SDGs) that since 2015 have established sustainable production and consumption as a strategic goal. In the meantime, countless frameworks across policy, industry, and academic sectors have been proposing particular roadmaps for the reduction of raw material sourcing and waste generation by recovering the "waste" as a resource and input.[2] Various think tanks at the nexus of industry and research, such as the Ellen MacArthur Foundation, for example, call for a radical rethink of production and consumption practices at government, business, and household levels, by designing out waste and pollution and keeping products and materials in use.

Significantly, considerable enthusiasm is being expressed in policy communities that deal with the intersection of the employment, environmental, and spatial policies for the promotion of circular economies (Schröder et al. 2020). And while the most crucial intervention and impact will have to happen at industrial scales, starting with the design stage of production, the advocacy and consumption practices of civil society play a significant role in seeing circular economies through. Spatially, circular economies reinforce the idea of localized geographies for production and consumption, thereby fundamentally subverting the current globalized value chains that anchor design, production, and consumption. Environmentally, circular economies reduce carbon-intensive production processes because a considerable amount of the carbon emissions associated with transportation is eliminated, and they radically reduce waste streams due to reuse and repurpose imperatives. Economically, circular economies are seen as the only way to guarantee long-term economic viability, because they are compatible with macroeconomic priorities of achieving a zero-carbon or low-carbon global economy by 2050 (Preston and Lehne 2017).

There are two important considerations here. First, we must be wary of overly celebratory accounts of circular economies as the bridge to transition from unsustainable to sustainable business practices, and must keep in mind that the efforts and investments in circular economies have to date been highly uneven. While countries in the Global South consume a fraction of what the Global North consumes (not to speak of carbon emissions), the transboundary waste flowing from wealthy countries to poorer ones has since the 1980s created an alarming "spatial fix" (Harvey 1996). In more recent years, this has often been narrated as integral to more-sustainable processes of recycling and reuse as we have seen with the offshoring of e-waste landing in countries like Ghana, Singapore, and many parts of China, for example, and generating a whole economy of waste sorting and recovery (Alexander and Reno 2012). The second consideration is that, while the recent attention to circular economies at policy and industrial scales is crucial, glossy reports and fancy visualizations of circular economy frameworks eclipse the long-standing, homegrown circular economies of under-resourced neighborhoods like Mathare, where the repair, reuse, and resource recovery of plastics, metals, car parts, and even clothing has been integral to everyday efforts to make materials and resources last longer and to retain (or reinsert) use and exchange value.

The main challenge is that these homegrown efforts in places like Mathare remain localized, and often highly fragmented. In some cases, digital platforms have played a potentially transformative role, connecting otherwise off-grid and underserved neighborhoods and micro-enterprises to potential networks and markets. The "I Got Garbage" app operating in India since 2014 provides a useful example of how digital mediation becomes a bridge between informal waste-pickers working in isolation and the rising demand for professional recycling services.[3] While the "uberization" of informal economies requires careful scrutiny and monitoring (Meagher 2018), we also see that the rapid increase of digital literacy in communities that lack formal educational hardware such as libraries and well-resourced secondary schools has shaped new and dynamic relationships between street-based knowledge and digital learning. Here, the "online" and "offline" social networks and economies create unforeseen outcomes for youth who may not have a job or a school certificate, but who have a smart phone, several digital profiles, and a lot to say. Here is where our frame, which we call *Radical Social Enterprise*, comes into play.

Radical Social Enterprise

As the labor market data presented in the introduction to this chapter indicate, the majority of urban and rural dwellers will face a future of so-called "non-standard," vulnerable work, which necessitates *both* continued activist scholarship to call out the various forms of structural and symbolic violence that perpetuate deep inequalities, *and* a more-attuned scholarship capable of *seeing* what is actually going on and *questioning* our own forms of knowledge production and familiar (perhaps outdated and problematic) conceptual categories. We are thus caught in an epistemic dilemma: motivated by the desire for "structural transformation," but equally compelled to "redescribe" and indeed to harness aspects of profoundly makeshift socioeconomic relations born out of the strategies and capabilities displayed by youth in under-resourced neighborhoods like Mathare, Nairobi.

Here is where we find that there is a generative relationship between two fields that have not, to date, tended to intersect in either theory or practice: social enterprise and social justice. We find that the pairing of *social+enterprise* offers a generative description of youth-led projects that incorporate a social mission into their income-generation activities aiming to benefit individual, household, and communal scales. But we remain constructively critical of premature celebrations of social enterprise as being an ahistorical and apolitical concept. Equally, we recognize the importance and positive contribution of social justice organizations, such as Slum/Shack Dwellers International, as well as countless other initiatives fighting for land and housing tenure and access to basic service provision in vulnerable communities. However, youth have not always been integral to the leadership and voice of these groups, so our focus is less centered on rights claims *tout court*, or what Partha Chatterjee (2004) calls "political society." A more apt redescription of the kinds of experiments taking place in urban neighborhoods such as Mathare requires us to insert politics into social enterprise, so as to examine and support grassroots initiatives that clearly articulate a linkage between *social enterprise* and *social justice* needs. We perceive the value and potential importance of diverse economic activities and ventures to addressing social justice issues, particularly related to uneven *access* to urban infrastructures and services. The intellectual and practical exercise of joining a social justice approach to social enterprise leads to an emergent framing we call "radical social enterprise." And so we ask: *How can urban reproduction be reimagined through a kind of contemporary urban archaeological "dig" for grounded accounts of radical social enterprise experiments at work?*

By *radical* we mean a timely point of departure from the status quo, one that is profoundly political in that it challenges structural inequality and violence but often in ways that are incremental and patient rather than pushing for total disruption to local systems (Pieterse 2007). "Radical" assumes the belief that change is possible, that it can come from anywhere and any direction, but that it never cedes to ambivalence because change is always reversible and fragile. "Radical" also speaks to the imperative to phase out an industrial and linear economic approach, recognize the prevalence of a post-wage era, and admit the driving force (for better or worse) of digital platforms.

We emphasize the *social* not to adopt the overused business idiom of "social enterprise" but rather to emphasize the social ties and networks of practice and communities that bind the resource elements of effective development action, in contexts where the legacies of uneven development and unequal resource allocation have marked neighborhood histories of provisioning, distribution, and power relations. To this end, we understand that what is deemed "social" can liberate but also imprison; it can oblige and obligate at the same time as strong social ties can form and stretch solidarities that lift people out of hard times. Everyday social life is, in part, transactional and is infused with deal-making, with codes being made and unmade, and with complicated ethics and rationalities at work.

There is always a risk of being "taken for a ride," but always potential for getting something out of the deal.

Finally, we refer to *enterprise* in the dual sense of the term: first (the most obvious and the one that elicits an in-built bias from the canon of the Left) as the organizational form and cultural logics that shape an enterprise. Second (and most relevant here), we consider *enterprise* to be the micro and individuated acts of "undertaking" (from the French word, *entreprendre*), as a set of practices embedded to a place and socially constituted. Enterprise connotes the possibility of income generation and experimentation with ways of making a living, but in a form that is continuously building toward particular imagined futures that hold a certain promise. Enterprise also describes the labor in *making* work, and is an overture to various readings of productivity, including preparation, setting the scene, and making connections. Our reading of *enterprise* is one that privileges local economic knowledge that is also open to external forms of support and collaboration. As well, it includes the skills to adapt to conditions of resource scarcity and adversity, to become adept at continuous course correction, and always to be open to iterative grassroots "research and development."

Conclusion

This chapter draws on our shared concern for understanding how residents living and working on the edges of legal, economic, and infrastructural legibility become incorporated and continuously (re)shape urban economies in African cities. We have aimed to respond to Ferguson and Li's call to rethink the presumed "telos of 'development'" that for so long has defined what is and should be "proper" work (Ferguson and Li 2018), and we point to the productive tensions between seemingly disparate lines of scholarship that merit more-conceptual articulation and friction: post-capitalistic politics (Gibson-Graham 2008; Mason 2015); circular economies (Preston and Lehne 2017); and informal urban livelihoods (Hart 1973; Rakodi 2002; Chen 2014). Empirically, we have drawn on longitudinal ethnographic research conducted in one of Nairobi's largest and oldest informal settlements to reflect on the incommensurate dynamics at play when protracted underinvestment and systematic uneven urban development (Parnell and Pieterse 2014) nevertheless operate in tandem with vital everyday experiments that produce emergent urban modes of life, work, service provision, and activism (Thieme 2017). These experiments are based on composites of commitments to social justice along with attempts to make a living that may appear ad hoc but are in fact rooted in local street knowledge and social investments (Thieme 2021). As a result, particular forms of place-making emerge, despite residents' often being accorded no place and no right to the city. These urban modes of life express particular economic relations that are inextricably linked to wider global economic terrains, but that often operate under alternative logics, simultaneously revealing shared solidarities, betrayals, uncertainty, unexpected support, and, most important, a sense of possibility, no matter how slight.

Giving ourselves some liberty to "imagine" through this written intervention, while remaining cautious and feeling humbled by the intimidating challenges that lie ahead, we do not seek to normalize, celebrate, or dismiss these forms of sociality and struggle. Instead, we argue that urban modes of life embedded in socially contingent economic relations merit affirmative vocabularies, rather than political scientists' falling back on familiar tropes that inevitably define by negation, absence, and dispossession. We therefore offer a provocation that signals (or thinks through) which levers might be pulled to better harness the potential of homegrown modes of urban life and labor that tend to be off-grid and yet could resonate with (or even propel) wider progressive policies and practices in African cities. We are aware that this chapter only gestures toward an alternative approach. But it should be read as the beginnings of a research agenda and dialogue with scholars and practitioners alike who share our curiosities and theoretical frustrations. By juxtaposing and articulating the concepts of social enterprise and social justice, we urge allied scholars and practitioners to consider the generative possibilities of urban-scapes where "radical social enterprise" might be more readily seen, documented, and perhaps also harnessed.

Notes

1. According to the International Labour Organisation 2018, "stable employment" includes wage and salaried employees as well as business owners. "Vulnerable employment" includes subsistence farming, informal self-employment, and work for family members and is characterized by low and erratic incomes.

2. https://www.ellenmacarthurfoundation.org/circular-economy/what-is -the-circular-economy.

3. https://www.igotgarbage.com/what-we-do/.

References

Alexander, Catherine, and Joshua Reno, eds. 2012. *Economies of Recycling: The Global Transformation of Materials, Values and Social Relations*. London: Zed Books.

AUC/OECD. 2018. *Africa's Development Dynamics 2018: Growth, Jobs and Inequalities*. Addis Ababa: African Union Commission and OECD Publishing.

Beall, Jo. 2004. "Surviving the City: Livelihoods and Linkages of the Urban Poor." In *Urban Governance, Voice and Poverty in the Developing World*, edited by Nick Devas, 53–67. London: Earthscan.

Chatterjee, Partha. 2004. *The Politics of the Governed*. New York: Columbia University Press.

Chen, Martha. 2014. "Informal Employment and Development: Patterns of Inclusion and Exclusion." *European Journal of Development Research* 26, no. 4: 397–418.

Ferguson, James, and Tania Murray Li. 2018. "Beyond the 'Proper Job': Political-economic Analysis after the Century of Labouring Man." PLAAS *Working Paper* 51. Cape Town: PLAAS, University of the Western Cape.

Friedmann, John. 1992. *Empowerment: The Politics of Alternative Development*. London: Blackwell.

Gibson-Graham, J. K. 2008. "Diverse Economies: Performative Practices for 'Other Worlds.'" *Progress in Human Geography* 32, no. 5: 613–632.

Hake, Andrew. 1977. *The Self-Help City: The African Metropolis*. Sussex: Sussex University Press.

Hamdi, Nabeel. 2004. *Small Change: About the Art of Practice and the Limits of Planning in Cities*. London: Routledge.

Hart, Keith. 1973. "Informal Income Opportunities and Urban Employment in Ghana." *Journal of Modern African Studies* 11, no. 1: 61–89.

Hart, Keith. 2009. "On the Informal Economy: The Political History of an Ethnographic Concept." *Working Papers* CEB, 09-042.RS, ULB—Universite Libre de Bruxelles. https://ideas.repec.org/p/sol/wpaper/09-042.html.

Hart, Keith, Jean-Louis Laville, and Antonio David Cattani. 2009. *The Human Economy*. Cambridge: Polity Press.

Harvey, David. 1996. *Justice, Nature and the Geography of Difference*. Oxford: Blackwell.

Heintz, James, and Imraan Valodia. 2008. "Informality in Africa: A Review." *WIEGO Working Paper No. 3*. WIEGO. https://www.wiego.org/sites/default/files/publications/files/Heintz_WIEGO_WP3.pdf.

ILO. 1972. *Employment Mission to Kenya Report: Incomes and Equality—A Strategy for Increasing Productive Employment in Kenya*. Geneva: International Labour Organisation.

ILO. 2016. *Non-standard Employment Around the World: Understanding Challenges, Shaping Prospects*. Geneva: International Labour Organisation.

ILO. 2018. *Paid Employment vs Vulnerable Employment: A Brief Study of Employment Patterns by Status in Employment.* Geneva: International Labour Organisation.

King, Kenneth. 1996. *Jua Kali Kenya: Change and Development in an Informal Economy 1970–1995.* London: James Currey.

Lopes, Carlos. 2019. *Africa in Transformation: Economic Development in the Age of Doubt.* London: Palgrave Macmillan.

Mason, Paul. 2015. *PostCapitalism: A Guide to Our Future.* London: Allen Lane.

Meagher, Kate. 2018. "Cannibalizing the Informal Economy: Frugal Innovation and Economic Inclusion in Africa." *European Journal of Development Research* 30, no. 1: 17–33.

Mo Ibrahim Foundation. 2015. *African Urban Dynamics: Facts and Figures.* London: Mo Ibrahim Foundation.

Monteith, Will, Dora-Olivia Vicol, and Philippa Williams. 2021. "Introduction: Work Beyond the Wage." In *Beyond the Wage: Ordinary Work in Diverse Economies*, edited by Will Monteith, Dora-Olivia Vicol, and Philippa Williams, 1–19. Bristol: Bristol University Press.

Moser, Caroline. 2008. "Assets and Livelihoods: A Framework for Asset-Based Social Policy." In *Assets, Livelihoods and Social Policy*, edited by Caroline Moser and Anis A. Dani. Washington, DC: World Bank.

Moulaert, Frank, and Oana Ailenei. 2005. "Social Economy, Third Sector and Solidarity Relations: A Conceptual Synthesis from History to Present." *Urban Studies* 42, no. 11: 2037–2053.

Myers, Garth. 2005. *Disposable Cities: Garbage, Governance and Sustainable Development in Urban Africa.* London: Routledge.

OECD, AFDB, and UNDP. 2016. *African Economic Outlook 2016: Sustainable Cities and Structural Transformation.* Paris: OECD.

Parnell, Sue, and Edgar Pieterse, eds. 2014. *Africa's Urban Revolution.* London: Zed Books and UCT Press.

Pieterse, Edgar. 2007. *City Futures: Confronting the Crisis of Urban Development.* London: Zed Books.

Preston, Felix, and Johanna Lehne. 2017. *A Wider Circle? The Circular Economy in Developing Countries.* London: Chatham House.

Rakodi, Carole. 2002. "A Livelihoods Approach—Conceptual Issues and Definitions." In *Urban Livelihoods: A People-Centred Approach to Reducing Poverty*, edited by Carole Rakodi and Tony Lloyd-Jones, 3–22. London: Earthscan.

Roitman, Janet L. 1990. "The Politics of Informal Markets in Sub-Saharan Africa." *Journal of Modern African Studies* 28, no. 4: 671–696.

Schröder, Patrick, Alexandre Lemille, and Peter Desmond. 2020. "Making the Circular Economy Work for Human Development." *Resources, Conservation and Recycling*, no. 156. doi: 10.1016/j.resconrec.2020.104686.

Schumacher, E. F. 1973. *Small Is Beautiful: A Study of Economics as if People Mattered*. New York: HarperCollins Books.

Simone, AbdouMaliq, and Edgar Pieterse. 2017. *New Urban Worlds: Inhabiting Dissonant Times*. Cambridge: Polity Press.

Thieme, Tatiana. 2017. "The Hustle Economy: Informality, Uncertainty, and the Geographies of Getting By." *Progress in Human Geography* 42, no. 4: 529–548.

Thieme, Tatiana. 2021. "'Youth Are Redrawing the Map': Temporalities and Terrains of the Hustle Economy in Mathare, Nairobi." *Africa* 91, no. 1: 35–56.

World Bank Group. 2015. *Addressing the Youth Employment Crisis Needs Urgent Action*, October 13.

DEFORMATION

Remaking Urban Peripheries through
Lateral Comparison

Introduction: Unsettling the Territory

A woman named Melani is the local secretary for the Maja district planning council in the hinterlands of Greater Jakarta, Indonesia. It is a council
that exists in name only, as there is not really a precisely defined district or
much planning of any kind, though there are frenetic building activities
seemingly everywhere and at every scale. The acquisition of land, as well as
its very status, remains largely opaque, as are the interrelationships among
scores of men and women who circulate across the landscape with briefcases
and hardhats, carrying the occasional surveyor's tools. At night convoys of
trucks come from all directions to clear away the debris of a successive string
of failed projects and replace them with the materials that will materialize yet other inflated imaginations. Melani constantly weaves in and out
of construction sites and rice fields on her motorbike, claiming to super-
vise the choreography of factories, apartment blocks, hostels, makeshift
shacks, abandoned interchanges, and leisure parks dancing their way to
each other on a seeming collision course of half-baked finance, overesti-
mated occupancy rates, bankruptcies, and discrepant jurisdictions. When
asked when the "real planning" will begin, when exactly systematic and
strategic development plans will be applied to this periphery replete with
the intense contiguities of both rational and irrational spatial products,
Melani shrugs and says that this would be a matter of *bad form*.

As increasing numbers of urban residents find themselves both volitionally and involuntarily ensconced in such landscapes, the matter of form once again comes to the fore. As the capacity for formatting, for rendering massive amounts of urban data into specific visual templates, constitutes the primary basis of *figuring* what to do with many urban peripheries, the harried and protracted negotiations over how to make hundreds of discrepant "urban projects" fit together would appear out of sync with the amount of computing power applied to smoothing out the jumbled up surfaces of the urban hinterlands. Calculations of the securitization of land value, of floor area ratios, equities, parametric designs, material flow footprints, risk exposures, cost sharing, cross subsidies, labor supply, capital repatriation, and externalities of all kinds can be *rendered* into a form that addresses a wide range of immaterial values, such as sustainability, resilience, environmental harmonization, due diligence, and good governance (Marvin and Luque-Ayala 2017; Lury and Day 2019; Willems and Graham 2019). These renderings are most frequently performed in vast computer-design rendering farms, most usually in China and mobilizing gigantic hard drives, and would appear to be aimed at the consolidation of the form most optimal to any given environment. Yet, despite the sweeping alterations of land and atmosphere, many peripheries seem to persist in their contiguities of discrepant uses and built environments. The viability of extended territories of urbanization does not rest in the replicability of the logics of the city or suburb, but rather of a protracted disentangling of any framework of relationality that might tie the multiple environments and functions of the periphery into a coherent form of appearance and rule (Kipfer 2018).

Deformation is a process of populating space, of continuous supplementing, adding things on, but doing so by means of subtracting the modalities of apparent organization that might tie them together in some clear sense of complementarity and reciprocity. Thus the modalities of "being together" most commonly associated with some of the most marginal of worlds come to predominate the operating systems of large megaregions, most often found, but not exclusively, across the Global South. These modalities actively refuse reciprocal exchange or the elaboration of common frameworks of belonging. Instead, they value exorbitant displays of expenditure, transgressions of apparent rules, raiding, theft, strange alliances, and incessant side-switching, which characterize many locales in Africa's Sahelian and Saharan worlds. They thus become salient points of reference in describing the deformations of contemporary urban peripheries.

While peripheries may have long embodied the proximities of various uses of land and people, their accelerated expansion brings with it the juxtapositions of competing administrative authorities cherry picking specific competencies and jurisdictions, as well as power vacuums in which no institutional structure takes responsibility to provide essential services (Keil 2018). This is a process aided and abetted by new transportation corridors, logistics systems, land seizures, the complicities and competitions among thousands of itinerant developers, state-subsidized megadevelopments, heavily leveraged buyouts of artificially inflated land, infrastructure rollouts, occupations by artisanal farmers, expulsions of polluting industries from urban cores, resettlements of the poor, and massive outlays of what is euphemistically called "affordable housing."

Yet, far from chaos, the multiplicity of these strands, these different inputs performed and funded at various scales and degrees of authorization, manage to provisionally work their way through each other in ways that provide a large measure of autonomy to individual actors and projects. At the same time, however, they necessitate varying experiments of intercalibration involving intricate architectures of brokerage and negotiation (Monte-Mór 2018; Schmid et al. 2018). Deformation, far from being a problem to be solved, is instead an enabling atmosphere of provisionality that suffices as agendas of different actors, *for now*. I emphasize the presentism of such sufficiency, since no actor claims that such a disposition is suited for the long run. But it is precisely that "long run" that remains vague for many actors.

Even for those major real estate developers whose capital sunk costs are high, despite being hedged across numerous kinds and locations of assets, their professed objective is less the short-term profitability of their investments than the need to put "facts on the ground" that advantageously position them to have something to say about what will eventually happen. The built environment, in this instance, then becomes a means of leveraging eventuality; it is imagined that eventually something will take place—its precise shape and function in the present remaining uncertain—and that the objective is to ensure the opportunity to take advantage of that eventuality when the time comes. Here, an active deformation of the terms of value and efficacy are concretized in spatial products, as their present form is simply an occasion or locus through which something, which now is impossible to define or even to speculate about, can be effectively addressed (Halbert and Attuyer 2016; Rutherford 2020).

For many nascent residents of the periphery, a not dissimilar orientation to provisionality also prevails. They often are simply looking for a place to "park"—an aged parent, a collection of belongings, or a set of kids—without spending too much, in order to have some money left to fund lives of more-extensive circulation across the urban region, looking for opportunities that they are unlikely to know of in advance. Here, itineraries of movement tend to supersede those of emplacement, even as nearly everyone needs a place to at least "park." In part, the periphery embodies a growing sense that livelihood is not secured through a continuous, incremental "upward" trajectory. It has less to do with piecing together a career or steady employment, but more with an opportunistic, often impulsive drive to "keep on going," to make one thing lead to another, all while holding in abeyance any sense of discretionary judgment about which thing is better than another. This does not mean that such judgments are not being made all the time, as jobs and situations can be quickly discarded as not being "enough." But the ability to dissociate particular trajectories of circulation or particular occupations, and to dissociate ways of making money and networks from overarching frameworks of value, is often seen as necessary in order to make the most of the situation at hand. For these frameworks are, too, often seen as *bad form.*

Finding a Proper Form

Urbanization has always been a matter of form. For in order to navigate the intensive relationalities of urban life, form was necessary as a delineation of space, as a means of precluding matters from simply becoming a blur, to maintain the sense of actors' being able to go from "here" to "there," and of crafting particular domains that enabled actors to know what was theoretically expected of them and what to actually expect.

For relationships are always moving across other relationships, turning themselves inside out and outside in, opening up possibilities and closing other ones down. At the same time, relations are twisting each other into particular kinds of knots. Sometimes they act as analogies or necessary contradictions for each other so as to prefigure particular kinds of relations as being essential to the exclusion of others. For example, there is no inevitable or necessary reason why kinship relations should be the predominant locus around which households are formed. But they become critical metaphors for each other. Kinship is turned into a household that continues to "turn" to kinship for its moral, expressive underpinning (Cooper 2017). Similarly, neighborhoods adapt "familial" feelings and obligations (Wagner 2018).

Yet, relations can unfold without overarching reasons for doing so (Strathern 2011). They can seemingly expand to encompass all kinds of actors and situations. But if relations are to be activated and recognized as operative in the day-to-day lives of given individuals and societies, there must be some means for them to be recognized. This occurs only if they assume a particular *form*, a particular aesthetic that enables them to properly appear, and to be properly recognized.

In cities, residents often initiate particular activities, such as making markets, improving the built environment, managing festivals, or undertaking small entrepreneurial activities as a way of signaling, of making visible a willingness to explore collaborations that go beyond the function of these activities themselves. These activities become devices for finding a proper form capable of eliciting an exchange of perspectives. They explore ways of being together that rely on making the relationships visible in the moment. But they also can serve as a platform for residents to feel out the possibilities of collaboration that are not yet and perhaps never will be visible. As such, what they have in common is the interplay of the visible and invisible. For it is not just vision that is at work, but also atmospheres of feeling and intuitive experimentation with relational devices and interfaces that will often lack permanence and solidity.

What are the contemporary implications of such relational economies whose definition and scope may never be fully known? How do they play out in conditions where the dispossession of belonging, identity, and assets are very concrete? How do urban inhabitants mediate between the compulsion to turn bodies and lives into logistical instruments—being at the "right place at the right time" unimpeded by history—and then to slow circulation down sufficiently to be able to reflect on their own actions? How do they maintain some ground in order to build a sense of memory and a narrative about where they come from? For such are the means to anticipate possible forward trajectories in order to decide to act, as opposed to succumbing to paralysis or constant anxiety.

The elaboration of the social that mediates these questions, then, cannot simply be the implementation of specific laws or structures of commonality. Rather, the social as an experiential milieu is an economic matter of combining whatever lies at hand, whether the elements seem to go together or not; of combining ways of tying some things down and letting other things go. So the form of things is something more provisional than fixed, more of a "setting up" of possibilities than a frame that holds and defines them.

Combinations, therefore, are not the products of prescribed formulas; they are not pieces of a puzzle predesigned to fit with others. Rather, combinations reflect expenditures of effort, of an often inexplicable affording of interest, enthusiasm, and patience on the part of individuals and groups to processes and events that they do not fully understand or view as relevant to them. In the context of urban life, with so many bodies, events, dimensions, and transactions to pay attention to, all of which touch human and nonhuman residents in so many varying ways, the dilemma is always one of alignment, of how one operates in the "crossfires" of intersecting agendas and built environments. To be sure, adaptations cannot rely on defensive or immunological maneuvers alone; they cannot simply retreat behind high walls, even as gated communities might act otherwise. Adaptations also require active assertions of emplacement, opportunism, belonging, and even risking in the face of all the things that can draw a person into various associations beyond their control. *It is matter of things extending themselves to each other.*

Strange Forms of Time

Extended urbanization as a process of urbanization extending itself to and through various modalities of existence also entails a reconsideration of the notion of "form."

For extension is not simply the expansionism of a coherent set of mechanisms for capital accumulation, not simply the incursion of the city on a periphery. It is not merely the reformatting of space according to a coherent set of regulations, investments, or spatial products. Not only the more-extensive captures and captivations of bodies along with their efforts and imaginations. Extension is a process of *figuring out(ward)*, beyond the familiar tropes of urbanization, beyond the city-form—a process of divergent histories, agendas, and practices "feeling each other out," albeit with discrepant resources and power available to them.

Form is the product of politics, of who gets to see and say what. The extensiveness of urbanization, then, also entails the ways in which it is extended across the perceptions and geographies of those who have long been either disqualified as insufficiently urban or who have, through the work they have done to support the reflexive consideration of urban form, implicitly generated other forms removed from visibility.

While it is inevitable that comparisons of *new territories* associated with our global urban age will revolve around efforts to maintain "the urban" as being a universal object of geographic focus and, as such, also to constitute the horizon-limit for any urban theory's revisability, any definitive identification of a given place or process as "urban" remains *both* elusive *and* possible. When Eduardo Kohn's indigenous Runa collaborators in Ecuador identify the vast surrounding rain forest, the domain of the spirit masters, as an underground "Quito" (referring to the country's capital), they are pointing to form as "a strange but nonetheless worldly process of pattern production and propagation . . . one whose peculiar generative logic necessarily comes to permeate living things (human and nonhumans) as they harness it" (Kohn 2013, 20). While this forest has long been important to rubber and oil extraction, and has in recent years become intensely financialized in terms of both its "subtraction from extraction" in carbon credits and the speculation on the politics of its continued extraction, its urbanization is not simply the degree of its articulation to various elsewheres. It also rests in its being experienced as "urban" by those who reside there.

Kohn emphasizes the spontaneous, self-organizing apperception and propagation of iconic associations in ways that can dissolve some of the boundaries we usually recognize between insides and outsides. These are not symbolic connections requiring conventions of cultural meaning that generate and pattern differences. Rather, form blurs the lines of distinction as each action and entity flows into the other without cause or effect, without knowing what happened first. The ways particular sounds are associated with images connoting danger, and the ways that subsequent reactions are signals for still others to alter their courses of behavior, in turn precipitate repetitions of the original sound.

Details here are less marks of distinction than they are conveyors of thoughts and feelings "passing through," of resonance or sympathetic charge. So, when Kohn says we no longer ask thought to produce a specific outcome or "return," our observations of things—what we "sense" in the world and in our minds—become self-similar iterations. Even as Amazonian forests were for centuries objects of extractions and ruination, the capture of wealth could only take place through accessing associations—that is, the conjunctions of physical and biotic patterning in which this wealth was ensconced. The ways in which Ecuador's rivers were shaped by the forest embankments were, in turn, shaped by the flows of the rivers' generating specific settings that enabled the growth of rubber trees. It is through this very logic of patterning that the Runa people experience the forest as an underground Quito, as an urban domain. While the "actual" Quito may look on this forest as a domain of resource exploitation that is crucial to its own urban development, the Runa look on that Quito as an undeveloped city, a rudimentary imitation of the forest's vast "urban fabric."

Here, the value of form is not that of a Platonic ideal, but instead a tendency of matter emerging from its own complexity; it is the way that embodied sense and potential is taken up as a kind of living archive, the propagation of self-similarity, constraints, and potentials (how we *inhabit form and generate form as a way to inhabit*—that is, how we are finding, dreaming, extracting something, and anticipating how the world anticipates me anticipating it) (see Amin and Thrift 2016).

How does this "cat and mouse game" of mutual anticipation play out in the peripheries of today's mega-urban regions? What are the terms of comparison through which city residents attempt to forge linkages between their pasts and their futures, so as to develop a sense of efficacy and purpose for their actions?

Emerging Situations of Comparison

In Indonesia, across the Jakarta urban region, residents are being uprooted, evicted, priced-out, and sometimes even volitionally relocating themselves in more affordable or more advantageous positions. In many instances the relocations are provisional in that they do not reflect even a medium-term commitment to specific places, but rather an interim platform from which to further assess and act on possible strategic engagements with work and other opportunities, themselves usually provisional. Even for those evicted from positions that reflected substantial expenditure of time and available resources to stabilize, many will return to these locations or elsewhere better situated for their livelihood practices, but with highly reduced capacities to deploy.

Across these situations inevitably multiple comparative moments arise when residents attempt not only to assess their present situations in terms of what has come before, but also to detach significantly and willfully from the affective qualities and cognitive understandings of those places of "origins." As a result, the objects of comparison for the future draw from a much more diffuse field of experiences and factors. In other words, in attempting to assess the terms of a viable future urban life, many Jakarta residents seek to constitute the terms of reference from their own ongoing and provisional itineraries across the region, deferring any rapid judgments on the value of particular residential locations, employment opportunities, and social affiliations for the moment—a moment that is often prolonged in order to experiment with yet another arrangement for commuting, job-sharing, forming a household, or taking advantage of an entrepreneurial opportunity.

This "short-termism" may be compensated by the reiteration of particular value orientations, such as are reflected in the surge of "traditional" Islamic practice currently under way in Jakarta, where residents sometimes talk about the need for having a "maximum exposure" to Islam. Events such as recent tsunamis in Indonesia are explained by the over-exposure of women's bodies to the *dunya* (earthly concerns rather than that of God). Or other residents cite chicken farms that play recorded Qur'anic verses 24/7 in the chicken coops so that every moment of their egg production is maximally exposed to God. Rather than unfolding a problematic that considers how particular things and facets of life are related to changing vectors of Islamic practice, much of the desire involved in the current demand for the Islamification of Indonesian society centers on finding an overarching form, a total subsumption of particularities, where there is a collapse of distinctions and thus of acts of relating.

On the other hand, reference is also made to another mode of "maximum exposure"—a process of deforming, in which things and events are treated as being detached from relational frameworks. To be maximally exposed to one's surrounds means deferring any tendency to tie details down to some ready explanation or practice of comparison. Grounded in a perception that multiple forces are at work in any particular situation, some Jakartans express the exigency of remaining open to the various and unanticipated ways in which these forces interact. This is particularly the case in extended regions of the city where the arrangement of the built environment and land uses are described as being "all over the place," making it difficult for residents to develop coherent narratives about where and how "things are headed." Characterized by different temporalities of development and decline, as well as retrofit and ruin at different rhythms, exposure here entails an openness to engage one's surrounds in experimental trial-and-error fashion, rather than placing a great investment of time and money into one way of doing things.

Here is a "wait and see" attitude that attempts to establish terms and convictions of viability from a series of improvisations generating a continuously shifting terrain of comparisons. The spatial and political economic transformations under way in Jakarta thus act on the sensoria of residents—the way they perceive, feel, and interpret their conditions in such a manner as to engage those conditions as a process that is "yet to clearly unfold." The details of their daily itineraries are less viewed as indicative of specifically defined futures that would suggest clear courses of action, based on what they knew from their prior residential situations, and viewed more as entities still in motion, yet to be "settled" within any framework. Instead of provoking stasis and an inability to take decisive courses of action, individual enactment in an environment of detached details is seen as a function of paying attention to the "background." In many discussions with residents in Jakarta, I, as both researcher and fellow resident, would often hear them refer to this notion of the "background" as the justification for their actions, as well as the object of their attentiveness.

Comparison's Plurality

For a still small, but not insignificant, number of middle-class residents, comparison is less the exigency of *relating* things, of determining what any given experience or situation has to do with others, but more a matter of keeping things out of fixed relationships—a refusal to provide accounts, either to oneself or to others, about how one's life course at any particular moment connects to those of others. Of course, in everyday conversations and transactions, individuals constantly offer their sense of things, relating what they have heard elsewhere to what is being reported by friends, neighbors, and other associates. The daily pragmatics of household management requires constant conventional comparisons in order to stay afloat. As such, these quotidian comparisons are essential to the performance of everyday life. But simultaneous with these performances is the figuring of a relationship to the intensely uncertain trajectories of urban change—about what kinds of practices are likely to work in the future (Bou Akr 2018).

Just as police usually call for backup before commencing an uncertain operation, city residents, too, sometimes invoke the need for "backup," not so much to confirm or legitimate their actions, but instead to have someone or something familiar, well-worn, in close proximity to stop them from inventing some outlandish explanation for their behavior.

There are also more "lateral comparisons" that cross apparently incommensurable domains from which are derived unanticipated potentialities of action that do not belong exclusively to any domain, even though they might seem to emerge from them. Such comparisons address the continuous question of "what *could* be done, what else *could* be taking place at this moment." As Maurer (2005) points out in his work on finance, "Islamic banking and Ithaca HOURS [an alternative currency] became necessary to one another in my own efforts to restage what I saw them doing. They do not 'represent' each other or 'shed light' on each other so much as they draw on each other—but only sometimes, contingently and laterally. They metastasize into one another, but that metastasis is not essential to either of them, nor is it causal. For each overlaps and interconnects with other things, too" (2005, 10). The domains that are brought together unfold according to their own logics and in a relationship of "non-taxonomic differentiation"—in other words, a process of individuating that is not identifiable through preexistent categories nor by the intervention of some external causal and explanatory force outside the relationship itself.

For example, as particular territories of religious expression extend themselves across Jakarta, consolidating the affective and temporal investments of some residents, and as identifications and livelihood practices, at the same time, become more dispersed and particular, the trajectories of these territories do not stand in opposition to each other. Neither can they be construed as either complementary or potentially conciliatory, even though all these dispositions may be at work within the relationship. Rather, there is a *disjunctive synthesis*. The attempts to subsume more and more aspects of life to a religious coding system, and the simultaneous tendencies of territories of identification to become more dispersed and diffuse, thus subverting existing interpretive frameworks, are two trajectories that play off each other in a simultaneous process of continuous becoming. What ensues in their relationship is not determined by some external "coordinator," even as both respond to events outside the relationship itself.

Of course, other domains could be engaged as facets of any such *multiplicity*—such as the continuously remade fabric of kinship relations, the complex calibrations of activities that constitute the "marketing" of essential commodities, and so forth. Relations may seem contradictory or complementary. Calling for Sharia law to be followed in everyday life throughout the city would seem to contradict advocacy of noninterference in how communities choose to compose relations of property and governance; individual entrepreneurship would seem to complement the belief in individual freedom of choice. Each object of advocacy views the relationship according to its own nature, which then has different implications for how each unfolds in relationship to the other and what it allows residents to do. Yet, at Jakarta's peripheries, this is often not the case. Seeming contradictions and complementarity become something else. Rather, they are characterized as relationships of internal presupposition, of intensive multiperspectival variations largely organized according to a series of refrains, ebbs, and flows—rhythms of engagement, deployment, and affiliation. Sharia will be more or less applied to varying situations; individual choice will be melded with experiments in collective ownership. Here it is the rhythm of alterations, as various agendas become intertwined and disentangled, that is important.

Again, such multiplicities coalesce around the question of "what could be done?" What enables knocking on doors, staying out late, facilitating or obviating the need for protracted circulations across the region, that provides space of anonymity or filiation? What defers or elicits obligations, or extends a sense of familiarity, so that invasive questions can be kept to a minimum? Moving back from the peripheries to some obdurate neighborhoods in the urban core, I want to take note of youth residing in the long-implanted districts of the center of Jakarta—those who live roughly grouped around the Senen rail station who have long been seen as the most problematic residents in the city. These districts are the most densely populated in Indonesia, and are thickly packed with the byproducts of many heterogeneous backgrounds, practices, and aspirations. These are tough places for tough people and to date have largely, though not exclusively, been immune to the enormous transformations of the city's urban core—transformations that push large numbers to Jakarta's peripheries.

Performing Multiplicity: A Counter-ethics of Comparison

For many years I have worked with a community theater group in Kampung Rawa, a neighborhood where family members take turns sleeping, where so-called informal sectors are equally overcrowded, and where having the name of this district on one's resident card practically guarantees being shut out of many kinds of employment. At the same time, Kampung Rawa is far from being a slum, and while many of its residents are poor, others self-describe themselves as "middle class" and are more than willing to publicize certain proof of it.

Although districts such as Kampung Rawa and the neighboring districts of Galur, Tanah Tinggi, and Sentiong are sites of vast, intertwined productive activity, a continuous influx of new residents, and the remaking of micro-developers, the people living there have a pervasive sense that their districts are being left behind. They are simultaneously positioned in a need to demonstrate broader articulations to the rest of the urban region and to intensify their own perceived singularities, as places apart where they can be considered capable of performing particular "jobs" that cannot be done elsewhere. Thus, there is the continuous elaboration of projects of normalization that attempt to demonstrate the ways in which residents of these areas are really just like others, while coexisting with projects that remake the compositions of the illicit, transgressive, and idiosyncratic. These are projects of inclusive disjunction—both equally necessary and spurring tensions that absorb a great deal of energy, not in terms of reconciling these tensions but in continuously recalibrating them.

Thus, the intensive Islamification of some neighborhoods can take place, bringing with it the exigencies of establishing standardized versions of normality but in contexts in which many nonmarried household heads continue to live. While neighborhoods everywhere are replete with various contradictions and exceptions to the rule, I am less interested in the existence of such contradictions than I am in the ways in which disparate territories of expression and becoming are inhabited, across different temporal sequences, so that residents can engage in comparative work that is oriented to identifying the possibilities of action within the domains that they must pass through each and every day.

As one of the subdistrict local authorities has donated space behind its main building for the community theater group, participants are subject to its scrutinizing gaze, imposing implicit limits on how participants gather with each other. The daily ritual of performing the Muslim late-afternoon prayer before holding rehearsals in the parking lot of the facility not only meets a daily requirement but also demonstrates fidelity to a religious ethos that provides a substantial amount of cover for what then ensues inside the rehearsal space. Not dissimilarly, the act of performing *dawah*—acts of popular religious dissemination—enables participants to go door to door to inform the other residents of a wide range of nonreligious events taking place there, as well. Their theater training has instilled a great deal of confidence in the participants that is often generalized in their mutual participation in meetings and events that have nothing to do with theater, enabling them to speak up about issues that they otherwise would not have the temerity or confidence to comment on.

The ability of these youth to move in and out of different territories of expression, each with its own incommensurable logics of operation, regarding the territories as multiple relations, enables them to configure possibilities of temporary autonomous actions that cover their vulnerabilities in terms of how they are perceived by various household, local, and institutional authorities. They ply the edges of sectoral divides, and have managed to entice young "religious enforcers," criminal syndicates, Islamic schoolteachers, retailers, and factory workers into the performance space to act out scenarios that on the streets would otherwise lead to violent confrontation. Perhaps more important, they conceptualize modes of theatrical intervention in a wide range of public spaces—deploying ways of questioning, demonstrating respect, or putting people in touch with each other—that are not recognizable as theatrical performance. Conversely, the operations of an important all-night produce market not far away have been staged as an explicit theater piece inside the gymnasium of a Catholic school.

All these activities are acts of comparison not aimed for the discernment of likenesses or divergence, nor for generalizability or interdependence. Rather, they are prospectively aimed for "what could be done" in circumstances that tend to render actions evaluable either in terms of the singularities they contribute to this area of Jakarta, the degrees of normalization attained, or their capacity to criticize and diminish a wide range of actions. Comparisons are not retrospective judgments in search of modulating existent dispositions, but instead are speculative practices aimed at inducing "strange compositions" of potentialities from within circumstances seemingly adverse to them and, alternately, at identifying ways of being "regular" at the margins of urban life.

In a city where many frequently talk about a limited horizon, of diminished aspirations in the face of their having reached the limit of their capacities to consume and feeling rampant uncertainty about where the region is headed in terms of its ability to provide work, housing, and basic services in the face of political and climate turbulence, many residents with whom I work or whom I personally know constantly invoke the need to keep their options open, to approach their situation in different ways. The comparisons they make, then, are less to the past, less to thinking comparatively across already semicongealed scenarios, and more toward ways of thinking across disparate landscapes and situations in order to provisionally piece together itineraries for fulfilling responsibilities and providing necessary degrees of stability while, at the same time, engaging their surrounds as a field of improvisations of sites and functions that could be composed in different ways. It is a form of subtraction, of saying "no" to that which is familiar, while at the same time not dispensing with familiarity altogether.

Here I am talking in terms perhaps similar to what Michel Foucault (1986) referred to as counter-memory: where what transpires in the present is not necessarily the coming-into-recognition and relation of the past. A useful example of this is when Foucault talks about a table across which various objects are spread. Rather than the deployment of the human sciences as a method of bringing things into relation, what needs to be thought is their non-relation. Whereas those sciences conceptualized the forces that generated relations, formed political arrangement, and then enabled the resultant polity to acknowledge itself as a living entity in order for it to invoke the necessity of taking care for its own endurance, Foucault talked about ungrounded arts of existence. These were arts not necessarily directed toward the sustenance of life, nor to the constitution of spaces that could be recognized or communicated, but instead to ways of existing that operate outside the proper functioning of the whole.

The Presuppositions of Comparative Maneuvers

I recall my neighbors in the working-class and lower-middle-class district of Tebet, in South Jakarta. There were clearly push factors that were at work in motivating the decisions of many residents there to move to the distant peripheries of the capital city. Rampant tensions between the maintenance of residential spaces and the conversion of those spaces into more-lucrative commercial uses brought a greater influx of flow-through traffic. The increasingly common practices of converting part of one's house into short-term rentals dissipated local social solidarities through the influx of migrant labor. The locational advantages of the district and its proximity to major transportation thoroughfares also made it subject to excessive speculative investment.

By contrast, the district was replete with interlocking small enterprises, markets, workshops, and social institutions, largely the products of the district residents' own efforts. The growth of incomes and a heightened sense of well-being across the district was largely a reflection of the residents' capacity to find multiple and innovative ways of working together. Thus, decisions to vacate their former homes, despite the pressures enumerated above, could be construed as self-defeating, as many households wound up purchasing small apartments in developments that were quickly built, provided uncertain ownership status, and sometimes lay at a great distance from work and services.

In conversations with many of my former neighbors, I sensed the need that many felt to reorient their attentions. They were spending too much effort attempting to resolve more-frequent local disputes. Neighbors were increasingly perceived as parasitic rather than cooperants. Increases in property tax, though usually not onerous, meant making too many small adjustments in household expenditures. In sum, residency was perceived as excessive work that deferred attention away from what was necessary in order to have a larger view about what viable livelihoods would look like for the future. Nearly all the residents who left their old neighborhoods behind believed that their present relocation was not going to persist for long; nearly all saw their present places of residence as a platform from which to maximize their engagement with the larger region. The need they felt was to find an affordable way to instantiate the bare necessities so as to invest time, effort, and resources in trying out several options. These might include various ways of commuting, of working, of moving through multiple short-term employment contracts, and of investing time in trying to rebuild social networks composed of more-heterogeneous actors and locations. To decenter one's focus away from local intensities, away from the details of how to thoroughly institutionalize one's presence within a given set of circumstances, was seen as necessary in order to expand one's focus and possible playing field. This expansion of field was then what was referred to as *"the background."*

These active attentions to background sit uneasily with those others that focus relentlessly on the vagaries of staying in place. Every afternoon two dozen middle-aged men huddle at one of the several coffee shops in the underground mall of one of the more infamous vertical housing developments in Jakarta, called Kalibata City. I myself moved here, like several of my neighbors, when my lease expired in Tebet. There are men in the area that all carry almost identical cheap, black shoulder bags that are never removed and opened only occasionally to retrieve a sheaf of random documents that is quickly perused and then put back in place. These are brokers often attempting to sell apartments under the table, part of an extensive network circumventing the management of official developers. A pervasive air of melancholy is punctured only by passing security guards, when everyone proceeds to the outdoor smoking area a few feet away or when the lines for KFC intrude on their space. Like so many Jakartans these days, these men are on standby, constantly browsing their WhatsApp accounts and appearing at the ready to disperse on "important missions" at a moment's notice. But these missions never seem to materialize, and so they appear stuck in an interminable wait. In fact, their attentions are usually centered on attaining a certificate of full ownership for their apartments—some of which they live in, while they rent out others.

Many people in the neighborhood experience interminable delays in this process. There often is uncertainty as to how many years remain on the developer's leasehold, doubt regarding the governmental jurisdiction under which the development falls, and legal ambiguities in terms of what full ownership might mean if, in all likelihood, authorization for continued residency in the complex is not renewed for an additional twenty-year period after 2030. In other cafés across Kalibata City it is not uncommon to see other men and women spending days with their laptops open, some engaged in actual renumerated work, but most using the screen as the primary interface with the city, searching for various "answers" to their everyday-life dilemmas.

So proclivities to reorient sensoria to a generativity of the *background* is certainly not a univocal trend, but is situated along with other "expressions of territory." Yet it is a significant stratum that introduces an orientation to comparison that it would be useful to think through, in terms of how certain residents navigate contemporary urban conditions.

What Is the Background?

So the question is, what is this *background* as both the seeming vanishing point of comparison as well as a field of continuous comparative becomings? Everything that takes form emerges from a background, and then form itself becomes a background. While processes of urbanization may seem to be governed through form, and through the formatting of multiple interactions among things, form is less the inscription of definition than a *modality of holding*. For the question is how to hold things in place long enough so that interaction might take place, so a relationship can occur. It also means how to hold things together so they do not veer in every direction and instead just wander off. If there is no overarching compulsion for things to relate to each other, if there is no grand design through which things would automatically take their place, if there is no inevitable disposition to which things are inclined, then holding things together for the time being becomes critical.

But each holding implicitly knows that its instrumentality is geared to the "time being," and that any composite being produced through the holding of things accorded momentary definition in the being-held is not sustainable in its own terms. The holding is to make something happen, to generate a resourcefulness that is to be deployed elsewhere, that finds its feet and existence in moving on. The need to hold is neither to confine nor to defend but rather to convey, translate, and extend (Gad et al. 2014).

Form, then, in line with Eduardo Kohn (2013), is a spontaneous, self-organizing understanding and propagation of iconic associations in ways that can dissolve some of the boundaries we usually recognize between insides and outsides. For when we no longer ask thought for a "return," we are left with self-similar iterations. *We are part of a vast web of interwoven tissue*, part of the stitch-and-weave. The value of form is not that of a Platonic ideal, but instead a tendency of matter emerging from its own complexity; it is the mimetic archives of embodied sense and potential, the propagation of self-similarity, constraints, and potentials. We are always *inside form*—that is to say, we are always finding, dreaming, and extracting something, as well as anticipating how the world anticipates me anticipating it.

The background is that space where and those moments when things are about to take form, things that are forming but have yet to coagulate into specific bounded constellations that can be definitively counted or that count for something in particular. *Deforming*, rather than being a process of taking things apart, is actually the process of things feeling themselves out, of reaching toward and away from each other, circling, extending, not knowing for sure what to make of any particular encounter, not dwelling in one place for very long but passing on, being passed on. Things indeed are taking shape, occupying form but in a way in which many different futures are possible. There is a sense of open-endedness that takes advantage of the potentials that past forms had posited but then were closed off, interrupted.

A city like Jakarta is a landscape of contours, vectors, gradations, and swirls. As the city took shape, the emerging density of things and encounters was based on both the opening out onto extended terrain as well as a folding back, a constant involution of inward and outward focus, of holding things in place long enough for a view, a perspective, to be constituted, but not so long that agencies atrophied or imploded. Urban form may have concretized a map of such centrifugal and centripetal movements, a representation of functions and sectors and how they were populated. But this necessitated a background of deformed things actively responding to each other, recalibrating their actions and maneuvers, of hedging their bets, of both luring and repelling.

It is clear that contemporary urban life such as that throughout Jakarta produces enlarged itineraries for many residents. Their search for work, shelter, and resources usually entails extended commutes, and infrastructural inputs provide platforms for heightened mobility. So even through the bodies of residents themselves, disparate dimensions, places, and sensibility are being intersected, despite the forces of segregation that also characterize contemporary urban life. Yes, cities are increasingly formatted, surveyed, and regulated through parametric and infrastructural design, preemptive governmentality, and official computation. Such formatting would seem to specify how distinct components and residencies are to be related to each other and how the outcomes will be measured. Yet there is also a surfeit of uncertainty as to what else might be taking (its) place in a process of urbanization that seems to compel everything to relate. While the formatting of space to maximize its logistical potentials appears totalizing, the preponderance of slippages, leakages, and chokepoints would also suggest other trajectories of forms in the making (Jensen 2011).

As a long-time collaborator whom I know in Jakarta, named Fadli, puts it: *"I think that in all of my train rides across Jakarta, all of the things I have to do and all of the things that I just end up doing for little reason at all, that I am being exposed to something I can't quite talk about clearly, but I know it will change my life, and this is what I want. Even if it is a wild ride full of risks at every turn, something out there holds it all together."* So the background I have in mind is that of incipience, but an incipience that is always there, in the background, of things leaning to and from, of veering toward and away, regardless of their current formatting, regardless of their participation in a forming underway and of a momentary holding off of sense.

People necessarily compare, but the comparison takes place among things and possibilities that are not on equal footing or in any clearly discernible relation to each other. The actualities of what is perceived as being a "concrete situation," as seeming to be the "situation at hand" that must be dealt with as "the reality," are upended by what else might be taking its place, some other arrangement of common sense, as this very potentiality is, itself, shaped by the purportedly empirical and verifiable rendition of the situation at hand. It is not that each qualifies the other or undermines the forcefulness of each's particular ontological status. Rather, the simultaneity generates an opening of comparative practice concretized in the small experiments that residents undertake in the variations, however slight, that they perform in their everyday itineraries. These constant adjustments of subjectivities enacted during commutes, errands, visits, and moving from one place to another—what Doreen Lee (2015) has called "absolute traffic"—constitutes a terrain of real citizenship, of people tending to each other without fixed preconceptions.

Conclusion: Already Gone

Residents of any city in the world may ask themselves "Why are we here and not there? Why are we facing the situation that we do? Why don't we have our basic needs met? Why are life and livelihood so uncertain?" Many different explanatory frameworks can be legitimately applied to such queries. Still, the pursuit of comparison that implicitly frames these questions seems always to fall short of engendering confidence in those who ask them. The ethos of neoliberalism emphasizes a practice of constant comparison—"how do I stack up in relation to others?"—as effectively being a motor for making the body a nonstop machine of effort and improvement. The more one compares, the more one falls short of attaining any sense of confidence in the present. Comparison may be deferred in celebratory acts of either self-inflation or self-effacement, though this maneuver simply amplifies the problem of rendering oneself comparable in a larger number of domains.

Another maneuver might be centered on *deformation*—that is, not to ask "why are we here and not there?" but instead to ask what does the "here" look like, now that we are already "there"? In other words, where situations are lived with as if they have already been vacated for somewhere else—a "somewhere else" that has not necessarily been made visible or even knowable within the terms that one would ordinarily apply to constituting a perspective on a "here," on a present situation. Here, comparison is not only more *lateral*—in terms of crossing fields of concern and sectoral domains—but is a means of curating provisional interstices among dispositions, trajectories, life situations, physical locations, and livelihood formations that permit a simultaneously retrospective and prospective view on things.

This is a way of mobilizing a past that is not yet over—at least not in the terms in which it was experienced up until now—and of offering a speculative view of something that has not yet concretized or formed into a solid destination, that is still coming into form. In this space, then, the extensivity of the urban is expressed as a "lending of hands," a disjunctive inclusion of elements—a yet-improvised past and an unformed future—that lend each other their own incommensurable perspectives as a kind of "decision-support system." Such a system provides a means to enable residents in volatile urban climates to hedge their bets, to attain momentary "holds" on fluid circumstances, and then to try to make the best of things. While not being a substitute for large-scale political mobilization and change, these are nevertheless important maneuvers to defer its foreclosure. As many residents of Jakarta express it, "they suffice for now." They enable them not to *settle for* anything on offer—anything "fronted" as secure, appropriate, or affordable. For now, peripheries are to remain unstable, deformed, even if prospects for long-term sustainability may be in question, or indeed may *be* question.

References

Amin, Amin, and Nigel Thrift. 2016. *Seeing Like a City.* London: Polity.

Bou Akr, Hiba. 2018. *For the War Yet to Come: Planning Beirut's Frontiers.* Stanford, CA: Stanford University Press.

Cooper, Melinda. 2017. *Family Values: Between Neoliberalism and the New Social Conservatism.* Brooklyn, NY: Zone Books.

Foucault, Michel. 1986. *The History of Sexuality, Volume 3: The Care of the Self.* Translated by Robert Hurley. New York: Random House.

Gad, Christopher, Casper Bruun Jensen, and Brit Ross Winthereik. 2014. "Practical Ontologies: Worlds in Anthropology and STS." *Naturecultures* 3: 67–86.

Halbert, Ludovic, and Katia Attuyer. 2016. "Introduction: The Financialization of Urban Production: Conditions, Mediations and Transformations." *Urban Studies* 53, no. 7: 1347–1361.

Jensen, Casper Bruun. 2011. "Comparative Relativism: Symposium on an Impossibility." *Common Knowledge* 17, no. 1: 1–12.

Keil, Roger. 2018. "Extended Urbanization, 'Disjunct Fragments' and Global Suburbanisms." *Environment and Planning D: Society and Space* 36, no. 3: 494–511.

Kipfer, Stefan. 2018. "Pushing the Limits of Urban Research: Urbanization, Pipelines and Counter-colonial Politics." *Environment and Planning D: Society and Space* 36, no. 3: 474–493.

Kohn, Eduardo. 2013. *How Forests Think: Toward an Anthropology Beyond the Human.* Berkeley: University of California Press.

Lee, Doreen. 2015. "Absolute Traffic: Infrastructural Aptitude in Urban Indonesia." *International Journal of Urban and Regional Research* 39, no. 2: 234–250.

Lury, Celia, and Sophie E. Day. 2019. "Algorithmic Personalization as a Mode of Individuation." *Theory, Culture and Society* 36, no. 2: 17–37.

Marvin, Simon, and Andrés Luque-Ayala. 2017. "Urban Operating Systems: Diagramming the City." *International Journal of Urban and Regional Research* 41: 84–103.

Maurer, Bill. 2005. *Mutual Life, Limited: Islamic Banking, Alternative Currencies, Lateral Reason.* Princeton, NJ: Princeton University Press.

Monte-Mór, Roberto Luís. 2018. "Urbanisation, Sustainability and Development: Contemporary Complexities and Diversities in the Production of Urban Space." In *Emerging Urban Spaces*, edited by Philipp Horn, Paola Alfaro d'Alencon, and Ana Claudia Duarte Cardoso, 201–216. Cham, Switzerland: Springer International.

Rutherford, Jonathan. 2020. *Redeploying Urban Infrastructure: The Politics of Urban Social-Technical Futures.* London: Palgrave.

Schmid, Christian, Ozan Karaman, Naomi C. Hanakata, Pascal Kallenberger, Anne Kockelkorn, Lindsay Sawyer, Monika Streule, and Kit Ping Wong. 2018. "Towards a New Vocabulary of Urbanisation Processes: A Comparative Approach." *Urban Studies* 55, no. 1: 19–52.

Strathern, Marilyn. 2011. "Binary License." *Common Knowledge* 17, no. 1: 87–103.

Wagner, Roy. 2018. "The Reciprocity of Perspectives." *Social Anthropology* 26, no. 4: 502–510.

Willems, Thijs, and Connor Graham. 2019. "The Imagination of Singapore's Smart Nation as Digital Infrastructure: Rendering (Digital) Work Invisible." *East Asian Science, Technology and Society* 13, no. 4: 511–536.

EDGE SYNTAX

Vocabularies for Violent Times

> A vocabulary is a specific kind of knowledge assemblage and interven-
> tion. Its etymological roots lie in the act of giving a name to things, just
> as its contemporary meaning underscores the need to expand the "range
> of words" available to us. Both are means to make a range of realities
> intelligible, visible and relevant. Vocabularies, in one sense, are maps of
> different life-worlds of knowledge, including their hierarchies.
>
> GAUTAM BHAN, "NOTES ON A SOUTHERN URBAN PRACTICE," 2019

Over the past ten years I've been part of research collaborations exploring
micro-economies on streets in urban peripheries across the United Kingdom, in places where jobs are hard to come by and the impacts of austerity governance are sorely felt. We've been compelled by questions of how
the asymmetries of global migration overlap with the ongoing ferocities of
urban marginalization, and which types of diverse economies emerge in
this multi-scalar constellation. It has been a tumultuous decade, marked
by the brutal intersection of human residualization and racialization that
has played out in the everyday life of urban peripheries with devastating
consequences. Streets in the "edge territories" (Hall 2021, 59) of U.K. cities make visible the compounded impacts of the state and market shatter-
ing of infrastructures of affordability, support, and dignity. The systemic
undermining of infrastructures that sustain meaningful and reasonably
secure prospects to make life and livelihoods has been propelled through
combined forces of residualization.

Profound urban inequalities across the U.K. have been heightened by dramatic reductions of public care forged through austerity governance, where the burden of state deficit following the 2008 financial crisis was disproportionately borne by the most deprived sectors of society. The exacerbation of inequality has been further advanced by the global financialization of urban property markets that capitalizes on the speculative potential of urban margins, evidenced in the sale of affordable public housing and assets by local authorities in an attempt to shore up their reduced budgets. Over the same period, we've witnessed the hurtling of the labor market toward casualization and self-employment, with impacts especially pronounced in racialized and minoritized groups. Such overlapping processes of diminution compel us to think about a lifeworld of work in the urban peripheries in which enduring borders, long working hours, and escalating rentals prevail (Hall 2021). The edge, therefore, regarded as an acutely precarious and lively assemblage, is not simply a physical location but also a structural, material, and psychological relation to power. We've explored the commonplace banality of the street in relation to what Stuart Hall encapsulates as its "improvised gestures" (Hall and Schwarz 2018, 7). This requires an engagement with the edge as neither a peripheral nor a minority condition, but instead as a space through which the violent syntax of multiple dispossessions occurs alongside lively acts of refusal.

From the street we learn of a variety of vocabularies of making work and repurposing space. In this chapter I pull to the foreground different ways of communicating or "giving a name" to the edge in order to contest processes of displacement and to "expand the range of words" (Bhan 2019, 640) available to us to think about work and the kinds of attainable space required to make a living. The research collaborations I've been a part of have been shaped by an ethnographic commitment to the life of street transactions. They have also been compelled by the possibilities of capturing and translating these diverse forms of exchange for an array of public audiences as a practice of rendering "a range of realities intelligible, visible, and relevant" (Bhan 2019, 640). Working within interdisciplinary research teams on a number of research projects focused on street livelihoods in urban peripheries between 2012 and 2018, we were to learn that the matter of gathering a syntax of edge economies and then transmuting vocabularies that might speak to traders, planners, politicians, and activists is an unstable process. In addition, edge territories are saturated with deep structural violence, and such vocabularies need to articulate not only *where* the effects of dispossession are most likely to be located, but also *who* is most likely to be affected (Gilmore 2002).

A violent milieu demands commensurate practices and strategies, in trying to keep open to effective ways of listening, in forging tactics of how to speak to various audiences, and in organizing the activation of language so that it might be heard. We were to learn that because dialogue is a process of assemblage, it too is unpredictable, and we often were caught between "that ambiguous space in which differences are permitted a hearing" and more-restricted idioms in which values are already presupposed (Chambers 1994, 31). In this chapter I briefly reflect on three different but related modes of syntax we evolved, each time learning about the limitations and occasional possibilities of composing vocabularies of "evidence" to intervene in processes of dispossession. I unpack how we engaged with the syntax of *counting*, of *detailing*, and of *activating*, as modes of speaking to established presumptions of what counts and, by implication, who matters. The elevation or relegation of what and who matters further brings into play "the wider environment of 'whiteness' in the dominant values and practices in planning processes," and raises questions about what forms we speak through and what is recognized or suppressed in the conventions or disruptions of vocabulary (Kobayashi and Peake 2000, 393).

I begin with a focus on Rye Lane in Peckham, south London, at the time of an intensive regeneration agenda encapsulated in the local borough council's redevelopment plan for the Peckham Town Centre. On the street, transactions emerge from crossovers of proprietors, hustlers, shops, internet cafés, beauty salons, money remittance services, butcheries, and markets. A number of evangelical churches, yoga groups, and performance scenes rent out the large spaces to the rear of the street, while religious and spiritual spaces, art venues, and food bars of varying types find a place above, below, and behind the street. The varied modes of exchange that compose the street include forms of self-interest and cooperation along with practices of profit-making, profiteering, subsisting, care, and counsel (Hall et al. 2017). Southwark Council's "Revitalise: Peckham and Nunhead Area Action Plan" of 2014 proclaims the prospects for a "Fairer future" and, like many area action plans across London, the document highlights "concentrations of large development opportunities" (Southwark Council 2014, 18). Since 2010, the Council has had its budget nearly halved (Southwark Council 2018, 6), and the impacts of austerity governance in this borough and across London have further propelled the sell-off of public assets, including council housing. This has further stimulated state-led forms of "regeneration" and, with it, the pronounced loss of affordable space for both housing and livelihoods. Over the past decade, Land Registry data and estate agent sites reveal a significant increase in property prices in Southwark, while between 2001 and 2011 there had been an overall decline in the proportion of households renting from the local authority, alongside an increase in private rental tenure (Southwark Council 2015, 13).

The combined processes of regeneration and dispossession continue to unfold across London, where racialized and minoritized groups are frequently disproportionately affected. This may occur through how the financialization of housing estates might be accompanied by policing (Perera 2019) as well as how affordable work space is eroded (King et al. 2018). Edge territories are therefore spaces where the conjoined violations of state and market have differential and differentiating impacts, surfacing the reach of dispossession in the intersections of "race," class, and locality. In order to claim space, citizens of the edge acquire improvisational repertoires to contend with prevailing precarity and discrimination. In the lively struggles to hold onto space, they draw on material and associational resources to challenge the vocabularies of redevelopment. On the street, an everyday politics of the edge is established through a "spatial dissensus" where self-organization is deployed to combat specific acts of regeneration, and where subjectivities declare their presence through practices of meaningmaking sustained in the arrangement of objects, surfaces, and contact (Vardy 2019). As researchers we are therefore engaged in multidirectional and at times disorienting processes of hearing multiple registers, and of communicating among and across multiple audiences. Doing this research can at times feel like an involvement in a dissonant process, trying to stay close to the dynamic expressions of the street, while at the same time attempting to infuse the procedures of planning with an edge syntax.

Counting: Do Numbers Matter?

Starting from the margins of Rye Lane in Peckham, south London, I explore how proprietors on the street form a "range of words" to circumvent a consortium of redevelopment initiatives to turn their margin into a center. In Southwark Council's regeneration plan for the Peckham Town Centre, detailed in its "Revitalise: Peckham and Nunhead Area Action Plan" of 2014, Peckham is identified as historically having a "negative reputation" arising from "high crime levels and feelings of the area not being safe." In contrast, the town center is identified as "a creative and cultural hub" well disposed for redevelopment, where the mechanism of the Area Action Plan is envisaged as having the directive capacity to alter the image of Peckham itself by enrolling developers, land owners, and the local authority in developing their respective sites (Southwark Council 2014, 28). The positioning of Peckham as a historically problematic area fits within the edict of "spatial liberalism," in which the instrumental nature of the market-state compact has placed a different kind of pressure on the margins, often relegating it in order to reconstitute it (Clarke and Cochrane 2013).

The format of state-led regeneration requires using the comprehensive vocabulary of master plans to assert the legitimacy of wide sweeping change, with a concomitant commitment to something being broken and requiring fixing. The regeneration rhetoric imbued in vocabularies of revitalization, job provision, and the creation of mixed communities needs to be placed adjacent to the crucial question of who is being valued or devalued. By thinking about how stigmatization occurs in relation to planning "as a cultural and political economy," Imogen Tyler and Tom Slater advance our understanding of the production of abjection in the coordinated reordering of urban space (2018, 721). Relegation is produced in structural and atmospheric entanglements, where surfaces, statistics, and vocabularies are invoked, thus overlooking grounded practices of city-making. When our research team started our fieldwork on Rye Lane in 2012, we were interested in its everyday formations of social and economic life forged within a context of durable marginality and unfolding multiculture. Over our three-year research period, we became aware of the differing ways in which a planned revitalization process for the Peckham Town Centre was being advanced. We were unaware of any detailed analysis of the street's economies that had been undertaken from the perspective of the shops, market stalls, and street vendors. Rather, user needs and consumer preferences had been engaged, leading to the identification of aspirations for a wider retail offer as core to the remaking of the center.

The risk in such processes of consultation is that the parlance of a familiar entertainment and retail cache of multinational chains is foregrounded within design and planning processes. "Clone Town Britain" speaks to the ubiquitous reliance on the formats of apparently predictable retail chains and franchises across streets and in town centers, one that has been revealed as a brittle corporatized model that is highly susceptible to economic and social crises (Cox et al. 2010). In contrast, the loose cohesion of independent shop proprietors and street vendors that comprise the street remains less legible to the highly formalized and professionalized circuits of regeneration expertise. When we spoke with Abdul, an independent street proprietor who has had a shop on Rye Lane for many years, he reflected on how he perceived the traders' lack of recognition in the planning process by stating, "The problem is, they don't see us." When I interviewed a planner involved with the redevelopment plans for the Peckham Town Centre, I asked him to comment on how he understood how Rye Lane fits within the Council's broader notion of economic value. Tim clarified, "The Council has an economic development strategy: to articulate a strong and inclusive economy. There are tensions between large-scale developments versus supporting existing economies to grow. These two things don't always meet well."

Questions of vocabulary are also questions of voice, and processes of planned regeneration can be underscored by the conformity of professionalized expertise. Streets like Rye Lane reveal a city-making that emerges through a choreography of sidesteps and subversions, a consortium of improvisational imperatives tuned by residents and small-scale operators. Throughout the street various proprietors rewire existing business and social circuits to divert and reconfigure otherwise unavailable infrastructures. Part of the work of this chapter is to engage with the contradictions we juggled, of how we could explore a respective makeshift epistemology, while still wanting to speak to those in the local authority. On Rye Lane we began our research process in what felt like a straightforward way, starting by walking the ground floor stretch of two-hundred-odd tightly packed retail units, engaging with respective shop proprietors. We designed a basic one-page survey, which was brief enough so as not to disrupt their entrepreneurial rhythm, but which allowed us a face-to-face entree into each shop and the start of a conversation.

After a couple of weeks of walking and talking, we had spoken to the majority of proprietors and had a sense of whom we could go back to for more-extended conversations, observations, and spatial mappings. Out of this fairly loose, tangible process, we formatted a stiffer set of survey results. A numeric dataset allowed us to incorporate the rudimentary details of 199 units of retail, with close to two-thirds of these retailers operating in independent, nonaffiliated retail. The spectrum of retail trade primarily included clothing, food with specialties in fish and Halal meat, beauty products largely comprising hair and nail bars, money remittances, and mobile phone products and services. Ground floor space was at a premium, testified to by the limited number of vacancies and charity shops. Just under half the proprietors had occupied their shops on the street for five years or fewer. For the most part, we used these numbers to raise a set of questions for ourselves, as well as to deploy a manner of speaking to engage with planners and local officials that we presumed might fit with the bureaucratic procedures of planning.

The street survey allowed us to locate global displacements in relation to urban emplacements, tracing the histories and geographies of proprietors from a wide array of countries: Afghanistan, England, Eritrea, Ghana, India, Iran, Ireland, Jamaica, Kashmir, Kenya, Nepal, Nigeria, Pakistan, Somalia, Sri Lanka, Tanzania, Uganda, Vietnam, and Yemen. Their co-presence points to urban multicultures forged through the "postcolonial continuum" of Britain's imperial history and its continued practices of political interventionism, which makes its way to the everyday life of cities across the U.K. (Jazeel 2019, 65). As part of our survey, we asked proprietors how many languages they spoke, and while almost two-thirds of proprietors told us they spoke two or three languages, close to a third said they spoke four languages or more. We were intrigued by how street proprietors used language, as well as by the ways in which multilingual proficiency is nurtured as strategic, cultural, and sociable, shaping varied forms of communication but also suggesting repertoires acquired in navigating multiple borders.

During our street research, a key challenge was to find ways of communicating the street's values to local authorities within the Council in the hope that this might influence planning considerations. One of our first tactics was to develop a form of montage: to take the practices of the street and in effect to translate them, using established languages of cultural and planning value in the hope that this would render the street legible to this authority. We took a printed plan of Peckham Town Centre in south London and placed it side by side with a plan of the acclaimed Westfield Stratford City shopping center in east London, highlighting how the granular infrastructure of the town center delivers more jobs. We then juxtaposed the multilingualism of the street with the multilingualism of "experts" at the London School of Economics and Political Science (figure 11.1) to suggest how language proficiency might be understood as a twenty-first-century-citizenship capacity, constituting a diverse social capital to interpret, to learn, to transfer, and finally to involve wider forms of communication (Hall 2013).

These visualizations always got a few nods and laughs in the meeting rooms with Council officials and planning professionals alike, but it also seemed that this kind of counting and translating could only take us so far and no further. It may be that the juxtapositions were indeed too close a fit with the master's tools, or perhaps even were a cultural conceit or amus-

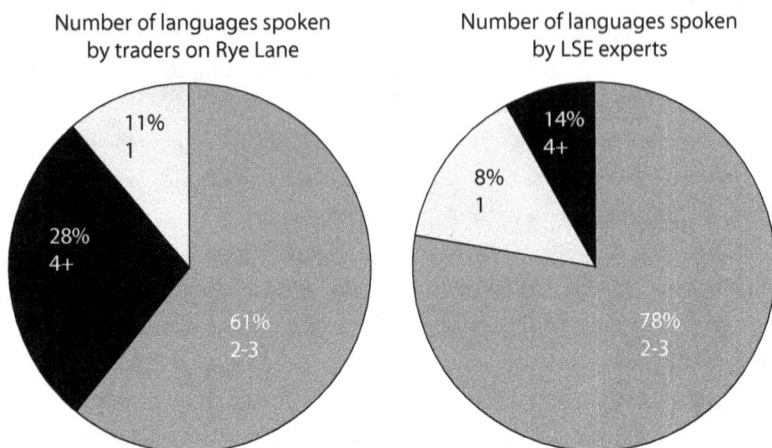

Number of languages spoken
by traders on Rye Lane

11%
1

28%
4+

61%
2-3

Number of languages spoken
by LSE experts

14%
4+

8%
1

78%
2-3

11.1 Multilingual citizenship: Number of languages spoken by shop proprietors on Rye Lane (left) and by LSE experts (right). Drawn by Adriana Valdez-Young

ing comparison, where the numbers themselves were interesting but not crucial. A regeneration process was already in motion, one reliant on large-scale investors who possibly had a more convincing or translatable set of numbers and narratives to portray. But our numbers did not fall completely by the wayside; they began to be picked up and used by various activist groups, contesting the specificities of the Peckham Plan either through locally organized action, or through collectives challenging the narrow articulations of the economy in the mayor's London Plan. Our numbers and drawings were put together with perspectives from other research on streets, markets, and industrial hives, where a combined narrative began to emerge not only about quantities of jobs but also about diverse economies as being extended networks of livelihoods, transactions, and forms of exchange and care. The account put forward by crucial alliances in London like the informal alliance, Just Space, argues for a variety of modes of making economies, and pointedly recognizes the everyday socio-spatial infrastructures required to sustain them.

Detailing: Capturing Spatial Practice

Teresa Caldeira refers to peripheries as "spaces that frequently unsettle official logics," and places that offer the possibilities of transformation without "erasing the gaps" forged by durable inequalities (Caldeira 2017, 3).

In this part of the chapter, I'd like to expand on the unheroic struggles of the edge shaped in the unspectacular forms of interior subdivisions and multiple occupations of space on Rye Lane. The suggestive possibilities of the directive of infrastructure put forward by AbdouMaliq Simone (2017) and James Holston (2009) foreground the tangible stakes of place and the convening powers of territory in procuring everyday politics. Affordable homes and affordable workplaces are elemental to life in the margins and are therefore the means of agency as well as the instruments of insurgency. This requires a regard for how a cultural street politics is shaped from the interior, apart from the historic possibilities of working-class districts collectively politicized and culturalized by wage labor and union representation. The self-employed and part-time workers and proprietors on a street such as Rye Lane have no singular affiliation. Moreover, their economic and cultural presence is increasingly questioned by the burgeoning border politics that perpetuates societal bordering in the U.K. and racialized comprehensions of value. Their unity is falling incomes and rising rents, as much as the bricks-and-mortar format of shop interiors that provide possibilities for experimentation and expression.

When we conducted our street walks, we noticed that as many as one in four of the ground floor shops practiced what we called "urban mutualism," an intense subdivision of shop space in which multiple activities are colocated and in which varied forms of tenure arise (Hall 2015). In mapping the minutiae of multiple subdivisions of shops along Rye Lane, we were able to explore the recalibrating of space that establishes a spatial realignment and repurposes more-brittle tenure arrangements. The reconfiguration of interiors is partly lodged within the logic of the market and dramatic increases in property values in Peckham, where the affordability of street space has to be secured through other means. Spatial subdivisions and sublettings have become a dynamic practice of contending with the urban premium of escalating markets across cities, and these emergent circuits are highlighted not without concern for what these densely orchestrated divisions and inhabitations mean for privacy, ritual, exploitation, and stress. Careful, grounded research has revealed these reappropriations of city space as being more than perfunctory or extractive responses to the ever-increasing weight of market impositions. In a stunning comparative collection, Margot Rubin et al. (2020) reveal this auto-densification as being a rewording of intimacy in the intensification of precarity and proximity, where new spatial practices forge the everyday struggles for alternatives.

Taking a closer look at the interiors of these reconfigured spaces on Rye Lane reveals a dense overlap of activities, aesthetics, and tenures, and over a period of three years we mapped several of these spaces by recording and visualizing their composition. In our mapping of a large double-story unit on the street, we marked the outer boundary of the shop with a dark outline that signifies the shop unit as a whole (figure 11.2). Within this unit are several visible internal subdivisions, resulting in a carving up and parceling out of space according to cultural and economic practices. Much of the designation of divisions in this large shop area was driven by a mixture of pragmatics and sociability. The shop's proprietor, Adofo, had arrived in the U.K. from Ghana some twenty-five years ago and had started out by selling products from a table in the Brixton market. We spoke with Kofi, Adofo's son-in-law, who explained how the shop space is apportioned:

> You see, if you enter here, everything can be got from here. If you come to buy a body cream you can also get a haircut, or have your clothing made or repaired, or book a flight to Ghana or send your cash back home. You kill five birds with one stone. There is no point of going elsewhere. The things we have here is just like being back home and it really reminds you of being in Ghana. We also make it feel like this in the way we've set up and arranged the shop.

Barbara, Adofo's daughter, oversees the ground floor area, largely committed to fresh produce and including a Western Union remittance store at the rear. The ground floor is arranged to "greet the street," pulling customers in through the arrangement of fresh food, jars of spices and herbs, and dried fish. These arrangements of crates, boxes, and trays of food gradually begin to narrow down, forming a single aisle leading to the remittance desk.

Winding up the staircase toward the rear of the shop, one enters a loosely subdivided space where a hairdresser, three tailors, a travel agent, and a cash exchange colocate. At one end the tailors each have their own cutting desk and sewing machine, and are reportedly "busy, busy, busy." A large sofa marks out their end of the upper room, making a delineation between the stacked piles of patterned cottons and silks that are arranged in the center of the room, not reaching more than seat height so that customers can stroll around the piles, perusing the variety of cloths. Cynthia's hair salon at the other end is a few meters squared, and she pays a low-risk, small rental of £80 for her chair per week. This chair rental arrangement, which spans across the city, is central to the viability of the expanding hair

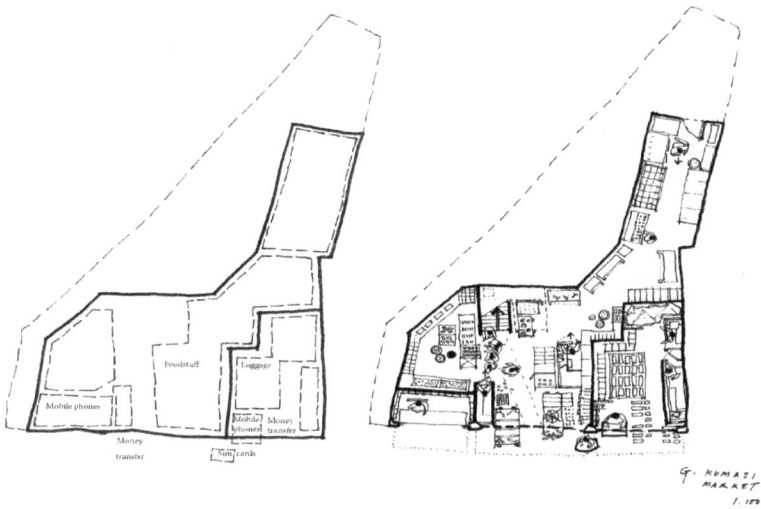

11.2 A subdivided interior on Rye Lane. Drawn by Thomas Aquilina
Legend: 1 Mobile phone, 2 Money transfer, 3 Foodstuff, 4 Luggage, 5 Money transfer,
6 Mobile phone, 7 SIM card

and nail sector, and is occupied largely by female stylists. These stylists work without job security, and flexibility is core to their precarious balance of variable working hours that can only be sustained though low-risk tenure arrangements. Balancing family commitments is a further consideration, and Kofi, who generally works upstairs, comments that, "After school I don't have to rush and can bring my kids here before we all head home."

Nonetheless, times are hard on the street, and Francesca, who has traded on Rye Lane for many years, talks about the constant struggle against difficult times, saying: "These days it's getting tough with us. Customers are bagging [buying] a little. The shops are divided by little, little, little. It's hard to make even £100 in a day." This stringent reality, produced by durable inequality and exacerbated by heightened periodic stress such as the financial crisis or the COVID pandemic, takes its toll on the residents and proprietors of the "edge." In the absence of meaningful structural distribution, affordable space remains a recourse to claiming life and livelihood, and the interior subdivisions of shops on Rye Lane are maintained through everyday practices that elude professionalized accounts of value (Tayob 2018). Detailing rental agreements and shared leases matters, because doing so captures the intricacies of practice that are impossible to comprehend through research encounters that privilege surveys and quantified representations. On Rye Lane, detailing reveals the rescaling of the edge—a carving up of space and time into ever-smaller increments to contend with external pressures and to incorporate internal meanings. This vocabulary of the edge is inherently about adaptation and assertion, accommodating forms of expression that entail survival and personhood, only just ahead of the relentless reach of the market and state.

Activating: Why Coalition Is Key

In the period following our research on Rye Lane, our project expanded to explore edge economies on streets in deindustrialized peripheries across several U.K. cities, where the impacts of punitive immigration acts were unfolding with brutal effect. Engaging in this larger comparative project had the effect of making us acutely aware of the pervasive nature of social injustice unfolding across urban peripheries. We continued to seek out vocabularies and strategies to engage in listening and mapping, but it was only in working more closely with an activist group that we saw other possibilities for grounded research practice. One example arose in 2018 when we were approached by Latin Elephant, an activist group that had evolved to "promote alternative and innovative ways of engaging and incorporating migrant and ethnic groups in processes of urban change in London" (https://latinelephant.org). The activists had been committed to working with traders within and around the Elephant and Castle Shopping Centre over many years, getting to know their needs, fears, and aspirations, coordinating support around legal rights and responsibilities, and linking together with campaigns against the unfolding displacement in the area. They were in the process of preparing evidence to object to a planning application for the redevelopment of the Elephant and Castle Shopping Centre, a strategic site in south London long occupied by traders alongside a steady stream of commuters who congregate to catch one of numerous buses or trains that converge in this busy hub. Nicolas, a shopkeeper, expands on the role of such a hub, remarking: "We are quite well-known for helping people. We have people coming from the airport with their luggage! Once the shopping center is gone, the commercial hub will be scattered."

The shopping center lies some three kilometers to the north of Rye Lane, and adjacent to another large-scale regeneration scheme incorporating the demolition of a total of 1,214 housing units on the former Heygate Estate. The newly developed Elephant Park introduces 2,704 housing units to the area, but with its minimal provision for affordable and socially rented housing, the regeneration translates into the significant displacement of affordability. A committed collective of advocacy and campaign groups in the area has actively supported a call for considered political engagement to determine, when affordable space is so vital to the lives and livelihoods of urban citizens, why it is being so substantially eroded. The particular purpose of Latin Elephant's evidence base was to challenge Southwark Council's approval of the developer Delancey's plan to demolish the Elephant and Castle Shopping Centre to develop a new town center and college campus. The existing advocacy by Latin Elephant called for the protection of the 130 independent and largely "Black, Asian and Minority Ethnic" traders (a term established by the state), who were currently within the red line designation for development. Our collaboration with Latin Elephant was meant to generate additional evidence to supplement their work in supporting their objection, which was to be lodged in the formal terms and formats determined by the due-planning process. The varied objections to the application were to be scrutinized by the Southwark Council and by the mayor of London and the Greater London Authority (GLA). Our project team, led by Julia King, developed a report on the "Socio-economic Value at the Elephant and Castle" (King et al. 2018) underscoring the need to protect affordable workspace in the context of current area regeneration and businesses' displacement. At stake were the livelihoods of the 130 traders who occupied the space inside and around the shopping center, and who were being offered substantially less space for immediate relocation, with additional affordable floor space promised by 2019. However, the affordable retail space would still leave a significant shortfall from the traders' original shop occupations.

The central narrative of our report was to push at what constitutes affordability in the redevelopment of the center, bringing issues of class and cultural diversity into the understanding of both the impacts of social change and the possibilities of diverse economies. We argued that "The systematic demise of affordability across London is a form of discrimination. Planning should actively regulate against the loss of genuinely affordable spaces to live and work, with regulation to protect affordable housing provision" (King et al. 2018, 11). Planning-based struggles over residents' right to the city accommodations are constituted by the concern for retaining space that is not only affordable in a pragmatic sense but also adaptable in a cultural sense. Class-based struggles are, as well, cultural struggles that incorporate lived experiences of gender and "race," in which affordable space is an essential infrastructure for these multifarious expressions and networks of support to be sustained. Indira, a long-standing tenant, qualified it this way:

> We are not just a food place. We are an information point. People come here and ask for a doctor or a bank. Some people even ask about other restaurants! It is kind of sad because if we moved to other places people may see it more difficult to come in.

In building on the original Latin Elephant survey of shop proprietors, we learned that many of the traders and shopkeepers were women, some of whom were holding down more than one form of work to make ends meet. Based on data available from thirty-six respondents, close to half of our respondents were in the age category of fifty-plus, and half the tenants had held their leases for ten years or more (figure 11.3). This speaks to the high levels of investment that proprietors had made over time, building their small businesses and actively contributing to the social life of the shopping center. In regeneration processes, tenants are often left in the invidious position of not being able to claim back this sweat equity or to formally capture the meaning of their contributions.

Final approval for the Delancey redevelopment plan was granted by the Greater London Authority on December 10, 2018. A coalition of research and activist organizations, including Latin Elephant and local grassroots groups working together with the area's traders and residents, had argued hard for a reconsideration of affordable space and the attendant dignity of secure tenure. In terms of an extension of affordable work and trading spaces in the new development, the initial proposal was expanded from a five-year to a fifteen-year commitment. The research had also presented dispossession as an ongoing process of wearing the infrastructure of the center down over a sustained period, including the gradual closure of retail units and the decline of maintenance. This was important in gaining reassurances about the continued maintenance and upkeep of trading activities during the transition period before the shopping center would be demolished.

This, however, is a story of small gains, and about the diminutive but important role of short and sharp action research, both of which tack onto much-longer and substantial processes of lively resistance. The battle for the Elephant and Castle has been sustained by a broad solidarity of multiple activist groups, legal challenges, marches and sit-ins, and even a host of exhibitions, films, and texts. Those multiple modalities that are committed, agile, and assertive might yield comparatively small concessions from

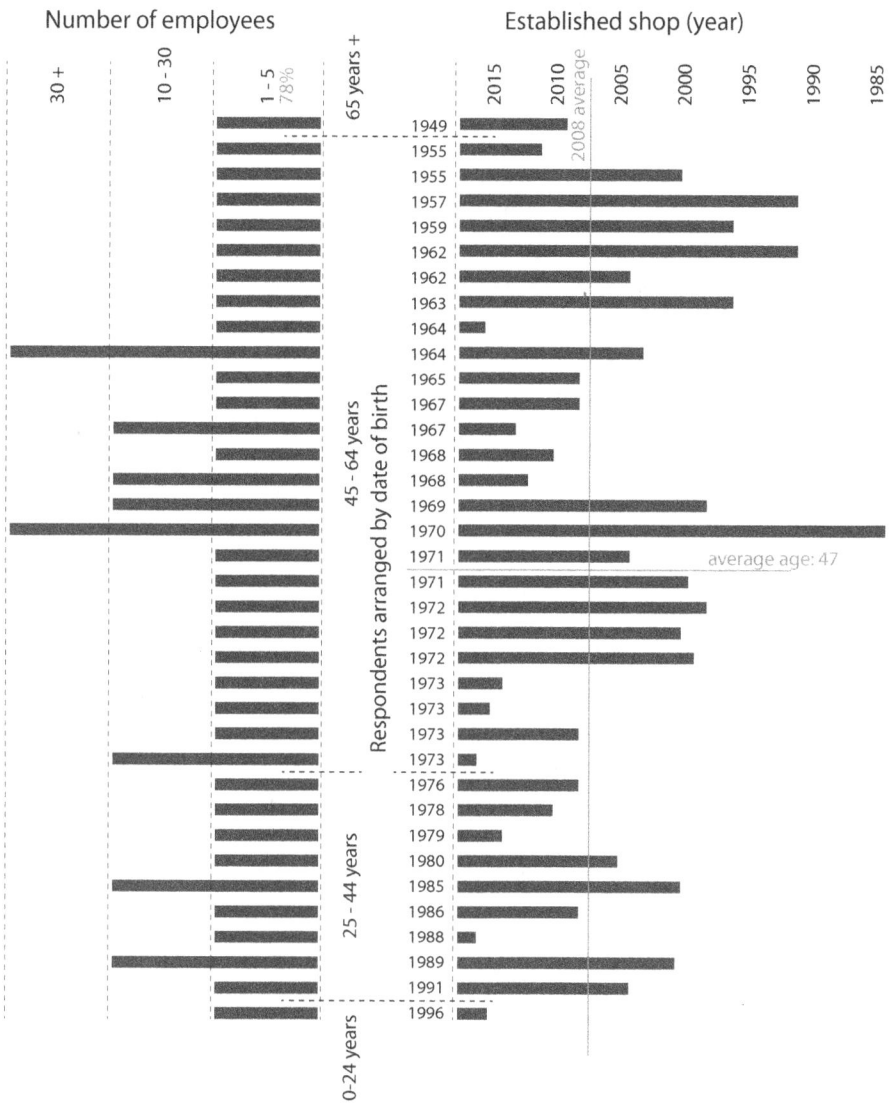

Number of employees

Established shop (year)

30 + | 10 - 30 | 1 - 5 78% | 65 years +

2015 | 2010 | 2008 average | 2005 | 2000 | 1995 | 1990 | 1985

Respondents arranged by date of birth

45 - 64 years

average age: 47

25 - 44 years

0-24 years

1949
1955
1955
1957
1959
1962
1962
1963
1964
1964
1965
1967
1967
1968
1968
1969
1970
1971
1971
1972
1972
1972
1973
1973
1973
1973
1976
1978
1979
1980
1985
1986
1988
1989
1991
1996

11.3 Graph showing relationships between proprietors, age, an approximate number of employees, and shop longevity. Drawn by Julia King

the virulent force of regeneration, but they do not fade and their strategies of intervention are continually sharpened. Our research, together with the report format of evidence that we sought to develop over the summer of 2018, in many ways signals the limited capacities of academic research. We have the privilege of sustained employment and funding that affords us the time to invest in the long trajectory of a research interest or passion, which then allows us to build up repertoires of listening, speaking, and writing. But most often, our available syntax is relatively staid and our communication remains constrained within predefined formats. An "edge syntax," by contrast, is sustained in other activations—in ways of speaking that encompass the violence of our time and place, the urgencies of intervention, and the recognition of *who* is at stake.

An Edge Syntax

Spaces like Rye Lane and the Elephant and Castle endure as an edge, not so much in the sense of a location but rather of a contestation, a set of experiments about claiming and holding onto space through repurposing meanings. On Rye Lane, the hybrid shop interiors combine intermixtures of precarity, dexterity, opportunism, and a litmus-like response to the needs and desires of time and place. The street, unlike the shopping center, is a disaggregated composition, under neither singular ownership nor corporate control, where a bits-and-pieces urbanism is possibly more porous to improvisation, though not impervious to regeneration. Because city-making in the edge territories of cities throughout the United Kingdom has been forged by long histories of migration, edge emporiums necessarily incorporate conjoined vocabularies of streets and markets across space, invoking affinities for highly social modes of exchange and adaptation. The edge emerges, then, as a lively space formed in and through the rewiring of the circuits of value, incorporating an Esperanto of both near and far worlds. Its evolving spatial grammar serves to circumvent property values and planning systems alike, and its densely invested interiors are a form of everyday cultural politics, sustained in the frictions and promises of interaction and expression.

The inhabitants of the edge invest in adaptations, sustained through a collage of paraphernalia and intention and rough-and-ready alterations, incorporating what Ash Amin and Michele Lancione articulate as "multiple sources of authority" (see editors' introduction to this book). Adaptation is not limited to being a responsive practice, but instead is an alternative resumption to claiming space through vocabularies that are simultaneously audacious and commonplace. One source of this authority is temporal: city-making at the edge is inherently emergent and therefore neither invested in a nostalgia for the past nor contemplating a future rendered as replacement. City-making's day-to-day authority can only exist through constant negotiation. Another source of this authority is material: it emerges through the expressive and immediate potential of moving and shaping of walls, objects, and thresholds that refer to grounded needs, rather than through the abstract grammar of action plans, vision statements, and projections. Authority is also collaborative, in which coalitions are frequently operationalized through spatial and sensory infrastructure. In tracing the formations of Black music in systems of racialized oppression, Katherine McKittrick engages with how music is a way of re*wording*, exploring how "inequitable systems of knowledge can be, and are, breached by creative human aesthetics" (McKittrick 2016, 81). The claiming of space on Rye Lane and at the Elephant and Castle is in practical terms a prosaic attention to the limits of available space, but in human terms is a re*forming* of the extant reality of exclusion and of the emergent possibility of space to affirm one's place in the world. Claiming, rewording, and reforming are conscious and emotive assertions of the right to difference forged in forms that are temporal, material, and collaborative.

How might *grammars of the urban ground* help us think more about processes of listening to the city—at, from, and through the edge? On reflection, perhaps some of the grammars we have engaged with in our research over the years are an illusion, in that they look to the ground in order to look to the authority of power. My sense is that our offerings are more compelling when they have stayed attached to the street, where we've taken time to detail its vocabularies and even worked within collectives that have long ties with respecting the nuances of everyday life in these violent times. From here the elemental syntax of recognition and redistribution needs to be called on insistently, proclaiming strong commitments to the elemental values of life within the fragile promise of secure place. With this comes an understanding of the edge as audacious, inventive, and relevant. I am struck by the emerging efforts of courageous and creative activists and "researchers" (for want of a better word) who in spirited ways stay grounded, working through rich collaborations, asserting their voice, and exploding the limited formats of prescriptive language.

References

Bhan, Gautam. 2019. "Notes on a Southern Urban Practice." *Environment and Urbanisation* 31, no. 2: 639–654.

Caldeira, Teresa. 2017. "Peripheral Urbanisation: Autoconstruction, Transversal Logics and Politics in Cities of the Global South." *Environment and Planning D: Society and Space* 35, no. 1: 3–20.

Chambers, Iain. 1994. *Migrancy, Culture, Identity*. London: Routledge.

Clarke, Nick, and Allan Cochrane. 2013. "Geographies and Politics of Localism: The Localism of the United Kingdom's Coalition Government." *Political Geography* 34: 10–23.

Cox, Elizabeth, Paul Squires, Josh Ryan-Collins, and Ruth Potts. 2010. "Reimagining the High Street: Escape from Clone Town Britain." *New Economic Foundation* (NEF).

Gilmore, Ruth Wilson. 2002. "Fatal Couplings of Power and Difference: Notes on Racism and Geography." *The Professional Geographer* 54, no. 1: 15–24.

Hall, Stuart, with Bill Schwarz. 2018. *Familiar Stranger: A Life between Two Islands*. London: Penguin.

Hall, Suzanne. 2013. "Multilingual Citizenship." *Discover Society*, no. 1: 1–3.

Hall, Suzanne. 2015. "Super-diverse Street: A 'Trans-ethnography' across Migrant Localities." *Ethnic and Racial Studies* 38, no. 1: 22–37.

Hall, Suzanne. 2021. *The Migrant's Paradox: Street Livelihoods and Marginal Citizenship in Britain*. Minneapolis: University of Minnesota Press.

Hall, Suzanne, Julia King, and Robin Finlay. 2017. "Migrant Infrastructure: Transaction Economies in Birmingham and Leicester, UK." *Urban Studies* 54, no. 6: 1311–1327.

Holston, James. 2009. *Insurgent Citizenship: Disjunctions of Democracy and Modernity in Brazil*. Princeton, NJ: Princeton University Press.

Jazeel, Tariq. 2019. *Postcolonialism*. London: Routledge.

King, Julia, Suzanne Hall, Patria Roman-Velazquez, Alejandro Fernandez, Josh Mallins, Santiago Peluffo-Soneyra, and Natalia Perez. 2018. "Socio-economic Value at the Elephant and Castle." London School of Economics.

Kobayashi, Audrey, and Linda Peake. 2000. "Racism out of Place: Thoughts on Whiteness and an Antiracist Geography in the New Millennium." *Annals of the Association of America Geographers* 90, no. 2: 392–403.

McKittrick, Katherine. 2016. "Rebellion/Invention/Groove." *Small Axe: A Caribbean Journal of Criticism* 20, no. 1 (49): 79–91.

Perera, Jessica. 2019. *The London Clearances: Race, Housing and Policing*. London: Institute of Race Relations.

Rubin, Margot, Alison Todes, Philip Harrison, and Alexandra Appelbaum. 2020. *Densifying the City? Global Cases and Johannesburg*. Cheltenham: Edward Elgar.

Simone, AbdouMaliq. 2017. "The Majority World and the Politics of Everyday Living in Southeast Asia." In *The* SAGE *Handbook of the 21st Century City*, edited by Suzanne Hall and Ricky Burdett, 339–415. London: SAGE.

Southwark Council. 2014. "Revitalise: Peckham and Nunhead Area Action Plan." November.

Southwark Council. 2015. *Southwark Key Housing Data 2015/16*, October.

Southwark Council. 2018. *Council Plan 2018/19-2021-22*, October.

Tayob, Huda. 2018. "Subaltern Architectures: Can Drawing 'Tell' a Different Story?" *Architecture and Culture* 6, no. 1: 203–222.

Tyler, Imogen, and Tom Slater. 2018. "Rethinking the Sociology of Stigma." *Sociological Review* 66, no. 4: 721–743.

Vardy, Sam. 2019. "Urban Dissensus: Spatial Self-Organisation at Wards Corner." In *Enabling Urban Alternatives*, edited by Jens Kaae Fisker, Letizia Chiappini, Lee Pugalis, and Antonella Bruzzese, 65–81. Singapore: Palgrave Macmillan.

ASH AMIN is professor of geography at Cambridge University and a Fellow of the British Academy, having held the post of Foreign Secretary and Vice-President from 2015 to 2019. His recent books include *Land of Strangers; Arts of the Political*, with Nigel Thrift (Duke University Press); *Releasing the Commons*, coedited with Philip Howell; and *Seeing Like a City*, with Nigel Thrift. He is currently writing a book on the politics of coexistence in Europe.

TERESA P. R. CALDEIRA is professor at the Department of City and Regional Planning at the University of California, Berkeley. Her research focuses on the predicaments of urbanization, such as spatial segregation, social discrimination, and uses of public space in cities of the Global South. She has analyzed the processes that generate these cities, such as peripheral urbanization and auto-construction, highlighting their inventiveness, political cartographies, and modes of collective life. Caldeira is the author of *City of Walls: Crime, Segregation, and Citizenship in São Paulo*. She was named a Guggenheim Fellow in 2012.

FILIP DE BOECK is a professor of anthropology at the University of Leuven, Belgium, and a writer, filmmaker, and curator. He lives and works between Brussels and the Democratic Republic of Congo. Over the past thirty years he has conducted extensive field research in both rural and urban communities in the DRC. Coauthored with photographer Sammy Baloji, his most recent book is *Suturing the City: Living Together in Congo's Urban Worlds*. De Boeck has also curated several international exhibitions and is the author of a long documentary film about Kinshasa.

SUZANNE M. HALL is an associate professor in sociology at the London School of Economics, where she codirects the Cities Programme. She is the author of *The Migrant's Paradox: Street Livelihoods and Marginal Citizenship in Britain*.

CAROLINE KNOWLES is professor of sociology at Goldsmiths, University of London, and director of the British Academy's Urban Infrastructures of Well-Being Programme. She has authored many books and papers on urban life in London, Hong Kong, Beijing, Fuzhou (China), Addis Ababa (Ethiopia), Daesan (Korea), and

Kuwait City, often focusing on migration and material translocal connections between cities. Her most recent books are *Flip-Flop: A Journey through Globalisation's Backroads* and *Serious Money: A Walk Through Plutocratic London*.

MICHELE LANCIONE is professor of geography at the Polytechnic of Turin, Italy, and a visiting professor of urban studies at the University of Sheffield, U.K. His work focuses on radical forms of inhabitation and housing struggles (through a five-year European Research Council project) and on the politics of life at the margins in the contemporary urban.

COLIN MCFARLANE is professor of urban geography at Durham University, U.K. His work focuses on the making and politics of urban life, including themes of density, infrastructure, poverty, and inequality. His recent books include *Fragments of the City: Making and Remaking Urban Worlds*, and a coedited volume with Michele Lancione, *Global Urbanism: Knowledge, Power and the City*.

NATALIE OSWIN is associate professor in the Department of Human Geography at the University of Toronto, Scarborough. Her work explores postcolonial queer geographies in the context of globalization and urbanization. She is the author of *Global City Futures: Desire and Development in Singapore* and managing editor of the interdisciplinary journal *Environment and Planning D: Society and Space* and the *Society and Space* online magazine.

EDGAR PIETERSE is founding director of the African Centre for Cities at the University of Cape Town and holds the South African Research Chair in Urban Policy. His research and teaching explore urban development politics, everyday culture, publics, radical social economies, responsive design, and adaptive governance systems. He publishes different kinds of text, curates exhibitions, and conducts difficult conversations about pressing urban problems. His current research is focused on a major exhibition—CompleXities—exploring urban futures. He is also working on an institutional framework to promote city-level innovation ecosystems in Africa that will promote the localization of sustainable infrastructure in low-income contexts.

ANANYA ROY is professor of Urban Planning, Social Welfare, and Geography and is the Meyer and Renee Luskin Chair in Inequality and Democracy at the University of California, Los Angeles. She is founding director of the UCLA Luskin Institute on Inequality and Democracy, which advances scholarship concerned with displacement and dispossession in Los Angeles and elsewhere in the world. Her current scholarship concerns the relationship among property, personhood, and police in the making and unmaking of racial capitalism.

ABDOUMALIQ SIMONE is Senior Professorial Fellow at the Urban Institute, University of Sheffield, U.K., and Visiting Professor of Urban Studies at the African Centre for Cities, University of Cape Town. His key publications include *For the City Yet to Come: Changing African Life in Four Cities* (Duke University Press); *City Life from Jakarta to Dakar: Movements at the Crossroads*; *Jakarta: Drawing the City Near*; *New Urban Worlds: Inhabiting Dissonant Times*, with Edgar Pieterse; *Improvised Lives: Rhythms of Endurance in an Urban South*; and *The Surrounds: Urban Life Within and Beyond Capture* (forthcoming, Duke University Press).

TATIANA THIEME is an associate professor in human geography at University College London. Her research projects have been funded by the Economic and Social Research Council, the British Academy, and a Cambridge Humanities Grant. Broadly, her ethnographic research and writing focuses on "hustle economies" among at-risk youth, people released from prison, and precarious migrants cut off from mainstream institutional support. Her research also intersects with urban political ecologies of waste and sanitation, and alternative development models. While she has worked in cities across the Global North and Global South, her primary field site remains Nairobi, Kenya.

NIGEL THRIFT is a visiting professor at Oxford University and an emeritus professor at the University of Bristol. His main research interests lie in the social and political uses of technology, international finance and financial exclusion, time and the history of timekeeping, cities and especially the violence to the planet caused by urban infrastructure, the contested dividing line separating sentience from nonsentience, and social theory more generally. His latest book, *Killer Cities*, addresses how cities are hastening the destruction of the planet and how they could be rehabilitated.

MARIANA VALVERDE is a socio-legal scholar specializing in urban governance and law. She recently retired from the University of Toronto.

Orangi Pilot Project (PPP), 65
overtourism, 86, 89

Park, Robert E., 13, 28–38
parking (term for housing solution), 131, 202
Peckham. *See* London (UK)
Peckham Town Centre, 225–27
people-scapes, 183–84
peripheral urbanization, 129–34, 199–202, 209–13, 219–22, 232
personhood, 53–54, 89
"Pic Sörensen," 150–52
Pixadores, 137
plutocracy, 17–19, 164–77
plutocratic domestic services, 173–74
plutocratic family life, 173
plutocratic women, 173, 175
plutocrats, 169, 171, 173, 177
Polish Peasant in Europe and America, The (Thomas and Znaniecki), 33
political economy, 9–11, 14
political-legal theories, 118
politics of fragility, 176–77
politics of the city, 176
politics of the composites, 12
population, 60, 82–97, 99–100, 103n2
post-categorical thought, 10–11
postcolonialism, 42, 51
posthumanism, 7
post-structuralist thought, 6
pousse-pousseurs (pushcart workers), 157
primaverism, 95, 97
private, the, 118
private contract, 111, 117
private equity, 170
private residential property, 111, 114
privatization, 118
privatized exclusive community. *See* private residential property
progress, 128–30
property, 54, 118
protest, 67–75, 119–21, 143–48, 177
provisional, the, 146n2

public, the, 118
public-private partnership. *See* arms-length conservancy
public rules, 121

Queer theory, 13, 27–29, 33–35, 38–39. *See also* LGBTQ+
Quito, 205–6

racial capitalism, 14, 42–44, 52, 54. *See also* capitalism
racism, 43, 45, 50, 110, 117. *See also* banishment
radical adjustment, 20, 65
radical geography, 42, 51
radical social enterprise, 18, 181, 192–94
Reclaiming LA, 54
regeneration, state-led, 225
relational device, 202–3
residential segregation, 116
residualization, 221
restrictive covenant, 110, 114–16
Revitalise: Peckham and Nunhead Area Action Plan, 223–24
reworlding, 14
rich pay less effect, 113–14
Right to Pee Movement, 70–72, 75
rolê, 137–38, 144
rolezinhos, 137
Rose, Nancy, 157
Rousseff, Dilma, 144
Royal Exchange, 168
Rubin, Gayle, 35–37
Runa (Indigenous population of Ecuador), 205–6
"run with the land," 114, 124n3
Rye Lane. *See* London (UK)

Saharan Africa, 200
Sahelian Africa, 200
São Paulo, Brazil, 16–17, 126–44, 147n12
self-help city, 184
sexuality, 29–35, 38, 134–36
Shelley v. Kraemer, 115

and labor, 194; life in, 1–6, 13–16, 20, 31, 44, 58, 94, 108–9, 114, 153–54, 195, 202–6, 212, 217; marginality and, 8; neoliberalism and, 160n3; policy of, 4, 62; politics of, 12–13, 20, 61, 74; poor, 45; and possession, 44–45, 54; praxis of, 9; projects, 199–200; Queer studies of, 13, 27–28, 35; racism and, 110; relationalities in, 202–3; residents of, 189; scholars of, 4, 7; and segregation, 116; and sexuality, 34; sexuality studies of, 38; social types of, 32, 37; Southern theories of, 14, 41; theory of, 1–15, 27–42, 51–52, 109, 118–22, 188; undercommons of, 13; welfare and, 11; and social types, 36–37. *See also* the city

urbanism, 2, 6–10, 16–20, 42, 61–77, 176, 236
urbanites, 8, 15, 64
urbanization, 31, 129, 200–205, 215–17
URBZ, 75–76

Vancouverism, 62
vocabularies, 18, 221–26, 232, 237

waster collectors, 184–86, 192
White, Peter, 51
whiteness, 44, 223
Wright, Jamaal, 43

zero (as in lack), 158